VOLUME I: THE WAY OF THE ANIMAL POWERS

PART 1

MYTHOLOGIES
OF THE
PRIMITIVE HUNTERS
AND GATHERERS

1. The God and his animal messengers. The god's feet rest on the beaks of a pair of birds portrayed upside down. Bronze plaque known as the Lafone luevedo Disk. Diameter, 4¼ inches; thickness, about ⅛ inch. La Aguada culture, Catamarca, northwest Argentina, C. A.D. 650 to 750. Thought by some to represent the pre-Incan divinity Viracocha with his servants, Imaymana and Tocapu.

JOSEPH CAMPBELL

HISTORICAL ATLAS OF WORLD MYTHOLOGY

VOLUME I

THE WAY OF
THE ANIMAL POWERS

PART 1

MYTHOLOGIES OF
THE PRIMITIVE
HUNTERS
AND GATHERERS

PERENNIAL LIBRARY
HARPER & ROW, PUBLISHERS   NEW YORK

CAMBRIDGE, PHILADELPHIA, SAN FRANCISCO, LONDON
MEXICO CITY, SAO PAULO, SINGAPORE, SYDNEY

TABLE OF CONTENTS

Library of Congress Cataloging-in-Publication Data: Campbell, Joseph, 1904–1987. Historical atlas of world mythology. Includes bibliographical references and indexes. Contents: v.1. The way of the animal powers. pt.1. Mythologies of the primitive hunters and gatherers. pt.2. Mythologies of the great hunt. 1. Mythology. I. Title. BL311.C26 1988 291.1'3 87-40007
ISBN 0-06-055148-8 (v.1, pt.1)   88 89 90 91 92 10 9 8 7 6 5 4 3 2 1
ISBN 0-06-096348-4 (v.1, pt.1) (pbk.) 88 89 90 91 92 10 9 8 7 6 5 4 3 2 1

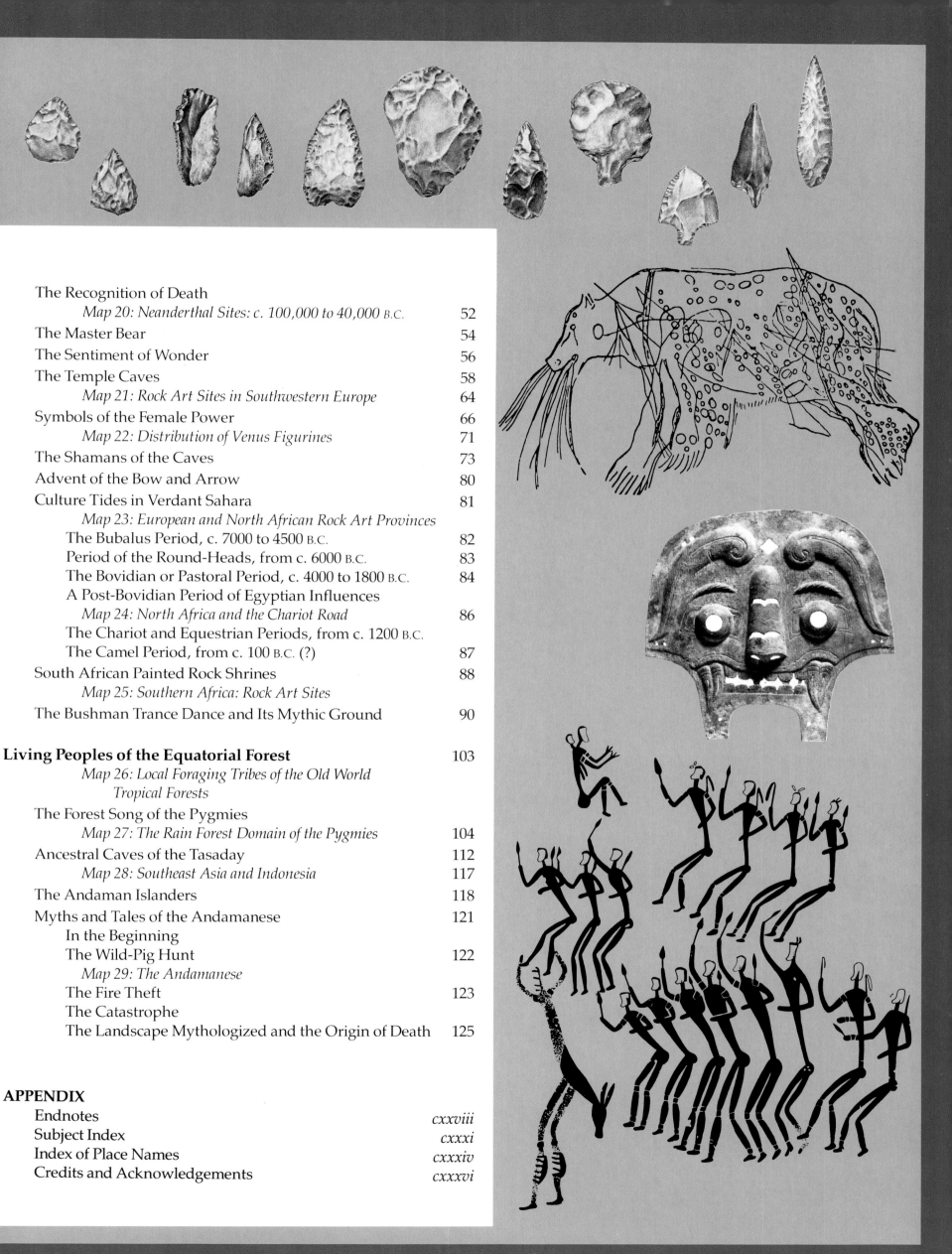

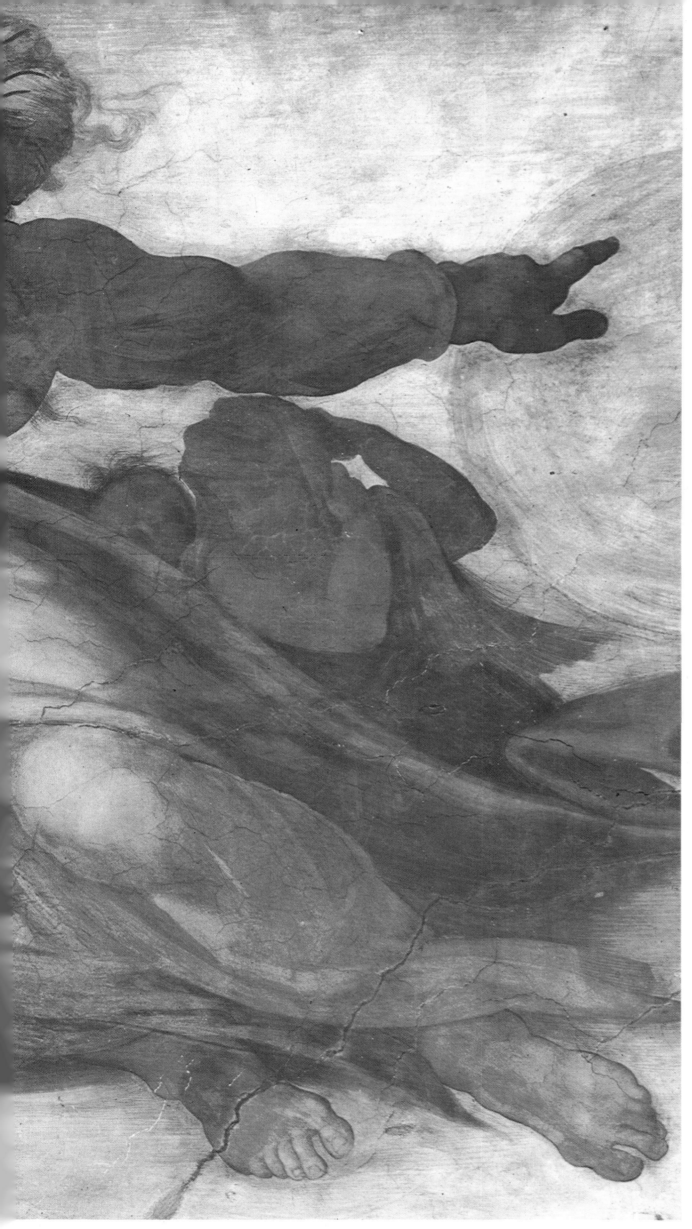

PROLOGUE

"In the beginning,
when the King's will began
to take effect,
He engraved signs
into the heavenly sphere."

(*Zohar* 1:15)

2. Michelangelo, *The Creation*, ceiling of the Sistine Chapel, the Vatican, Rome. Detail. Painted 1508 to 1512.

In the beginning of all things,
wisdom and knowledge were with the animals;
for Tirawa, the One Above, did not speak directly
to man. He sent certain animals to tell men that he showed
himself through the beasts, and that from them,
and from the stars and the sun and the moon,
man should learn. Tirawa
spoke to man through
his works.

CHIEF LETAKOTS-LESA OF THE PAWNEE TRIBE TO NATALIE CURTIS, C. 1904.

THE MYTHOLOGICAL DIMENSION

We live, today, in a terminal moraine of myths and mythic symbols, fragments large and small of traditions that formerly inspired and gave rise to civilizations. Our prevailing, Newtonian world view is of a three-dimensional space, "always similar and immovable," within which changes occur through a dimension of time that is also continuous, absolute, and enduring. Here material bodies, drawn and held together by a mysterious force called "gravity," are moved according to mechanical laws of cause and effect, the cause of the world itself being represented as the act of a deity generally envisioned as an anthropomorphic "spiritual" body, intangible, yet capable of functioning physically as a "First Cause"—such a one as appears in Michelangelo's representation of The Beginning, on the ceiling of the Sistine Chapel in Rome. As Newton himself wrote of this imagined moment:

"It seems probable to me that God in the beginning formed matter in solid, massy, hard, impenetrable, movable particles, of such sizes and figures, and with such properties, and in such proportion to space, as most conduced to the end for which he formed them; and that these primitive particles being solids, are incomparably harder than any porous bodies compounded of them; even so very hard, as never to wear or break in pieces; no ordinary power being able to divide what God himself made one in the first creation."[1]

But this hard-and-fast mythology is now itself breaking in pieces. Newton's "impenetrable particles" have exploded, and in the realm of subatomic physics that is opening to the mind's eye—beyond reach of direct scrutiny and to be known only by way of observed dynamic effects—the entire universe appears (to quote one recent interpreter) "as a dynamic web of inseparable energy patterns" that always includes the observer in an essential way.[2] This is to say that in what we think we know of the interior of the atom, as well as of the exploding stars in millions of spinning galaxies throughout an expanding space that is no longer, as in Newton's view, "always similar and immovable," the old notion of a once-upon-a-time First Cause has given way to something more like an immanent ground of being, transcendent of conceptualization, which is in a continuous act of creation now.

The first function of a mythology is to waken and maintain in the individual a sense of wonder and participation in the mystery of this finally inscrutable universe, whether understood in Michelangelo's way as an effect of the will of an anthropomorphic creator, or in the way of our modern physical scientists—and of many of the leading Oriental religious and philosophical systems—as the continuously created dynamic display of an absolutely transcendent, yet universally immanent, *mysterium tremendum et fascinans*, which is the ground at once of the whole spectacle and of oneself.

The second function of a mythology, then, is to fill every particle and quarter of the current cosmological image with its measure of this mystical import; and in this regard, mythologies differ as the horizons, landscapes, sciences, and technologies of their civilizations differ. Such a hunting tribe as the Pawnee of the North American plains, for example, would have known a world very different from that of the mid-Pacific Polynesians; nor can any of the experiences of such nonliterate, hunting, planting, and fishing folk compare with those of the peoples of the Roman, Achaemenid, and Chinese empires.

Adolf Bastian, a world traveler as well as a major ethnologist of the nineteenth century, recognized in the myths and ceremonial customs of mankind a significant number of essential themes and motifs that were apparently universal. He termed these *Elementargedanken*, "elementary ideas." But he perceived, also, that in their appearances they were clothed always in local forms, which he termed *Völkergedanken*, "ethnic ideas." One determinant of the folk inflections was, as just remarked, the landscape. Another, no less influential, was the local moral order; for, if the first function of a mythology is the mystical, as just described, and a second the cosmological—that of converting every feature of the locally envisioned order of nature into, as it were, an icon or figure revelatory of Tirawa, Yahweh, Shiva, Huracan, or the Tao—a third function, no less important, is the sociological one of validating and maintaining whatever moral system and manner of life-customs may be peculiar to the local culture. Indeed, one of the most striking features of mythologies everywhere is their reference to mythological beginnings even of such indifferent customs as, for example, the shape of a hat, color of the border of a shawl, or way of parting one's hair.

A fourth, and final, essential function of mythologies, then, is the pedagogical one of conducting individuals in harmony through the passages of human life, from the stage of dependency in childhood to the responsibilities of maturity, and on to old age and the ultimate passage of the dark gate. And it is in its service to this function that the most evident of its elementary ideas, or universal themes and motifs, are to be recognized; for a human life, after all, whether in the Andaman Islands or in the city of New York, will have to pass from infancy to engagement in the world and on to disengagement in old age, after which the mystery occurs of death, the ultimate term to the no less tremendous *mysterium* of birth—between which terms there will have been so many minor cycles of sleep (with dreams) and waking.

The principal method of mythology is the poetic, that of analogy; in the words of Ananda K. Coomaraswamy, it is "the representation of a reality on a certain level of reference by a corresponding reality on another:"[3] death by sleep, for example, or vice versa; and the experiences of sleep, then, as the (supposed) experiences of death; the light of the sun as of consciousness; the darkness of caves, or of the ocean depth, as of death, or of the womb; the waning and waxing moon as a sign celestial of death and rebirth; and the serpent's sloughing of its skin as an earthly sign with the same sense. There are many analogies of this kind that are recognized everywhere in the world. Others, however, are local or culturally specific: the majesty of

the elephant as an earthbound cloud, for example, or the seven days of a seven-day week as the days of the Creation and God's Rest.

The history and geography of the rise and diffusion of specific myths and mythological systems can be readily reviewed in broad lines today and represented in such a way as to convert the rubble of the great moraine that is about us into a laboratory of revelations. For we have present in our libraries a prodigious literature of information, explication, and interpretation, as well as, still among us, living representatives of many of the most typical or imposing of the rapidly disintegrating traditions of belief: popes, lamas, and other learned churchmen; sheiks, shamans, rishis, rabbis, roshis, and rimpoches; even Stone Age tribesmen like the Tasaday of the Philippines, the Bushmen of the Kalahari, and the Nambikwara of Brazil.

The first and most important historical distinction to be recognized is that between literate and nonliterate orders, and among the latter, that between primary and regressed mythologies, that is, those of isolated tribes, uninfluenced by literate neighbors, and those, on the other hand, of tribes whose myths and customs have been derived in large measure from the Bronze or Iron Age or even later high-culture systems. Geographically, an important distinction is to be seen, furthermore, between the mythologies of Old Stone Age tribes inhabiting the great animal plains of postglacial Europe, Siberia, and North America, and those of the jungles of the tropical equatorial belt, where plants, not animals, have been the chief source of sustenance, and women, not men, the dominant providers.

The landscape of the "Great Hunt," typically, was of a spreading plain, cleanly bounded by a circular horizon, with the great blue dome of an exalting heaven above, where hawks and eagles hovered and the blazing sun passed daily; becoming dark by night, star-filled, and with the moon there, waning and waxing. The essential food supply was of the multitudinous grazing herds, brought in by the males of the community following dangerous physical encounters. And the ceremonial life was addressed largely to the ends of a covenant with the animals, of reconciliation, veneration, and assurance that in return for the beasts' unremitting offering of themselves as willing victims, their life-blood should be given back in a sacred way to the earth, the mother of all, for rebirth.

In contrast, the environment of jungle tribes is of a dense and mighty foliage, the trunks and branches of prodigious trees; no horizon; no dome of the sky; but above, a ceiling of leaves populated by screeching birds, and underfoot a rough leafage, beneath which may lurk scorpions and lethal fangs. Out of the rot of fallen wood and leaves, fresh sprouts arise—from which the lesson learned appears to have been that from death springs life, out of death, new birth; and the grim conclusion drawn was that the way to increase life is to increase death. Accordingly, there has been endemic to the entire equatorial belt of this globe what can be described only as a frenzy of sacrifice, vegetable, animal, and human: from the African Guinea Coast and the Congo, across and throughout India, Southeast Asia, and Oceania, to Middle America and the jungles of Brazil. Moreover, in variously modified forms, the influence of this order of primitive rites entered and inspired much of the mythology of the higher cultures, where it survives in myths and rituals of sacrifice and communion with which many of us, of whatever religious affiliation, have been long familiar.

The beginnings of the world development toward higher, literate, and monumental civilizations are now generally recognized as having had as their seeding ground the fertile mudlands of the lower Tigris-Euphrates valleys. A mysterious people of unknown provenance known to scholarship as the Sumerians began settling there in the earlier part of the fourth millennium B.C., and by 3500 B.C. had established a cluster of little, brick-built city-states, organized around monumental temple compounds: Ur, Kish, Lagash, Shuruppak, Uruk, Ubaid, Nippur, and the rest, the first cities of their kind in the world. Moreover, it was by the priests of these temple compounds, ever increasing in size, that the arts of writing and mathematical reckoning were invented, together with an early science of exact astronomical observation, which had been made possible by recorded notations. The measured movements of the seven visible celestial spheres—Sun, Moon, Mercury, Venus, Mars, Jupiter, and Saturn—along an apparently circular way through the constellations, led to the realization, altogether new to the world, of a cosmos *mathematically* ordered; and with this awareness, the focus of mythic concern radically shifted from the earlier animal and plant messengers to the night sky and its mathematics, with the ever dying and self-resurrecting moon as its lord and the five visible planets as the dominant members of a court. This cosmic order, illustrated in the heavens, was to be imitated on earth, where the festivals of the religious year still follow the seasonal signs of sun and moon, kings and queens wear radiant celestial crowns, and to the God whose glory the heavens proclaim, there is daily lifted the Christian prayer: "Thy will be done, on earth as it is in heaven." The

idea was carried to Egypt and appears there with the First Dynasty, circa 2850 B.C.; to Crete and eastward to the Indus Valley, around 2000 B.C.; to China with the Shang Dynasty, circa 1500 B.C.; and to Mexico, some four or five centuries later.

Today, as already remarked, the focal center has again shifted—to the patterns, not of the planetary courses, but of subatomic energy traces—with mathematics still providing the key to the reading of the messages. Yet, mankind is no closer to the mastery of that golden key than were the Indians of the North American plains to immediate knowledge of that One Above, who, "in the beginning," as the Pawnee chieftain Letakots-Lesa told Natalie Curtis in the first years of the present century, "did not speak directly to man, but sent certain animals to tell man that he showed himself through the beasts, and that from them, and from the stars and the sun and the moon, man should learn. . . . For all things speak of Tirawa." [4]

It has always been the business of the great seers (known to India as "rishis," in biblical terms as "prophets," to primitive folk as "shamans," and in our own day as "poets" and "artists") to perform the work of the first and second functions of a mythology by recognizing through the veil of nature, as viewed in the science of their times, the radiance, terrible yet gentle, of the dark, unspeakable light beyond, and through their words and images to reveal the sense of the vast silence that is the ground of us all and of all beings. Gods that are dead are simply those that no longer speak to the science or the moral order of the day—like Michelangelo's and Newton's God, for example, whose hypothetical act of creation occurred at some moment in an imagined past no longer recognized. And the formulae of a science remain dead unless there is someone like Letakots-Lesa around to read them as tokens, not only of practical information, but also of life's mystery: our biological schedule of the evolution of all living things, for example, to be viewed (as the atom is now being viewed) as denoting some kind of "dynamic web of inseparable energy patterns," in which all of us, whether knowingly or unknowingly, are included.

The unfolding through time of all things from one is the simple message, finally, of every one of the creation myths reproduced in the pages of these volumes—including that of our contemporary biological view, which becomes an effective mythic image the moment we recognize its own inner mystery. By the same magic, every god that is dead can be conjured again to life, as any fragment of rock from a hillside, set respectfully in a garden, will arrest the eye. This *Historical Atlas of World Mythology* is to be as a garden of thus reanimated gods.

3. Visionary mask from Spiro Mound, Leflore County, Oklahoma. Wood, 11½ by 7 inches, c. A.D. 1200 to 1600. The surface of the face was originally painted; shell inlays have been lost from the earlobes.

"Let There Be Light!"

(Genesis 1:1 to 2:4)

The Bible opens with two distinct creation myths: that of Genesis 1:1 to 2:4 (here given), and that of the Garden of Eden and Man's Fall, verses 2:4 to 3:24. The myth of Eden dates from the period (930 to 721 B.C.) of the Two Kingdoms, Israel and Judah; this of the Seven Days of Creation, on the other hand, is from the period of the Second Temple. It is a work of the Priestly School, of the prophet Ezra's time, fourth century B.C., and, with its assignment of the seventh day to God's rest, confirms the institution of the Sabbath. The earlier myth knew nothing of this institution and described a different order of creation: first, man; then, a garden for him to cultivate; next, the animals for his entertainment; and finally, woman, from his rib; after which, the Fall.

In the beginning God created the heavens and the earth. The earth was without form and void, and darkness was upon the face of the deep; and the spirit of God was moving over the face of the waters.

And God said, "Let there be light"; and there was light. And God saw that the light was good; and God separated the light from the darkness. God called the light Day, and the darkness he called Night. And there was evening and there was morning, one day.

And God said, "Let there be a firmament in the midst of the waters, and let it separate the waters from the waters." And God made the firmament and separated the waters which were under the firmament from the waters which were above the firmament. And it was so. And God called the firmament Heaven. And there was evening and there was morning, a second day.

And God said, "Let the waters under the heavens be gathered together into one place, and let the dry land appear." And it was so. God called the dry land Earth, and the waters that were gathered together he called Seas. And God saw that it was good. And God said, "Let the earth put forth vegetation, plants yielding seed, and fruit trees bearing fruit in

which is their seed, each according to its kind, upon the earth." And it was so. The earth brought forth vegetation, plants yielding seed according to their own kinds, and trees bearing fruit in which is their seed, each according to its kind. And God saw that it was good. And there was evening and there was morning, a third day.

And God said, "Let there be lights in the firmament of the heavens to separate the day from the night; and let them be for signs and for seasons and for days and years, and let them be lights in the firmament of the heavens to give light upon the earth." And it was so. And God made the two great lights, the greater light to rule the day, and the lesser light to rule the night; he made the stars also. And God set them in the firmament of the heavens to give light upon the earth, to rule over the day and over the night, and to separate the light from the darkness. And God saw that it was good. And there was evening and there was morning, a fourth day.

And God said, "Let the waters bring forth swarms of living creatures, and let birds fly above the earth across the firmament of the heavens." So God created the great sea monsters and every living creature that moves, with which the waters swarm, according to their kinds, and every winged bird according to its kind. And God saw that it was good. And God blessed them, saying, "Be fruitful and multiply and fill the waters in the seas, and let birds multiply on the earth." And there was evening and there was morning, a fifth day.

And God said, "Let the earth bring forth living creatures according to their kinds." And it was so. And God made the beasts of the earth according to their kinds, and the cattle according to their kinds, and everything that creeps upon the ground according to its kind. And God saw that it was good.

Then God said, "Let us make man in our image, after our likeness; and let them have dominion over the fish of the sea, and over the birds of the air, and over the cattle, and over all the earth, and over every creeping thing that creeps upon the earth. So God created man in his own image, in the image of God he created him; male and female he created them. And God blessed them, and God said to them, "Be fruitful and multiply, and fill the earth and subdue it; and have dominion over the fish of the sea and over the earth." And God said, "Behold, I have given you every plant yielding seed which is upon the face of all the earth, and every tree with seed in its fruit; you shall have them for food. And to every beast of the earth, and to every bird of the air, and to everything that creeps on the earth, everything that has the breath of life, I have given every green plant for food." And it was so. And God saw everything that he had made, and behold, it was very good. And there was evening and there was morning, a sixth day.

Thus the heavens and the earth were finished, and all the host of them. And on the seventh day God finished his work which he had done. So God blessed the seventh day and hallowed it, because on it God rested from all his work which he had done in creation.[5]

IT·LVMINARIA·IN
MAMTO·CELI·

4. Mosaic of the Fourth Day of Creation, from the cathedral of Monreale, built by the Norman King William II ("the Good") of Sicily, last quarter of the twelfth century A.D.

5. This serene triadic image of *Shiva Mahesh-vara, "The Great Lord"*—23 feet high, 19½ feet across, carved in the eighth century A.D. on the back wall of an immense hand-hewn cave on an island in the harbor of Bombay—is symbolic of the immanent ground of all being and becoming. The profile at the beholder's left is male, that at the right, female; the presence in the center is the mask of Eternity, the ever-creating *mysterium*, out of which all pairs of opposites proceed: female and male, love and war, creation and annihilation. Though beheld externally, this mystery is to be known internally, as the indwelling Source and End of all that has been or is to be. "Not female nor yet male is it; neither is it neuter. Whatever body it assumes, through that body it is served." *(Shvetashvatara Upanishad 5.10)*

Out of One, the Many
(Brihadaranyaka Upanishad 1.4.1–5)

The following text is from the earliest of the Upanishads, the *Brihadaranyaka*, which is of a date somewhere about the ninth century B.C., and thus about contemporary with the biblical legend in Genesis 2 of God producing Eve from Adam's rib.

In the beginning, there was only the Great Self in the form of a Person. Reflecting, it found nothing but itself. Then its first word was: "This am I!" whence arose the name "I." Which is why, to this day, when one is addressed one first says, "I," then tells whatever other name one may have. . . .

That one was afraid. Therefore anyone alone is afraid. "If there is nothing but myself," it thought, "of what, then, am I afraid?" Whereupon the fear departed. For what was there to fear? Surely, it is only from a second that fear derives.

That Person was no longer happy. Therefore, people are not happy when alone. It desired a mate. It became as large as a woman and man in close embrace; then caused that Self to fall in two: from which a husband and wife arose. (Therefore, as the sage Yajñavalkya used to say, this body is but half of oneself, like the half of a split pea; which is why this space is filled by a wife.) He united with her; and from that human beings were born.

She thought: "How can he unite with me, after producing me from himself? Well, let me hide." She became a cow, he a bull, and united with her. From that cattle were born. She became a mare, he a stallion; she a she-ass, he a he-ass; and united with her. From that one-hoofed beasts were born. She became a she-goat, he a he-goat; she became a ewe, he a ram; and he united with her. From that goats and sheep were born. In this way he projected all things existing in pairs, down to the ants.

Then he realized: "I, indeed, am this creation; for I have poured it forth from myself." In that way he became this creation. And verily, he who knows this becomes in this creation a creator.[6]

Forbidden Fruit
(A Bassari Legend, Togo)

6. Ancestral figure of the Bakoa of Gabon. Wood covered with copper strips.

Throughout Black Africa the "living dead," that is the remembered dead, are the principal intermediaries between the living of the tribe and the Invisibles. For, though themselves now invisible, they are still engaged in the world of the living, can even be expected to return, in time, reborn, and so, against the anonymous background of the absolutely unknown—the distant unforeseeable future and the long-forgotten distant past, as well as those mysteries of nature and being that lie beyond comprehension—they constitute an enclosing, familiar company of favoring powers. Those dead who have been forgotten, on the other hand, pass into the unknown, and may return as dangerous spirits.

Generally an anthropomorphic Creator God is recognized—"Without father or mother, wife or children," say the Kenya Kikuyu. He once walked on earth, like the God of Genesis 2–3, but is now the ultimate Invisible, surrounding and including all.[7] The following legend is of the Bassari tribe of northern Togo.

Unumbotte made a human being. Its name was Man. Unumbotte next made an antelope, named Antelope. Unumbotte made a snake, named Snake. At the time these three were made there were no trees but one, a palm. Nor had the earth been pounded smooth. All three were sitting on the rough ground, and Unumbotte said to them: "The earth has not yet been pounded. You must pound the ground smooth where you are sitting." Unumbotte gave them seeds of all kinds, and said: "Go plant these." Then Unumbotte went away.

Unumbotte came back. He saw that the three had not yet pounded the earth. They had, however, planted the seeds. One of the seeds had sprouted and grown. It was a tree. It had grown tall and was bearing fruit, red fruit. Every seven days Unumbotte would return and pluck one of the red fruits.

One day Snake said: "We too should eat these fruits. Why must we go hungry?" Antelope said: "But we don't know anything about this fruit." Then Man and his wife took some of the fruit and ate it. Unumbotte came down from the sky and asked: "Who ate the fruit?" They answered: "We did." Unumbotte asked: "Who told you that you could eat that fruit?" They replied: "Snake did." Unumbotte asked: "Why did you listen to Snake?" They said: "We were hungry." Unumbotte questioned Antelope: "Are you hungry, too?" Antelope said: "Yes, I get hungry. I like to eat grass." Since then, Antelope has lived in the wild, eating grass.

Unumbotte then gave sorghum to Man, also yams and millet. And the people gathered in eating groups that would always eat from the same bowl, never the bowls of the other groups. It was from this that differences in language arose. And ever since then, the people have ruled the land.

But Snake was given by Unumbotte a medicine with which to bite people.

"It is important to know," states Leo Frobenius, from whose *Volksdichtungen aus Oberguinea* this legend has been taken, "that as far as we know there has been no penetration of missionary influence to the Bassari. . . . Many Bassari knew the tale, and it was always described to me as a piece of the old tribal heritage. I have heard it told by a number of people at various times and have never been able to detect any significant variations. I have therefore to reject absolutely the suggestion that a recent missionary influence may lie behind this tale."[8]

The Light Within
(A Polynesian Chant, Society Islands)

Two types of creation myth are known from Polynesia: one in which the universe emanates in stages from the void; the other in which the world-generating divine power is personified, as it is here in the sea-god known in the Society Islands as Taaroa, Tangaroa in the Austral Group, Tanaoa in the Marquesas, and Kanaloa in Hawaii. The "land of Hawaii," named at the close of the Society Island chant here quoted, is not the geographical Hawaii, but an imagined, ideal sourceland of the Polynesian race after which the island chain has been named.

He existed, Taaroa was his name,
In the immensity.
There was no earth, there was no sky,
There was no sea, there was no man.
Taaroa calls, but nothing answers.
Existing alone, he became the universe.
Taaroa is the root, the rocks.
Taaroa is the sands.
It is thus that he is named.
Taaroa is the light. Taaroa is within.
Taaroa is the germ. Taaroa is the support.
Taaroa is enduring. Taaroa is wise.
He erected the land of Hawaii,
Hawaii, the great and sacred,
As a body or shell for Taaroa.
The earth is moving.
O, Foundations, Rocks,
O, Sands, hither, hither,
Brought hither, pressed together the earth.
Press, press again. They do not unite.
Stretch out the seven heavens, let
    ignorance cease.
Create the heavens, let darkness cease.
Let immobility cease.
Let the period of messengers cease.

It is the time of the speaker.
Completed the foundations.
Completed the rocks.
Completed the sands.
The heavens are enclosing.
The heavens are raised.
In the depths is finished the land of
    Hawaii.[9]

7. *Tangaroa Generating Gods and Men.* Wooden image from a temple on Rurutu Island of the Austral Group. One of the very few Polynesian figures to have survived the nineteenth-century destruction of images, the figure, 44½ inches high, is now in the British Museum.

Song of the World
(A Pima Legend, Arizona)

From Hovering Hawk, an old chief of the Pima tribe of southern Arizona, Natalie Curtis received this song and its myth, about the year 1904. "I will sing an old, old song," he told her, "a song sung by the Creator at the beginning of the world."[10]

In the beginning there was only darkness everywhere—darkness and water. And the darkness gathered thick in places, crowding together and then separating, crowding and separating until at last out of one of the places where the darkness had crowded there came forth a man. This man wandered through the darkness until he began to think; then he knew himself and that he was a man; he knew that he was there for some purpose.

He put his hand over his heart and drew forth a large stick. He used the stick to help him through the darkness, and when he was weary he rested upon it. Then he made for himself little ants; he brought them from his body and put them on the stick. Everything that he made he drew from his own body even as he had drawn the stick from his heart. The stick was of greasewood, and of the gum of the wood the ants made a round ball upon the stick. Then the man took the ball from the stick and put it down in the darkness under his foot, and as he stood upon the ball he rolled it under his foot and sang:

I make the world, and lo!
The world is finished.
Thus I make the world, and lo!
The world is finished.

So he sang, calling himself the maker of the world. He sang slowly, and all the while the ball grew larger as he rolled it, till at the end of his song, behold, it was the world. Then he sang more quickly:

Let it go, let it go,
Let it go, start it forth!

So the world was made. And now the man brought from himself a rock and divided it into little pieces. Of these he made stars, and put them in the sky to light the darkness. But the stars were not bright enough.

So he made Tau-muk, the Milky Way. Yet Tau-muk was not bright enough. Then he made the moon. All these he made of rocks drawn forth from himself. But even the moon was not bright enough. So he began to wonder what next he could do. He could bring nothing from himself that could lighten the darkness.

Then he thought. And from himself he made two large bowls, and he filled the one with water and covered it with the other. He sat and watched the bowls, and while he watched he wished that what he wanted to make in very truth would come to be. And it

8. Pima basketry tray from Sacaton, Arizona. Diameter, 9½ inches. A.D. 1900 to 1905. The figure entering the maze is Siuhu, Elder Brother, a character from the creation myth here recounted. When the world had been created, he emerged from the center of the earth and later led his people from under the ground. But they turned against him, killing him several times, once even pulverizing him; yet, he always returned to life and at last departed. The maze design is called *Siuku Ki*, "Siuhu's House." It shows him going far into the mountains where the trails became so confused no one could follow.

SIUHU'S SONG

Here I have come to the center of the earth;
Here I have come to the center of the earth.
I see the central mountain;
I see the central mountain.

was even as he wished. For the water in the bowl turned into the sun and shone out in rays through the cracks where the bowls joined.

When the sun was made, the man lifted off the top bowl and took out the sun and threw it to the east. But the sun did not touch the ground; it stayed in the sky where he threw it and never moved. Then in the same way he threw the sun to the north and to the west and to the south. But each time it only stayed in the sky, motionless, for it never touched the ground. Then he threw it once more to the east, and this time it touched the ground and bounced and started upward. Since then the sun has never ceased to move. It goes around the world in a day, but every morning it must bounce anew in the east.[11]

"Let It Thus Be Done!"
(The Popol Vuh, Guatemala)

The *Popol Vuh*, the Sacred Book of the Quiché, a people of the Mayan race of Guatemala, was copied, c. A.D. 1701 to 1703, from an original manuscript (now lost), by Father Francisco Ximénez, who was at that time pastor of the little parish of Santo Tomás of Chichicastenango. The original had been written in the Quiché tongue in the Latin script, c. A.D. 1550, some years after the holocaust of 1524, when the Conquistador Alvarado razed to the ground the Quiché capital, Utatlán, executed its princes, and scattered its people, some of whom arrived in Chichicastenango.

And it was apparently a princely priest of these refugees, already become Christian, who composed this precious, sole surviving document of a mythology otherwise lost. Father Ximénez's copy and translation remained unknown until the middle of the nineteenth century, when the Abbé Charles Etienne Brasseur de Bourbourg acquired it from "a noble Indian of Rabinal" and, in 1861, published the full Quiché text with a French translation. Ximénez's manuscript now reposes in the Edward E. Ayer Collection of the Newberry Library, Chicago.

All was in suspense: calm, silent, motionless, and at peace: empty, the immensity of the sky. There was as yet neither man nor beast. There were no birds, fish, crabs, trees, rocks, caves, ravines, meadows, or woods: there was only sky. Not yet to be seen was the face of the earth; only the peaceful sea and a vast emptiness of sky. Nothing was yet formed into a body, nothing joined to anything else. There was nothing moving, nothing rustling, not a sound in the sky. There was nothing upright; nothing but the peaceful waters of the sea, quiet and alone within its bounds. For nothing as yet existed. In the darkness, in the night, there were immobility and silence, but also, the Creator and the Maker, Tepeu and Gucumatz: those that engender, those that give being, alone in the waters, like an increasing light.

They are enveloped in feathers, green and blue: hence the name, the Feathered Serpent, Gucumatz. Great wisdom is their being. Behold the sky, how it exists! how, also, the

THE END OF AN EON

9. Last page of the pre-Columbian "Dresden Codex" of the Maya. Along the top of the page are two rows of "serpent numbers," signs representing the prodigious sums of the Mayan astronomical cycles: the *kinchiltun* of 1,152,000,000 days, for example, or the *alautun*, of 23,040,000,000 days. Below, the rain-serpent sends a deluge. The old goddess, patroness of floods, with a snake crowning her head and crossbones decorating her skirt, overturns the bowl of the heavenly waters. And at the bottom of the scene the black god crouches, an owl screeching from his head, and with downpointed spears.[1]

This marks the end of such a cycle of time as that described in its beginning in the *Popol Vuh*.

Heart of Heaven exists! For such is the name of God. 'Tis thus He is called.

And it was then that the word came. Tepeu and Gucumatz talked together in the darkness, in the night. They consulted, deliberated, meditated, matching words and counsels. And it was then, as they reflected, that they understood that when dawn broke man should appear. They planned creation: the growth of trees, of lianas, life, humanity. Thus it was arranged—in the darkness, in the night—by the Heart of Heaven, who is called Huracán. The first sign of Huracán is lightning; the second sign is the short flash of lightning; the third sign is the long flash. And these three are the Heart of Heaven.

Together, Tepeu and Gucumatz deliberated, considering life and light: what to do to bring about light and dawn; who should furnish food and sustenance. "Let it thus be done! Be filled!" they said. "Let the waters recede and cease to obstruct! Let the earth appear and harden! Let the dawn illuminate sky and earth; for neither glory nor honor will be ours in all that we shall have created and formed until a human creature exists, the creature with reason endowed!" It was thus that they spoke while the earth was taking form through them. It was thus, truly, that creation took place and the earth came into being. "Earth!" they said; and immediately it was formed. Like a mist, a cloud, a gathering of dust, was this creation when the mountains appeared from the waters. In an instant there were great mountains. Only a marvelous power and magic could have brought about this formation of mountains and valleys with forests of cypresses and pines instantly upon them.

And Gucumatz was then filled with joy. "Welcome, O Heart of Heaven! And you, Huracán! And you, Short Flash and Long Flash!" "This that we have created and formed," they replied, "shall be finished."

Thus were first formed the earth, the mountains and the plains. And the watercourses were divided, rivulets running serpentine through the mountains, when the high mountains were unveiled. Just so was the earth created, when it was formed by those who are the Heart of Heaven and Heart of Earth: for so are those called who first made fruitful the sky suspended and the earth from the midst of the waters. Such was its fecundation, when they gave it life while meditating on its composition and completion.[12]

THE LIVING GROUND

The Universe, The Earth, and Earth's Life

The initial condition of the universe, according to one modern theory, was of a supercondensate of primeval hydrogen, which exploded 10 billion years ago with a "big bang." This produced an expanding hydrogen cloud within which galaxies condensed myriadfold while flying apart, as they must fly forever. A second theory has it that this state of expansion will be followed by a contraction, which in turn will end in a vast collision, again such an explosion, with galaxies then condensing anew while again flying to all sides. Nor will this cosmogonic oscillation of diastole and systole, in cycles of some 60 billion years, ever end; neither had it a beginning. A third view is of a steady state universe where there is occurring, throughout space, a continuous creation of hydrogen atoms, out of which new galaxies are condensing as the old, continuing to fly apart, pass out of range of astronomical observation.

Whether life exists within any galaxy but our own, or on any planet within our own solar system other than this earth, is a question unresolved. The earth, along with the other planets and moons, became solid some $4\frac{1}{2}$ billion years ago, and the earliest signs of life appeared in its oceans at least $3\frac{1}{2}$ billion years ago in the form of threads and spheres of one-celled, blue-green algae and bacteria.[13] The question of the origin of these earliest signs has been approached by experiments showing that when a sample atmosphere such as initially enveloped our planet—a mixture of hydrogen, ammonia, water vapor, and methane—is subjected to electric discharges and ultraviolet light, large numbers of organic compounds are obtained: fatty acids and amino acids, which are the building blocks of proteins. It is thought that phosphates, enzymes, and nucleic acids could have been formed in this way on the primeval earth under ultraviolet light energy. Enzymes catalyze the synthesis of compounds out of simple substances, and nucleic acids replicate. These being the fundamental processes of life, it is supposed that the earliest condition of life on this planet must have been as a watery "soup" of prebiological organic compounds, which became differentiated when quantities became enclosed in membranes, forming cells. It is all enormously mysterious and already wonderfully alive. The primordial, one-celled threads and spheres of blue-green algae and bacteria then produced the oxygen of our atmosphere as a byproduct of their living on the carbon dioxide and methane of their environment; and out of them all the known forms of life on earth to this day have evolved along the courses represented in our chart.

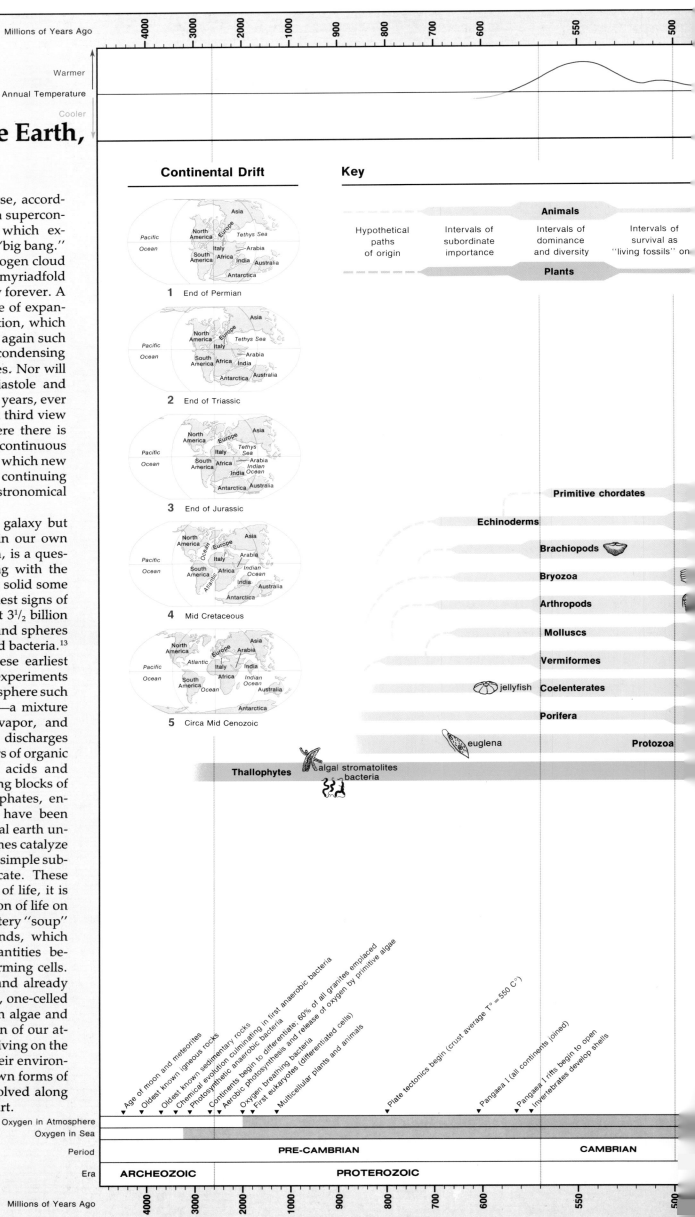

Millions of Years Ago

Present Mean Annual Temperature · Warmer · Cooler

Continental Drift

1 End of Permian
2 End of Triassic
3 End of Jurassic
4 Mid Cretaceous
5 Circa Mid Cenozoic

Key

Animals

Hypothetical paths of origin | Intervals of subordinate importance | Intervals of dominance and diversity | Intervals of survival as "living fossils" on

Plants

Primitive chordates
Echinoderms
Brachiopods
Bryozoa
Arthropods
Molluscs
Vermiformes
jellyfish Coelenterates
Porifera
euglena Protozoa

Thallophytes
algal stromatolites
bacteria

Age of moon and meteorites
Oldest known igneous rocks
Oldest known sedimentary rocks
Chemical evolution culminating in first anaerobic bacteria
Photosynthetic anaerobic bacteria
Continents begin to differentiate; 60% of all granites emplaced
Aerobic photosynthesis and release of oxygen by primitive algae
Oxygen breathing bacteria
First eukaryotes (differentiated cells)
Multicellular plants and animals
Plate tectonics begin (crust average T° = 550 C°)
Pangaea I (all continents joined)
Pangaea I rifts begin to open
Invertebrates develop shells

Oxygen in Atmosphere
Oxygen in Sea

Period: PRE-CAMBRIAN | CAMBRIAN

Era: ARCHEOZOIC | PROTEROZOIC

Millions of Years Ago

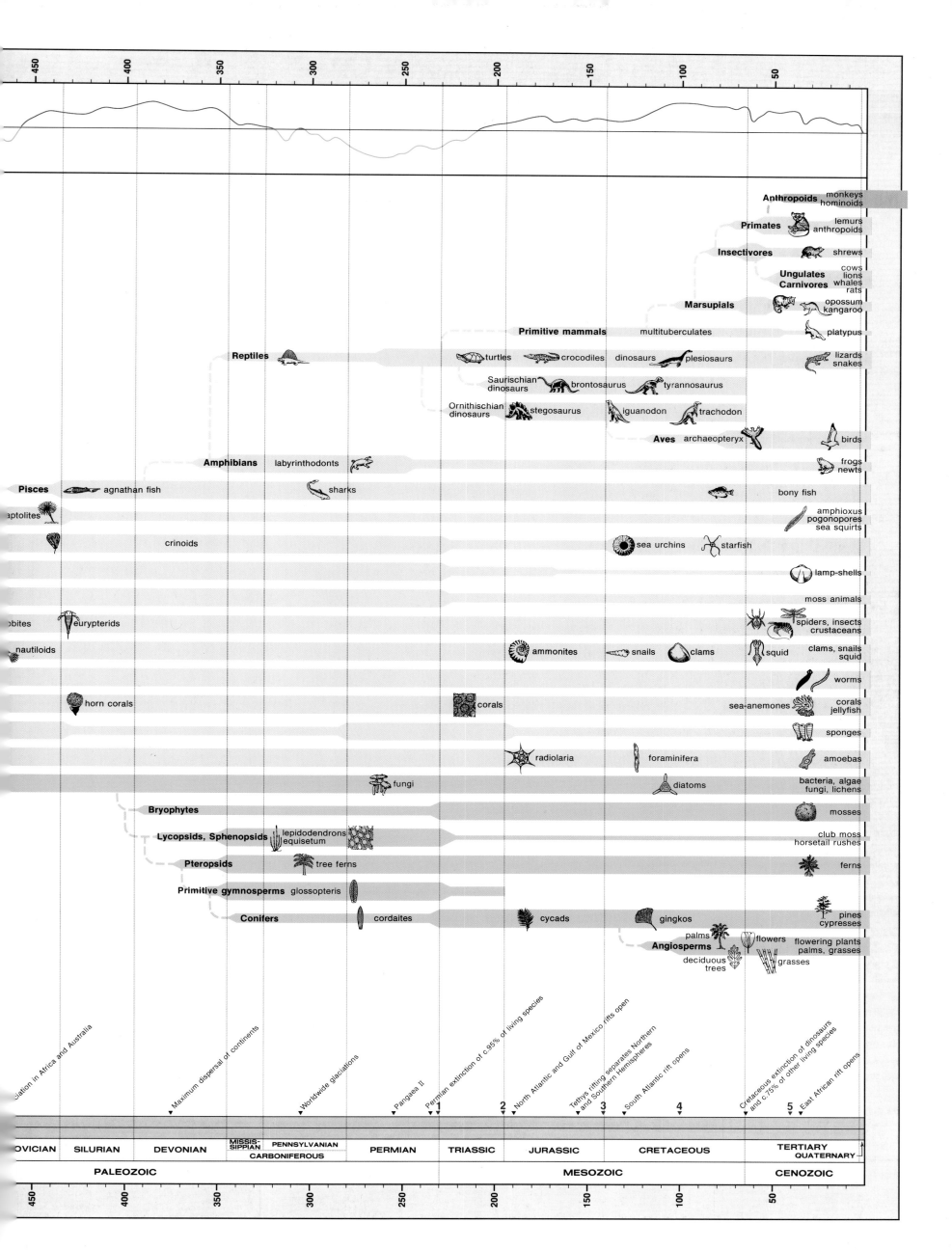

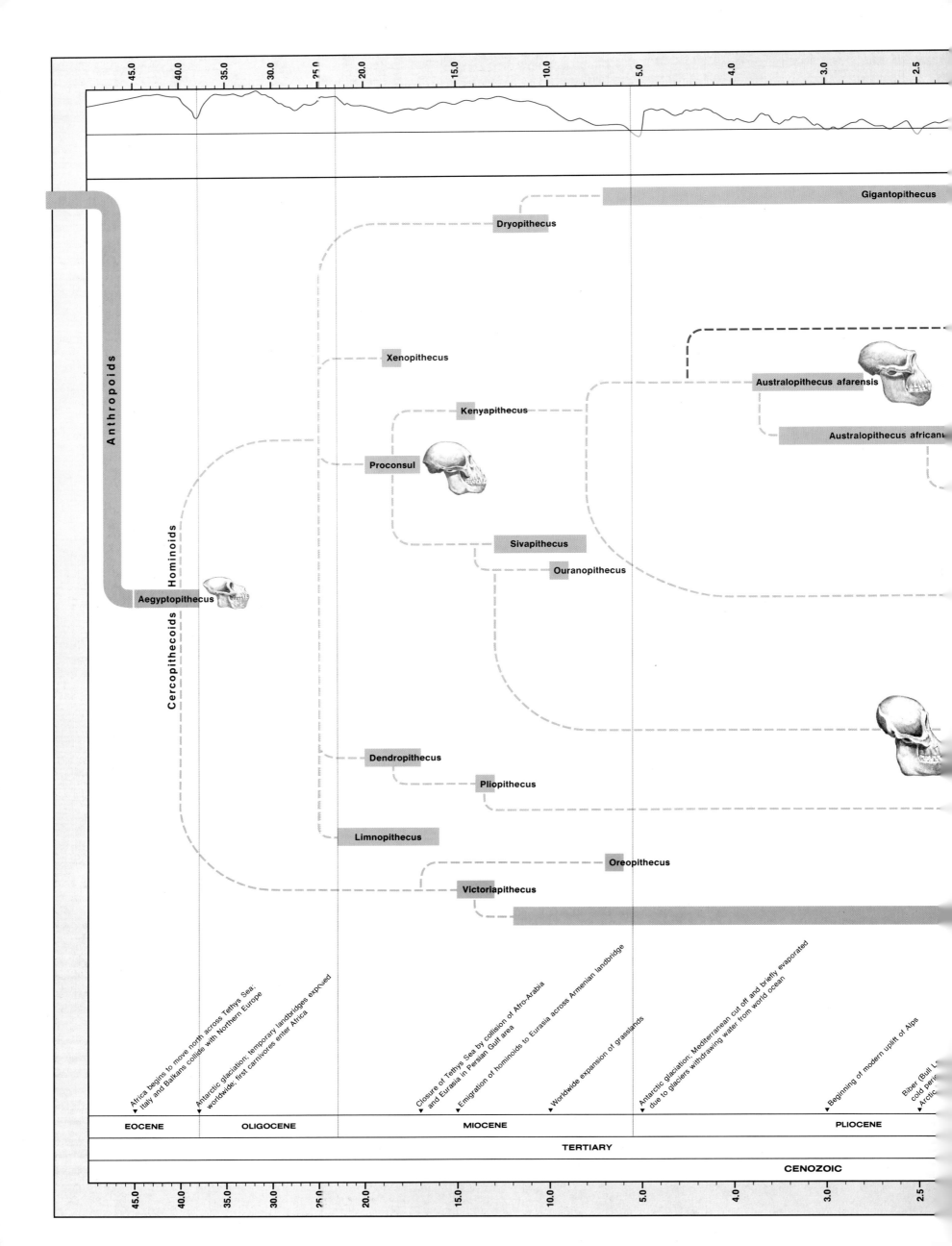

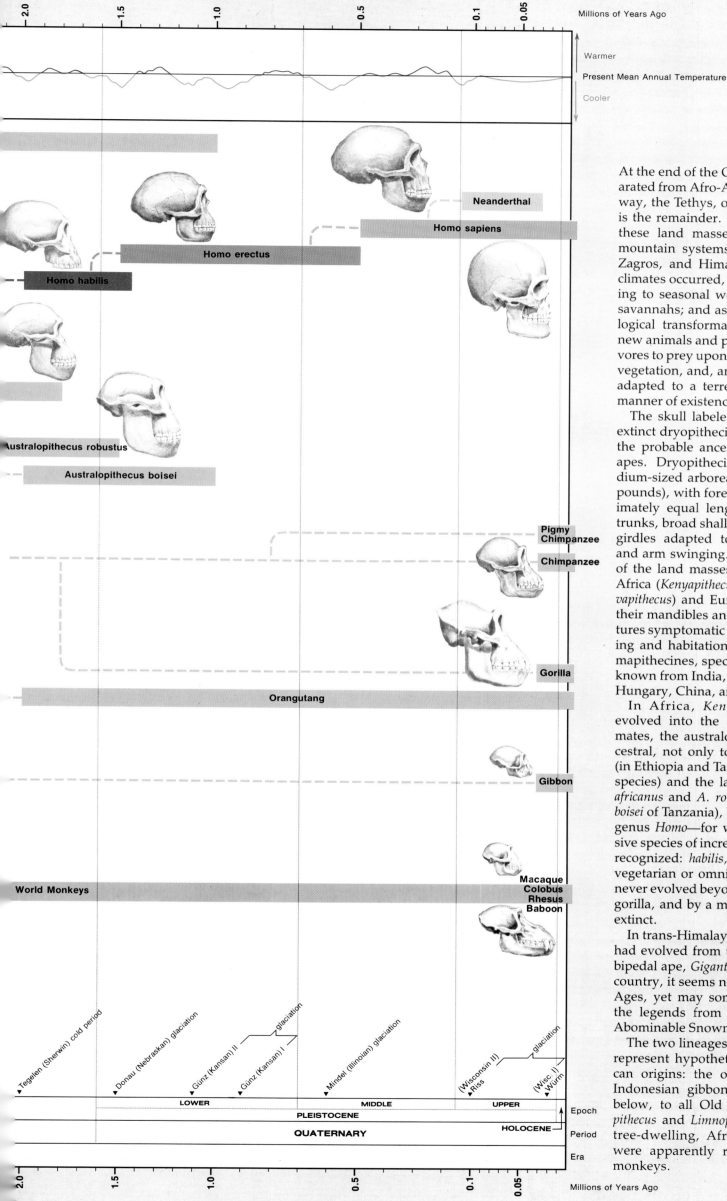

Warmer

Present Mean Annual Temperature

Cooler

Neanderthal

Homo sapiens

Homo erectus

Homo habilis

Australopithecus robustus

Australopithecus boisei

Pigmy Chimpanzee

Chimpanzee

Gorilla

Orangutang

Gibbon

World Monkeys

Macaque
Colobus
Rhesus
Baboon

Tegelen (Sherwin) cold period

Donau (Nebraskan) glaciation

Günz (Kansan) II

Günz (Kansan) I

glaciation

Mindel (Illinoian) glaciation

(Wisconsin II)
Riss

(Wisc. I)
Würm

glaciation

LOWER   MIDDLE   UPPER   Epoch

PLEISTOCENE

QUATERNARY   HOLOCENE   Period

Era

| 2.0 | 1.5 | 1.0 | 0.5 | 0.1 | 0.05 | Millions of Years Ago |

The Primate Connection

At the end of the Oligocene, Eurasia was separated from Afro-Arabia by a west-to-east seaway, the Tethys, of which the Mediterranean is the remainder. During the early Miocene, these land masses drifted together; major mountain systems arose (the Alps, Tauros, Zagros, and Himalayas); later, a cooling of climates occurred, with tropical jungles yielding to seasonal woodlands, grasslands, and savannahs; and as always happens with ecological transformations of such magnitude, new animals and plants appeared, new carnivores to prey upon herbivores adapted to new vegetation, and, among the primates, species adapted to a terrestial, instead of arboreal, manner of existence.[14]

The skull labeled *Proconsul* represents the extinct dryopithecine group now regarded as the probable ancestor of both man and the apes. Dryopithecines were "probably medium-sized arboreal apes (weighing 30 to 50 pounds), with fore- and hindlimbs of approximately equal length, relatively short stout trunks, broad shallow thoraxes, and shoulder girdles adapted to suspensatory posturing and arm swinging."[15] Following the juncture of the land masses, this group spread from Africa (*Kenyapithecus*) to northwest India (*Sivapithecus*) and Europe (*Ouranopithecus*), and their mandibles and teeth began to show features symptomatic of a turn to terrestrial feeding and habitation. Roughly grouped as ramapithecines, specimens of this later kind are known from India, Pakistan, Greece, Austria, Hungary, China, and Kenya.

In Africa, *Kenyapithecus* descendents evolved into the earliest fully bipedal primates, the australopithecines, and were ancestral, not only to *Australopithecus afarensis*, (in Ethiopia and Tanzania, the earliest known species) and the later australopithecines (*A. africanus* and *A. robustus* of South Africa, *A. boisei* of Tanzania), but also to the meat-eating genus *Homo*—for which, then, three successive species of increasing cranial capacities are recognized: *habilis*, *erectus*, and *sapiens*. The vegetarian or omnivorous australopithecines never evolved beyond the cranial capacity of a gorilla, and by a million years ago they were extinct.

In trans-Himalayan Asia, meanwhile, there had evolved from the dryopithecines a large bipedal ape, *Gigantopithecus*; adapted to open country, it seems not to have survived the Ice Ages, yet may somehow be responsible for the legends from that area of the Yeti, or Abominable Snowman.

The two lineages at the bottom of the chart represent hypothetical sequences from African origins: the one above leading to the Indonesian gibbon and siamang, and that below, to all Old World monkeys. *Dendropithecus* and *Limnopithecus* were lightweight, tree-dwelling, African dryopithecines that were apparently replaced by the evolving monkeys.

Men and Tools of the Old Stone Age

HOMO HABILIS   5,000,000(?) to 1,600,000 B.P.*

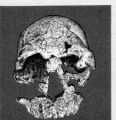

10. *Homo habilis* skull from Lake Turkana site, northern Kenya, c. 2,000,000 B.P. Cranial capacity c. 800 cc. *H. habilis* range: 480 to 800 cc. The earliest known stone tools (from Hadar in Ethiopia) were the work of *H. habilis*.

14. Mankind's earliest stone tools, "pebble tools" and "choppers," first made by *Homo habilis*, 2,750,000 or more B.P., continued in use in China and Southeast Asia to the end of the Paleolithic. Similar tools are today being used in the Philippines by the Tasaday. They are simply water-worn cobbles crudely flaked on one side to form a jagged cutting edge and may be hafted to a stick.

HOMO ERECTUS   1,600,000 to 75,000 B.P.

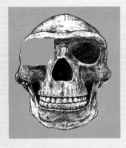

11. *Homo erectus* skull (*Sinanthropus*, "Peking Man"), from Choukoutien, near Peking (Beijing), c. 360,000 B.P. Capacities of four "Peking" skulls: 1015 to 1225 cc. *H. erectus* range: 774 to 1250 cc. One relic, from Vértesszöllös, Hungary: 1400 cc. +.

15. Bifacial hand axes, shaped by thinning down nodules on two faces to form an edge, are of two orders: the Abbevillian (earlier forms) and the Acheulian (more finished). Early specimens of both appeared 750,000 to 430,000 B.P. Though named for the European sites where first found, the industries are well known, with little or no change, in Africa, Northwest India, and the Near East—indicating a broad diffusion of learned skills.

Archaic HOMO SAPIENS   500,000 to 40,000 B.P.

12. *Homo sapiens neanderthalensis* (Neanderthal), from Shanidar, Iraq, 60,000 B.P. Cranial capacity: 1700 cc. Neanderthal ranges: ♀ 1300 to 1425 cc., ♂ 1525 to 1700 cc.; mean heights: ♀ 4 feet 10 inches, ♂ 5 feet 5 inches.

16. Levalloisian flake tools, in contrast to bifacial hand axes, were struck from nuclear cores, then "retouched" to various uses. The Mousterian, flake-tool industry distinguished by fine retouching, originated possibly c. 240,000 B.P., but became associated with *Homo sapiens neanderthalensis*. It is found distributed from western Europe through the Near East. In some areas Levalloisian techniques combined with it to constitute a mixed Levalloiso-Mousterian style, which spread down East Africa to the Cape. In Northwest Africa, a local flake culture, the Aterian, followed the Acheulian.

Modern HOMO SAPIENS   from 40,000 B.P.

13. *Homo sapiens sapiens* (Cro-Magnon Man) from Dordogne, France, c. 20,000 B.P. Cranial capacity: 1580 cc. Fossil-*sapiens* means: ♀ 1370 cc., ♂ 1580 cc.; mean heights: ♀ 5 feet 1 inch, ♂ 5 feet 3 inches to 6 feet.

17. Blade industries first appeared with modern *Homo sapiens*. From prepared cores of obsidian or flint, parallel-sided strips were struck and shaped to specialized uses. Originating in the Near East, the technique spread, both north into Asia and west into Europe, whence, turning south to Northwest Africa in two waves (Mouillian and Capsian), it was carried eastward to the Nilotic zone and southward to the Cape. Blade industries are of many styles and display a spectacular assortment of new tools and hunting weapons of bone, horn, and stone.

*before present

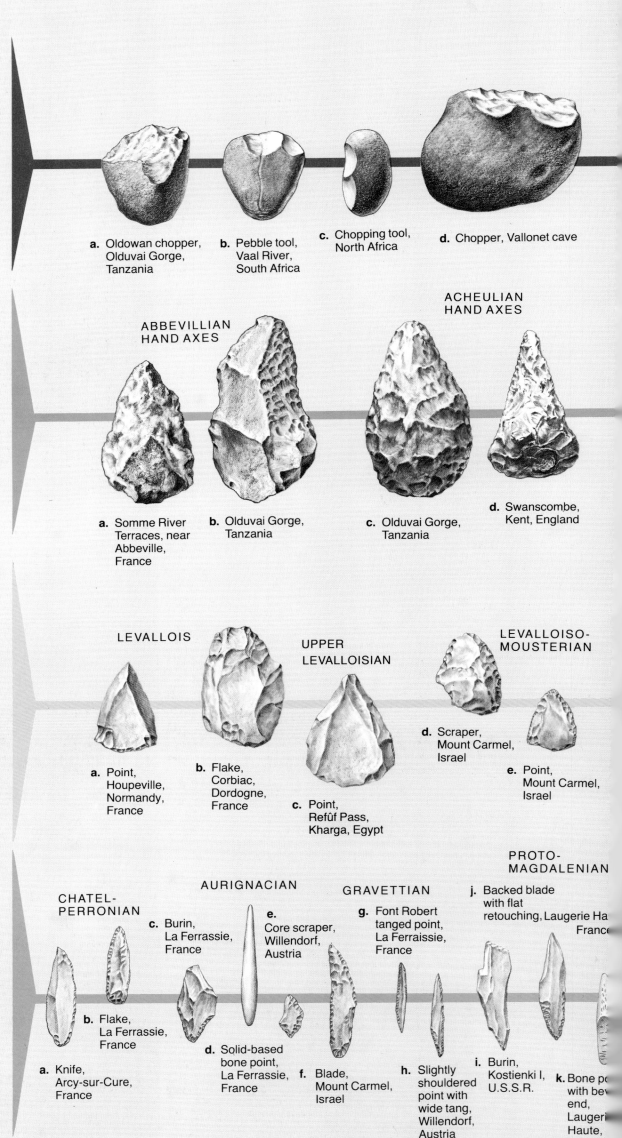

a. Oldowan chopper, Olduvai Gorge, Tanzania
b. Pebble tool, Vaal River, South Africa
c. Chopping tool, North Africa
d. Chopper, Vallonet cave

ABBEVILLIAN HAND AXES
ACHEULIAN HAND AXES

a. Somme River Terraces, near Abbeville, France
b. Olduvai Gorge, Tanzania
c. Olduvai Gorge, Tanzania
d. Swanscombe, Kent, England

LEVALLOIS
UPPER LEVALLOISIAN
LEVALLOISO-MOUSTERIAN

a. Point, Houpeville, Normandy, France
b. Flake, Corbiac, Dordogne, France
c. Point, Refûf Pass, Kharga, Egypt
d. Scraper, Mount Carmel, Israel
e. Point, Mount Carmel, Israel

PROTO-MAGDALENIAN
CHATEL-PERRONIAN
AURIGNACIAN
GRAVETTIAN

a. Knife, Arcy-sur-Cure, France
b. Flake, La Ferrassie, France
c. Burin, La Ferrassie, France
d. Solid-based bone point, La Ferrassie, France
e. Core scraper, Willendorf, Austria
f. Blade, Mount Carmel, Israel
g. Font Robert tanged point, La Ferraissie, France
h. Slightly shouldered point with wide tang, Willendorf, Austria
i. Burin, Kostienki I, U.S.S.R.
j. Backed blade with flat retouching, Laugerie Ha France
k. Bone po with bev end, Laugeri Haute, France

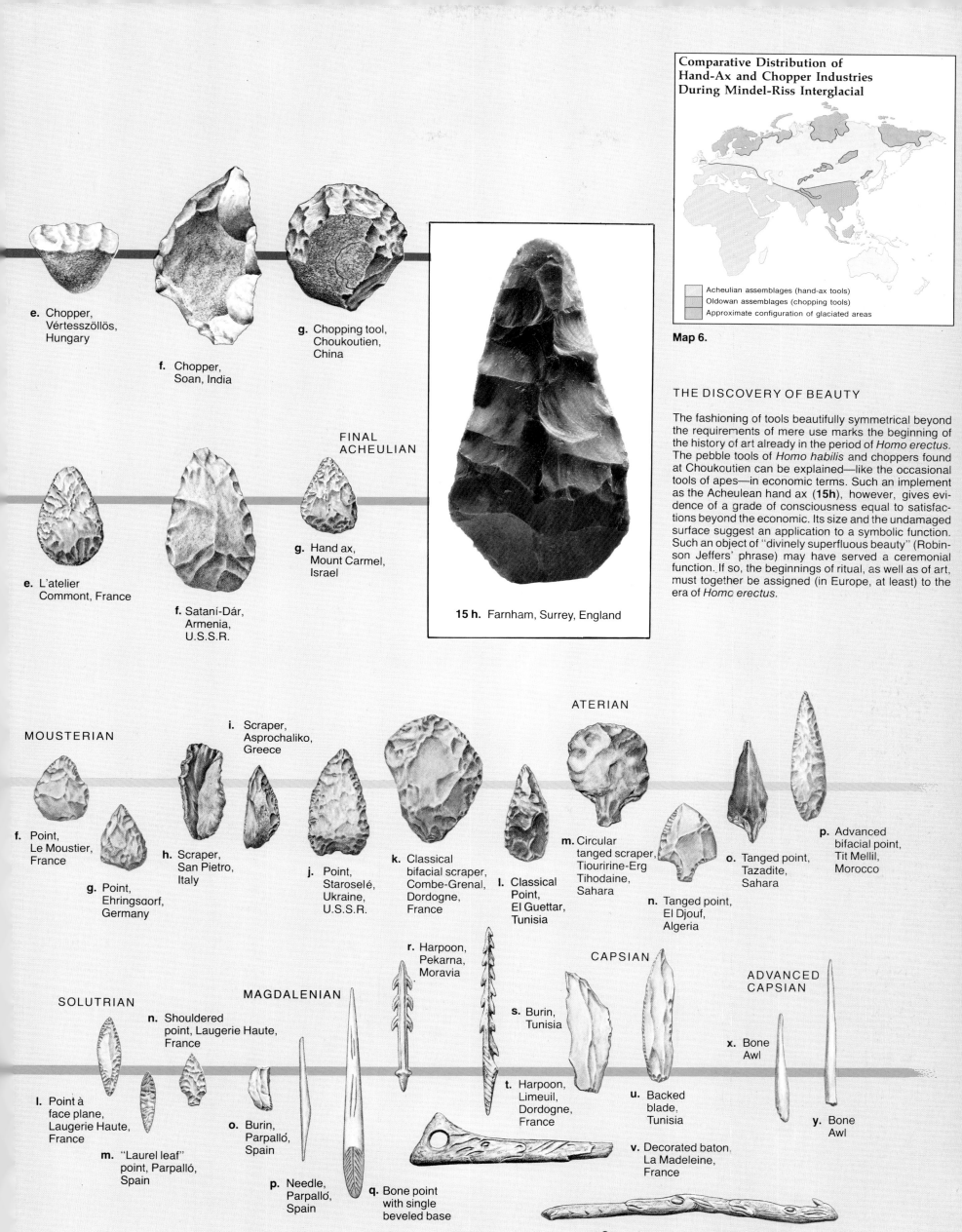

e. Chopper, Vértesszöllös, Hungary

f. Chopper, Soan, India

g. Chopping tool, Choukoutien, China

FINAL ACHEULIAN

e. L'atelier Commont, France

f. Sataní-Dár, Armenia, U.S.S.R.

g. Hand ax, Mount Carmel, Israel

THE DISCOVERY OF BEAUTY

The fashioning of tools beautifully symmetrical beyond the requirements of mere use marks the beginning of the history of art already in the period of *Homo erectus*. The pebble tools of *Homo habilis* and choppers found at Choukoutien can be explained—like the occasional tools of apes—in economic terms. Such an implement as the Acheulean hand ax (**15h**), however, gives evidence of a grade of consciousness equal to satisfactions beyond the economic. Its size and the undamaged surface suggest an application to a symbolic function. Such an object of "divinely superfluous beauty" (Robinson Jeffers' phrase) may have served a ceremonial function. If so, the beginnings of ritual, as well as of art, must together be assigned (in Europe, at least) to the era of *Homo erectus*.

15 h. Farnham, Surrey, England

MOUSTERIAN

f. Point, Le Moustier, France

g. Point, Ehringsdorf, Germany

h. Scraper, San Pietro, Italy

i. Scraper, Asprochaliko, Greece

j. Point, Staroselé, Ukraine, U.S.S.R.

k. Classical bifacial scraper, Combe-Grenal, Dordogne, France

l. Classical Point, El Guettar, Tunisia

ATERIAN

m. Circular tanged scraper, Tiouririne-Erg Tihodaine, Sahara

n. Tanged point, El Djouf, Algeria

o. Tanged point, Tazadite, Sahara

p. Advanced bifacial point, Tit Mellil, Morocco

SOLUTRIAN

l. Point à face plane, Laugerie Haute, France

m. "Laurel leaf" point, Parpalló, Spain

MAGDALENIAN

n. Shouldered point, Laugerie Haute, France

o. Burin, Parpalló, Spain

p. Needle, Parpalló, Spain

q. Bone point with single beveled base

r. Harpoon, Pekarna, Moravia

s. Burin, Tunisia

t. Harpoon, Limeuil, Dordogne, France

CAPSIAN

u. Backed blade, Tunisia

v. Decorated baton, La Madeleine, France

ADVANCED CAPSIAN

x. Bone Awl

y. Bone Awl

w. Spear thrower, La Madeleine, France

THE AWAKENING OF AWE

Man is the only being that knows death;
all others become old, but with a
consciousness wholly limited
to the moment, which must
seem to them eternal.
They see death, not
knowing anything
about it.

OSWALD SPENGLER, *The Decline of the West*

"In a child," says Spengler, continuing this thought, "the awakening of the inner life is often associated with the death of some relation. The child *suddenly* grasps the lifeless corpse for what it is, something that has become wholly matter, wholly space, and at the same moment it feels itself as an individual *being* in an alien extended world." And he quotes Tolstoi to this point: "From the child of five to myself is but a step. But from the new-born baby to the child of five is an appalling distance."[16]

We have to ask: When was it in the long course of the evolution of our genus that this awakening to the knowledge of death set man apart from the beasts and plants? From the moment of life's first appearances, some 3½ billion years ago, in the briny oceans of our planet, the innocence of Eden had prevailed until, at some point in time, the eyes which along the lines of animal life had evolved as agents of the quest for nourishment were opened to a dimension within, beyond, and behind what in India is termed "the sheath of food," the tangible, visible forms of phenomenality. At that instant the consciousness of man fell in two, separated in the awakened mind from the innocence, not only of the beasts without, but also of the beast within, by which the body is shaped, plantlike, in the mother womb, and through which it has maintained itself for millenia by killing, eating, and digesting other living things.

"When a man sought to know how he should live," Natalie Curtis was told by the Pawnee chief Letakots-Lesa, "he went into solitude and cried until in vision some animal brought wisdom to him. It was Tirawa, in truth, who sent his message through the animal. He never spoke to man himself, but gave his command to beast or bird, and this one came to some chosen man and taught him holy things. Thus were the sacred songs and ceremonial dances given the Pawnees through the animals.

"So it was in the beginning."[17]

In the relatively short period of mankind's attempts to reconcile what may be termed our "second mind," that of our knowledge and fear of death, with the "first," that of our animal innocence, there have been stages, the earliest of which was of such animal messengers—encountered both in life and in dream—as those of which Letakots-Lesa told. For the life-structuring force cannot safely be disregarded of that primal tide which for the past 3½ billion years has been evolving forms of ever-increasing complexity and beauty, such as have lately culminated in those "two noble appearances" (as Goethe terms them in his *Morphology of Plants*) of the tree and the human body.

It can only have been at some unrecorded moment in the course of the last 3½ *million* years of these developments that in the human line the crisis occurred of that awakening to the mystery of death, and therewith of life, which—more than any physical transformation—elevated man above the level of the beasts "that live but know nothing of life, and that die and see death," as Spengler remarks, "without knowing anything about it."[18]

The brains of the australopithecines, according to Carleton S. Coon, were "a little larger for their body size than the brains of the living great apes, but not enough larger to indicate, without supplementary evidence, a substantial difference in intelligence. It is unlikely that they could speak."[19] The cranial capacities of the higher apes range from about 325 to 685 cc; those of the australopithecines, from about 435 to 700 cc; and those of *Homo habilis*, from about 643 to 800 cc.[20] But size is not the whole story. What structures of the brain do we find?

Konrad Lorenz makes the point that humans, in contrast to apes, can think beyond an immediate need and use when fashioning a tool. It is one thing to pick up a stick or a stone, or even to shape it to a present end, and quite another to let the stone or stick itself suggest procedures, or to fashion a tool for the fashioning of tools. "When a man goes to work on something," Lorenz writes, "he takes into account, continuously, *during* his performance, the 'responses' of the object, and by these governs the following acts. For example, in driving a nail every blow of the hammer has to be made to compensate for the imperceptible bend given the nail by the stroke before it. . . . Indeed," he adds, "it appears that this very close tie between action and perception, *praxis* and *gnosis*, depends upon the existence of a special central organ, which only man possesses, in the *Gyrus supramarginalis* of the left inferior temporal lobe of the brain. Injury to this part, in which, significantly, the 'speech center' is seated, leads in man, not only to speech disturbances, but also to certain malfunctions in both action and perception, *apraxia* and *agnosia*; and it has not as yet been possible to identify in apes comparable centers or to produce in them any such malfunctions."[21] Richard Leakey reports evidence of the existence of this organ in a *Homo habilis* skull.[22]

We know that *Homo habilis* made tools—"pebble tools" of the simplest kind—and that australopithecines did not. We do not know what *Homo habilis* used them for; nor do we have evidence from his campsites of any ritual practices, amulets, or even ornaments. Leakey believes that his successor in the evolutionary series, *Homo erectus*, had a brain and vocal apparatus that "would have enabled him to speak in a slow and rather 'clumsy' fashion."[23] And indeed, the evidence of *Homo erectus*'s finest tools suggests an order of consciousness approaching the *Homo sapiens* range. However, it is not until the period of Neanderthal Man in Europe, toward the close of the great Ice Ages, during the Riss-Würm interglacial, that the first indubitable signs appear anywhere—namely, in burials of the dead and in reliquary shrines to the animals slain—of that recognition of the *mysterium* which marks the waking of the mythologically inspired "second mind."

18. Neanderthal skull.

25

THE PEOPLING OF THE EARTH

Africa and Eurasia

The first long season of human habitation of the earth was of tribes moving apart, losing contact with each other, entering new territories, and there coming to know as neighbors only the local animals and plants, waters, rocks, valleys and hills, all experienced as living presences with powers and interests of their own. The motherland had been the beautiful high plain of equatorial East Africa, Mount Kenya on the horizon, northward to Ethiopia and southward to the Cape,

19. The high East African plain; in the background, Mt. Kenya, sacred peak of the gods of the Kikuyu tribe, 17,058 feet high.

where, as early as 4 to 5 million years ago, there were at large among the grazing herds an increasing number of manlike/ apelike bipeds: some, in the way of beasts of prey, running down and tearing apart their quadrupedal neighbors; others, vegetarians themselves, wearing down their teeth on gathered roots, nuts, fruits, and leaves.

Among the remains of from 2 to 3 million years ago the crudest possible, deliberately-shaped stone tools begin to appear, fit for the preparation by cutting and pounding of meat and vegetable foods: possibly, also, for the preparation of skins for clothing, blankets, or the coverings of crude shelters.[24] At the Fifth International Congress of Anthropological Sciences, held at the University of Pennsylvania in 1956, the original discoverer of the first australopithecine relic, Raymond Dart of Witwatersrand University, Johannesberg, South Africa, exhibited a series of slides showing what were obviously implements, not of stone, but of bone and of horn: the lower jaws of large antelopes cut in half to be used as saws or knives;

gazelle horns with parts of the skulls attached, showing evident signs of use, possibly as digging tools; australopithecine palates with the teeth worn almost away, as though through constant use as scrapers, as human palates are used today by some of the natives of the area. The most sensational slides, however, were of baboon and australopithecine skulls that had been fractured by the blows of a type of bludgeon having two nubs, or processes, at the hitting end, and, as Dart was able to demonstrate, such dents could have been caused only by the double knob at the upper end of the humulus of an ungulate, the leg bone of a gazelle.[25]

It is now generally agreed that all such primitive implements, whether of stone, of bone, or of horn, were not of the vegetarian bipeds, the australopithecines (*Australopithecus afarensis*, *A. africanus*, *A. boisei*, and such), but of the earliest species of man, "able, handy, or competent man," *Homo habilis*. The australopithecines were the larger breed, up to 150 pounds, about the size of a gorilla, whereas the remains of *Homo habilis* are of a race of hardly 60 pounds, no larger than a pygmy chimpanzee, some 4 to 4½ feet tall. But the cranial capacities of even the largest australopithecines never surpassed 500 cc, the maximum of the largest now-living apes; whereas the capacities of *Homo habilis* skulls range to as high as 800 cc.

"Man," as Spengler has reminded us, "is a beast of prey,"[26] or, as is more usually said, "a hunter." L. S. B. Leakey, who

was the first to unearth and identify a *Homo habilis* relic (at Olduvai, 1960), recognized through a contrast-study of its teeth with those of an australopithecine skull which his wife had discovered the year before (*Zinjanthropus*, known today as *Australopithecus boisei*) that, whereas that other had been a herbivore, his new find was of an omnivore, a meat-eater and hunter. In other words, just as there are, throughout the natural world, among the insects and the fishes, the reptiles and the birds, as well as among mammals, genera shaped to feed on plants and others to feed on the eaters of plants, so at the opening moment of the primate mutation to human rank, two contrasting genera were let loose on the African plain: the one to eat plants and to flee when threatened, the other to pursue, to attack, and to kill. And is it not remarkable, that, although both *Homo habilis* and the australopithecines had forelimbs and hands released from quadrupedal bondage to the earth, it was only the hands of *Homo habilis* that took charge of the pebbles of the earth to break them into tools? Between the instinctive attitude toward the environment of a creature whose body and nervous system are programmed to alarm and flight, and that of one who lives, on the contrary, by stalking and attacking, there is an irreducible contrast. All the eyes, nostrils, and ears of the great herds on the Serengeti Plain of Tanzania today are ever on the alert for the first sight, scent, or signal of the lion at whose roar they will scatter. The lion's eyes are focussed forward. Those of the grazing cattle are at the sides of their heads, to right and to left, on the watch all around, their ears ever turning to catch the first sound, and their nostrils scenting the wind. The broad plain is for them a refuge; for the lion, a banquet table. The attitude of mastery and attack, which in the animal kingdom is the first life-principle of all carnivores, became in the human hunter extended and addressed to the whole environment. Chimpanzees can pick up, hurl, or make use of occasional sticks and stones for immediate purposes, as both Wolfgang Köhler in *The Mentality of Apes* and Jane Goodall in her *In the Shadow of Man* have shown with many examples.[27] Indeed, one of Köhler's capital examples, an especially clever male named Sultan, on finding that he could not reach with his hand a banana placed as bait outside his cage, walked about searchingly, and finally turning to a shoe-

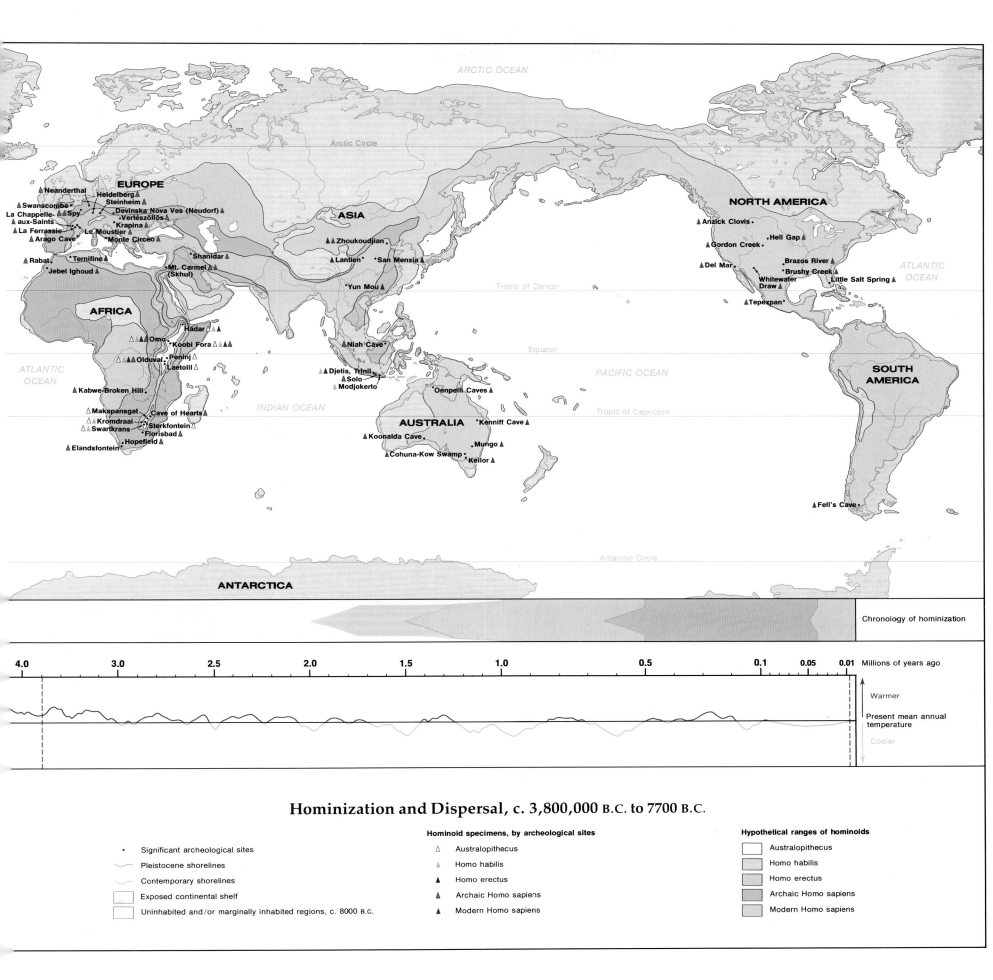

Hominization and Dispersal, c. 3,800,000 B.C. to 7700 B.C.

Chronology of hominization

4.0   3.0   2.5   2.0   1.5   1.0   0.5   0.1   0.05   0.01   Millions of years ago

Warmer

Present mean annual temperature

Cooler

Legend:

- Significant archeological sites
- Pleistocene shorelines
- Contemporary shorelines
- Exposed continental shelf
- Uninhabited and/or marginally inhabited regions, c. 8000 B.C.

Hominoid specimens, by archeological sites

- △ Australopithecus
- ▲ Homo habilis
- ▲ Homo erectus
- ▲ Archaic Homo sapiens
- ▲ Modern Homo sapiens

Hypothetical ranges of hominoids

- Australopithecus
- Homo habilis
- Homo erectus
- Archaic Homo sapiens
- Modern Homo sapiens

Map 7. Chronology of the evolution, and geographic ranges of the global expansion, of the genus *Homo,* to about 7700 B.C., in five stages: (1) from about 3,800,000 B.C., evidences in Africa of Australopithecus (immediate forebear of the genus *Homo);* (2) range of *Homo habilis,* to about 1,250,000 B.C.; (3) extended range of *Homo erectus,* to about 500,000 B.C.; (4) additional extensions by "archaic" *Homo sapiens* (Neanderthal Man in Europe and the Near East; "Solo Man" in Java; and, in Africa, specimens indicated, variously named), to about 40,000 B.C.; and (5) from about 50,000 B.C., occupation of the habitable earth by "modern" *Homo sapiens* (*Homo sapiens sapiens*).

Noteworthy is the coincidence of periods of accelerated evolution with glacial advances (indicated on temperature curve by blue valleys): about 1,500,000 B.C., *Homo habilis* to *Homo erectus* during the Donau–Nebraskan glacial peak; about 600,000 B.C., *Homo erectus* to archaic *Homo sapiens* during the Mindel–Illinoian peak; and about 50,000 B.C., archaic to modern *Homo sapiens* during the Riss–Würm–Wisconsin peak. The double naming of each glacial period correlates standard Old and New World glacial nomenclature. Map and scale after data provided by John A. Van Couvering of the American Museum of Natural History on evidence available March, 1983.

scraper made of iron bars in a wooden frame, worked at it until he had pulled out one of the bars, and with this then made for the object of his zeal to draw it to within reach.[28] A female ape named Chica, chasing another in a mock fight, saw a stone, stopped to pick it up, and when it did not immediately come away, scratched and dragged until it broke loose, then resumed the chase and flung the stone at her playmate.[29] We can perhaps credit as much to the australopithecines. But such an object, employed briefly as a tool and dropped, is not properly comparable to even the crudest industry of stones intentionally shaped for repeated use, which, moreover, in the

20. Fragments, possibly 4 million years old, of an australopithecine skull and femur discovered, 1981, in the valley of the Awash River in Ethiopia. We are here very close to the moment of separation of the hominid line of descent from that of the African pongidae, or apes.

hands of *Homo habilis* represented the first condition of a hominid technology that, without interruption through the next 2 million years, was to advance and expand to an age of rockets to the moon, computerized information banks, and oil drills 20,000 feet into the earth. "Technology," as Spengler perceived, "is the very strategy of life: the essential form of action in

21. This famous skull of an australopithecine child (*Australopithecus africanus*)—found in Taung, South Africa, in 1924—was one of the first recognized australopithecine discoveries. Its milk dentition is complete and the upper and lower first permanent molars are in process of eruption. The dating is disputed, ranging from 3 to 0.87 million years ago.

the battle that is life itself."[30] And in the history of the genus *Homo*, which made its first appearance as the little beast of prey, *Homo habilis*, the peculiar form of

action was of the indirect attack, not immediately on the intended aim, but mediately, through the fashioning of a tool.

No relics of *Australopithecus* have been found outside of Africa, and by 1.4 million years ago the genus was extinct. Remains identified as probably of *Homo habilis*, on the other hand, possibly from as early as 3 to 4 million years ago, have been recognized as far afield as Java,[31] the evident implication being that, already in its earliest years, the species *Homo habilis* enlarged its range to include not only Africa, but the entire Old-World equatorial belt.

22. An adult skull of *Australopithecus boisei*, formerly called *Zinjanthropus*. Discovered, 1959, in the Olduvai Gorge of Tanzania, c.1.8 million years old.

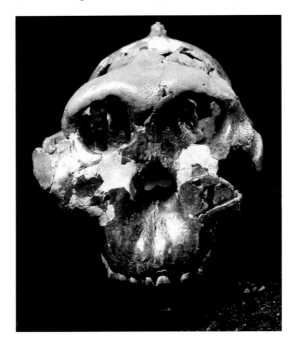

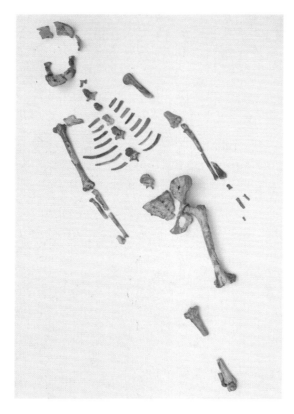

23. The possessor of this little female skeleton walked fully erect, 4 feet tall, some 3.5 million years ago in the Hadar region of Ethiopia. Of the species *Australopithecus afarensis*, which some regard as ancestral to all the later hominids, she is known affectionately as Lucy, was discovered in 1974, and can be thought of by those still interested in coordinating science and the Bible as the great-great-great-great grandmother of Eve.

24. Classified as *Homo habilis*, yet more than 2.8 million years old, this earliest relic ancestral to mankind, known simply as "skull number 1470," was unearthed in 1972 at Lake Turkana in northern Kenya.

Homo habilis disappeared with the glacial advances of the first Ice Age, when even in equatorial Africa the snow line descended to below 9000 feet and misty, cold, cloud-saturated forests spread from the highlands to all but a few protected enclaves on the coastal plains. By the time the clouds had lifted and the chill receded, members of the second human species, *Homo erectus*, were encamped on the shores of Lake Turkana (in Kenya), where formerly *Homo habilis* had lived alongside the last of the australopithecines. Indeed, by that time, other members of this second species had already spread, not only along the earlier way

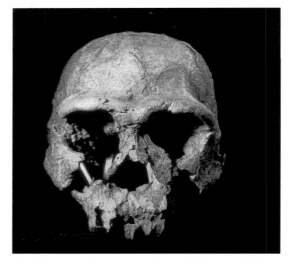

25. The prominent brow ridges of this typical *Homo erectus* skull (from China, c. 700,000 B.C.?) are characteristic over the whole domain and throughout the more than million years of the unknown history of this Glacial-Age pre-*sapiens* race.

to Java, but also north into both China and southern Europe.

The season of *Homo erectus* endured for nearly a million years—a longer stretch of time than that between its close (at the peak of the Mindel glaciation) and today. Furthermore, it was during that long season that the differentiation of Paleolithic industries (illustrated in Map 6, page 23) occurred, the eastern races continuing with pebble and chopper tools (complemented, no doubt, by implements of bamboo and other perishable materials), while in the west the hand ax came into use. Invented in Africa about a million years ago, the manufacture of this versatile bifacial core-tool spread both north into Europe and eastward into India, beyond which it never passed. In its earlier, cruder forms (called Abbevillean), and in the later, more craftsmanly (Acheulean), it remained the principal stone implement of western Paleolithic mankind until about the middle of the Riss-Würm glacial age, when the Mousterian flake technique was introduced.

Cranial Capacity and Tool Manufacture

The apparent relationship of the quality of stone-tool manufacture to cranial capacity is interesting. Cranial variations are considerable, of course, over the wide range and during the long season of the second species of our genus. The earliest African, Lake Turkana specimens (twenty or more at last count), dating from c. 1.6 to 1.3 million years ago, are of volumes around 900 cc, while from nearby Olduvai (Bed II), c. 1.2 million years ago, a specimen known as Chellean-3 Man has turned up, which already registers 1150 cc. Java Man (the original *Pithecanthropus erectus*, Figure 39, page 34), now dated to c. 1 million years ago, had a cranial capacity still at the 900 cc level, and Peking Man (*Homo erectus sinensis*, known also as *Sinanthropus*), who is represented by six skulls from c. 700,000 years ago, shows a range from 780 to 1225 cc, with a mean of 1020 cc; whereas, from eastern Europe, at that time, from Vértesszöllös (near Budapest), we have an occipital fragment judged to represent a cranial capacity exceeding 1400 cc.

We are here at the brink or threshold of the evolutionary transit from *Homo erectus* to "archaic" *Homo sapiens* and the large hand ax of Figure 15h (page 23), from the banks of the river Thames, testifies to the quality of mind, as well as to the skill of hand, of the inhabitants of that region at that time. It is a consummate example of the Acheulean bifaced hand ax. The only known relevant cranial specimens—besides the extraordinary Vértesszöllös fragment of c. 700,000 years ago—are two female skulls: one from Steinheim (near Stuttgart), of around 1175 cc; the other from Swanscombe (Kent, above Gravesend, unearthed near the Thames), around 1325 cc. The dates given for these two specimens range from c. 300,000 to c. 150,000 years ago.

Outside of Europe, comparable volumes at such dates have been identified only in Africa and Java; notably: at Jebel Ighoud (Morocco), an undated skull of 1480 cc; from the Omo River (Ethiopia), a cranial vault of roughly 130,000 years ago

and about 1435 cc; from Kabwe (Broken Hill) in Zambia (Northern Rhodesia), 125,000 years ago (formerly dated 40,000), a much-studied skull, now in the British Museum, of 1280 cc; and from Elandsfontein (Hopefield, South Africa), a cranial vault of uncertain age, 1200 to 1250 cc. The Javanese examples are eleven mutilated skulls, placed by some authorities at 500,000 years ago and by others at about 40,000, which were found together at Ngandong, a site on the Solo River, and have been variously classified either as *Homo erectus* or as *Homo sapiens*, their volumes ranging from 1035 to 1255 cc.

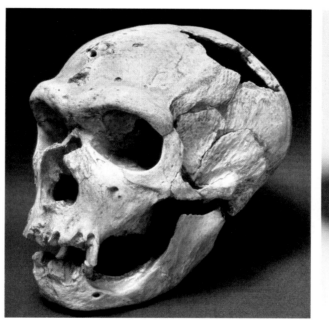

The appearance in northern Europe of the Mousterian flake technique during the middle of the Riss-Würm glacial age was directly associated with the appearance in that frigid region at that time of *Homo sapiens neanderthalensis*—a physically prodigiously powerful, local archaic *sapiens* race, which entered the prehistoric scene about 150,000 years ago. The cranial capacities of this distinctive race ranged from c. 1400 to 1600 cc; and since the average range of European man today is from 1450 to 1500 cc, it is evident that *Homo sapiens neanderthalensis* could not have been the half-brained ape-man of popular belief. Indeed, it now seems to have been in some province within the range of his dominion that the next major advance of the genus *Homo* occurred, namely, to the status of *Homo sapiens sapiens*.

A Locus for Eden

The question is still under debate, but the evidence is accumulating in favor of northeast Africa and the Near East as the critical area of what David Pilbeam has described as the likely "Garden of Eden" out of which "modern" *Homo sapiens* went forth between 50,000 and 30,000 years ago and "through a process of swamping and replacing older and more archaic subspe-

cies of *Homo sapiens* . . . inherited the earth."[32]

A number of notable finds have been lately made that seem to have about settled the argument. Their datings fall between 60,000 and 40,000 years ago. The racial affinities are Neanderthaloid, and the tool kits, Mousteroid. The most interesting is the male skeleton of the now-famous "suttee and flower burial" at Shanidar in northern Iraq, which is discussed on page 53. The date is c. 60,000 years ago, which marks it as one of the earliest ceremonial burials on record. Two other important specimens are from sites

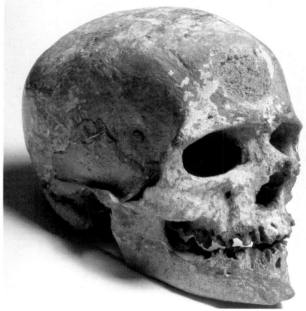

26. Neanderthal Man, *Homo sapiens neanderthalensis*, now known also as "archaic" *Homo sapiens*, is here represented in a skull from the last phase of his hundred-thousand-year existence. Taken from the cave burial at La Chapelle-aux-Saints (described on page 51), it has been roughly dated c. 45,000 to 35,000 B.C.

27. *Homo sapiens sapiens*, fully modern paleolithic man (with a brain capacity, however, somewhat larger than that of fully modern twentieth-century man) is supremely represented by the artists of the great Cro-Magnon caves of southern France and northern Spain. This noble skull from the Dordogne, c. 40,000 B.C., is of the same terminal glacial period as the "archaic"-*sapiens* skull of Figure 26.

at Mount Carmel, Israel, which have been variously dated betweeen 47,000 and 40,000 years ago: the earlier, from Mugharet et Tabun, a skull with a capacity of 1271 cc, and the later, from Mugharet et Skhul, a skull of from 1450 to 1518 cc.

The argued implications are that it was here, in the Near East, in the period of the Riss-Würm interglacial, that the evolutionary passage was accomplished from archaic *sapiens* rank to modern; and along with this, a dramatic advance in technology from the Mousteroid flake to the Aurignacoid blade tool technology. The cranial capacities, then, of those earliest representatives of our own proud stage of the evolutionary course, as typified in Cro-Magnon Man (the artist of the great Paleolithic painted caves of southern France and northern Spain), was between 1500 and 1800 cc.

Old Melanesia

In the period of the entry of Cro-Magnon Man into Europe, at the height of the Würm glaciation, so much of the earth's water was locked in ice that the ocean levels were from 200 to 400 feet lower than today, and lands now under wave were high and dry. Animals and their hunters passed from Siberia to Alaska across a landbridge as broad as the nation of France (see Maps 9 to 12, pages 34–35), while in the south the Asian mainland was joined by the exposed continental Sunda shelf to what are now the separate islands of Hainan, Borneo, Sumatra, Java, and Bali (see Map 8). Beyond Bali the ocean floor drops abruptly; but beyond this break (known as the Wallace line, or Wallacea) there is another shallow called the Sahul shelf, by which New Guinea was at that time joined to the augmented continent of Australia, with land where there is now the Great Barrier Reef and in the south a landbridge to Tasmania.

Thus, wherever the homeland—the Garden of Eden—may have been of *Homo sapiens sapiens*, it is at least evident that already before the end of the last Ice Age, members of this fourth species of the genus *Homo* were moving, not only out of the Near East into Europe, but also, at the other two extremities of the Asian continent, across Beringland into Alaska, and across Sundaland to the Wallacean brink, there to gaze across shark-infested waters toward the appealing islands beyond.

The earliest tangible evidence of the presence in Sundaland of a modern *Homo sapiens* population is in the form of a shattered skull that was unearthed in 1959 from a depth of 8 feet 4 inches beneath the floor of the great Niah Cave in Sarawak, Borneo (Figure 32 and Map 8). Radiocarbon dated to 37,600 ± 1000 B.C., below it were culture-bearing deposits going back to at least 50,000 B.C. Chopping tools and coarse flakes were the characteristic artifacts all the way down, suggesting, as William Howells, Curator of Somatology at the Peabody Museum, Harvard, has remarked, that in this part of the world, "wood was the real basis of implements and weapons, the stone flakes serving only to scrape and sharpen wood javelins, or bamboo points to be hafted with thongs, or digging sticks, and so on. If we remember," he continues, "the simple but dangerous javelins of the Tasmanians; the copious use by Australian aboriginals of equally simple spears, as well as completely barbed ones, made entirely of wood; similar things in recent Melanesia;

Map 8.

and the bamboo-pointed arrows of some Negrito groups in the Philippines, then the idea is appealing."[33]

The racial type of the Niah skull is recognized by both Carleton Coon and Howells as suggesting the modern Tasmanian Negrito.[34] In a related find, in the Tabon Cave on the western shore of the Philippine island of Pelawan (see Map 8), there were unearthed in 1966 a frontal bone and an almost toothless jaw, likewise of Negrito or Tasmanian type; and although their dating is c. 20,000 B.C., these remains were associated with the same crude type of chopping tool as had been found with the Niah skull of a date 20,000 years earlier. Howells has named the remarkably conservative Old Stone Age assemblage represented in these two related finds, the Old Melanesian Culture, with a dating from c. 50,000 to between 8000 and 5000 B.C.—by which time the seas, augmented by the melting of the glaciers, had risen to their present levels; so that, not only had Sundaland dissolved

into the Indonesian archipelago, but the continent of Sahulland had separated into Australia, Tasmania, and New Guinea.

Then in 1971, still another 20,000 years after the period of the Tabon skull, in a high mountain jungle on the neighboring Philippine island of Mindanao, there were discovered the now-famous "gentle Tasaday," still using the same Stone Age tools and, as reported, "wearing only orchid-leaf g-strings when they appeared at the mouth of their cave." In the words of the leader of the discovering expedition, "It was almost unbelievable—a shock—like suddenly going back into time thousands of years."[35]

Indeed, no more spectacular demonstration of the conservatism of an Old Stone Age people could have been desired. "Our fathers and grandfathers told us," said a Tasaday male about twenty years old, "that we could go out into the forest in daytime, but must always return to the caves at night."[36] And the words ring true: one hears their like in every part

of the primitive world, where the ancestors of an imagined past are revered as having established, once and for all, the norms and forms for life in a timeless present. Any change in the ways of life, or even in the shape of a tool is fraught with danger. The Tasaday were food gatherers, not hunters, surviving on palm piths and various flowers and fruits foraged from their mountain. They declared that they loved their place in the forest and never wanted to leave. "They are extremely gentle," was the finding of the first report, "and move through the jungle with what to outsiders is extraordinary ease—leaping from tree to tree, sliding down vines, bounding down grassy trails." In other parts of the same high mountain retreat, some 4000 feet above sea level, there were other, more numerous, and more advanced peoples, practicing horticulture. Nevertheless, this little cluster of old-timers, no more than twenty-four individuals when discovered, had held onto the ways, not only of their fathers and grandfathers, but also of their ancestors back for at least 50,000 years.

The Fossilized Past

One of the most interesting features of the richly fascinating lands and islands now remaining above water of the once-united

28/29. The "gentle Tasaday," discovered in 1971 still dwelling in their ancestral caves, readily fashioned whatever stone tools they required from pebbles taken from a nearby stream, some of which were fixed with rattan wrappings to crude handles.

30. Examples of an advanced pebble tool industry, dating possibly as early as 15,000 B.C., from Kenniff Cave, Queensland, Australia (see Map 8).

31

The fossils of this region reveal abrupt population changes through the greatest reaches of time. That there were already pre-*sapiens* inhabitants of Java we know from specimens recently found there of *Homo habilis*, 3 to 4 million years ago, as well as from the nineteenth-century finds of Java Man *(Pithecanthropus erectus)*, who is now thought to have lived 2 million years ago (Figure 39, page 34).

31. A composite reconstruction of the skull of a people on the *H. erectus/sapiens* cusp as represented in a cluster of eleven skulls uncovered at Ngandong on the Solo River (see Map 8), which are now dated to c. 500,000 years ago—the period of the Vértesszöllös, Swanscombe, and Steinheim skulls of Europe (see page 29). The Solo-skull cranial volumes range from 1035 to 1255 cc.

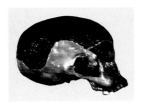

32. The earliest *H. sapiens* relic yet unearthed in Old Melanesia is the skull "of a youth," to quote Carleton C. Coon, "between fifteen and seventeen years old, probably female, definitely *sapiens*, and equally definitely Australoid."[2] It was found in 1959 in pieces beneath the floor of the huge Niah Cave in Sarawak on the northwest coast of Borneo (see Map 8). The reconstructed skull, according to Coon's judgment, most closely resembles the skulls of the (recently extinct) aborigines of Tasmania. The cranial capacity is undetermined. Its date, between 38,600 and 36,600 B.C., exactly matches that of Cro-Magnon Man's appearance in Europe.

33. From a site at the opposite, southern extreme of the Old Melanesian subcontinent, at Keilor, Victoria, Australia, in the valley of the Marybyrnong River, (see Map 8), a skull, likewise of Tasmanian Negrito type, variously dated as of 13,000 B.C. or of 11,000 B.C., testifies to the presence throughout the area for a season of some 30,000 years of a people ancestral to the aborigines of both Tasmania and New Guinea. The cranial capacity of this specimen is variously estimated at 1464 to 1593 cc.

34. A very different skull, from the Cohuna-Kow Swamp which is also in Victoria (see Map 8), shows a sloping forehead, prominent brow (reminiscent of the Solo skulls), and extreme prognathism. The cranial capacity is 1450 cc.; the date, c. 7000 B.C.; and the racial type, Australian.

world of Old Melanesia is their harborage, here and there, not only of living peoples, such as the Tasaday, who have carried into the present ancestral forms dating from Old Stone Age times, but also, in the same territories, the bones and tools of those very ancestors who first brought the preserved forms from elsewhere to these parts of the earth.

Judging from the findings in the Niah Cave, Howells dates the arrival of *Homo sapiens* in old Sundaland to 38,000 B.C. at the latest, and estimates that the crossing, then, of the deep-water trench beyond Bali into Sahulland—by way of Lombok, Sumbawa, Sumba, and Timor—must have occurred no later than 30,000 B.C.; and the findings of human remains at two very early sites in southernmost Australia support him in this judgment. The first, at a place called Keilor, in the valley of the Marybyrnong River, yielded for a scattering of crude stone tools the somewhat questionable date of c. 70,000 B.C., and for a second deposit, on a later level, the less questionable date of c. 30,000 B.C. After which there followed two skulls, an earlier, classed as Tasmanian, c. 13,000 B.C.(Figure 33) and a later, strikingly similar to the first, of c. 4500 B.C.[37]

At the second of these early sites, on the Lake Mungo plain east of Darling in New South Wales, there were found not only fire hearths from 30,000 to 22,000 B.C., but also a cremated skeleton of c. 14,000 B.C., the charred bones and skull of which had been buried in a shallow depression in a way still practiced by Tasmanians until their extinction in the middle of the nineteenth century.[38]

From a number of other finds of roughly comparable age, one in eastern New Guinea and the others in various, widely separated parts of Australia, crude pebble, flake, and chopper-type tools have been found that bear testimony to the same general order of culture for old Sahulland that we have already seen represented, not only in the Sundaland caves, but also in the hands of the living Tasaday. The date for the New Guinea site, known as Kosipe, high in the Papuan Highlands (see Map 8), is c. 25,000 B.C. Representative Australian stations are the Koonalda Cave on the Nullarbor Plain and the Burrill Lake Cave near Sydney, the Kenniff Cave in Queensland, and the Oenpelli Caves in Arnhem Land (all to be found on Map 8). Judging from the evidence of the uniformly Tasmanian character of the Mungo and Keilor skeletal finds, and comparing these with the physical traits of the modern aborigines of both New Guinea and Tasmania, Howells and others have concluded that the first inhabitants of Old Melanesia must have been of this racial strain.[39]

But then, from a date of c. 10,000 B.C.—when the seas had mounted and Old Mel-

anesia had been drowned—there appeared on the continent of Australia a new people, whose skeletal remains, from two widely separate stations, are clearly different from those of the earlier, Keilor-Mungo, Tasmanoid race, and more like the modern Australian. From Talgai, west of Brisbane, came the first of these finds: the flattish, heavily constructed cranium of a youth with a cranial capacity of about 1300 cc, which is hardly greater than that of a Solo skull, and with a large palate showing a straight line of front teeth, in the way of a pithecanthropoid jaw.[40] A second skull of the kind was unearthed in 1925 at the Cohuna-Kow Swamp in Victoria. (See site on Map 8 and Figure 34.) Since then a researching team in the area has uncovered no less than forty burials in which the specimens, according to the reports of their discoverers, are all clearly different in structure from the Keilor and Mungo skulls, and of

35. Australian, hurling a javelin with the aid of an atlatl, or spear-thrower: an instrument already in use during the Late Stone Age of Europe, Magdalenian period, c. 15,000 B.C.

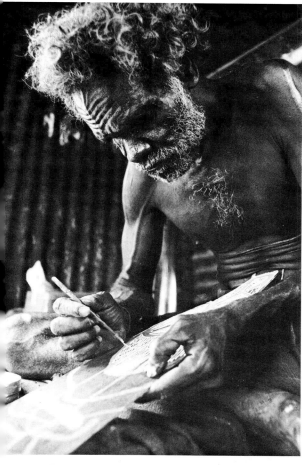

36. Bark painter, Arnhem Land, Australia, rendering a legendary design.

37. Arnhem Land bark painting, showing an imagined scene from the mythical isle, Bralku, to which souls go after death. Two spirits are welcoming an arrival. A fire has been lighted and four snakes are to be cooked in celebration. Two dingos attend. Jabirus and spoonbills dance.

radiocarbon datings between 8000 and 6000 B.C.[41] Howells suggests that a company of late Tasmanian-like immigrants may have mixed with a strain of Solo descendants and so produced this subrace, which then became the dominant people of Australia.

In any case, no matter what the genealogical backgrounds of these Talgai-Cohuna people may have been, Tasmania had already been populated by tribes of the earlier Keilor-Mungo race. So also had New Guinea. And when, then, with the rising of the waters, Sahulland became separated into three distinct islands, the Tasmanians were cut off with no more than the primitive equipment of that time, only pointed wooden javelins, no hafted tools, no stone-tipped spears, no spear throwers or boomerangs, no dogs and, worst of all, no boats. They could only collect shellfish humbly along the shores, not even venturing to catch fish.

In Australia, however, after a dateline of c. 5000 B.C., a variety of dog, the dingo, appeared, of which the closest known relative is an Indian wolf; and simultaneously came spear throwers, boomerangs and shields, fine pressure flaking, unifacial and bifacial points, microliths, and blades. Notable sites of these later industries are at Devon Downs and Fromm's Landing, both on the Murray River, while at Kenniff Cave and the Tombs Shelter, in Queensland, stenciled hands and other painted motifs are to be seen, depicting the use of boomerangs, spear throwers, and shields.[42]

There can be no doubt that this whole new industry had arrived from elsewhere, probably from India, because, as Howells has remarked, "only God can make a dingo." To which, then, the question arises as to why the practice of horticulture, which in due time became of such importance in New Guinea and throughout the island world of New Melanesia, never put down a single taproot in Australia. Westward, in the neighboring islands of Indonesia which had been left above the waters when Sundaland submerged, not only horticulture after 8000 B.C., but also full rice culture (after 5000 B.C.) were practiced, along with significant developments in the seafaring arts. A new people of Mongolian race, with a developing civilization from the north, was at that time moving down massively into those islands; and yet, in Australia, as though in a museum, the arts and ways of the "fathers and grandfathers" of an epi-Paleolithic hunting age have remained preserved to the present day.

38. Acheulean hand ax representative of the lithic industry of *Homo erectus*, the species of the genus *Homo* first to emigrate into Europe and East Asia. **39.** W. K. Gregory reconstructed this *H. erectus* head based on studies of the skullcap and molars of *Pithecanthropus erectus* found at Trinil, Java, in 1891 (see page 29).

40. Early Mousterian tools of *Homo sapiens neanderthalensis*. One facet of a core, prepared by flaking, was struck off so that one side of the tool was flat. **41.** W.K. Gregory' reconstruction of Neanderthal Man, based on the origina skull cap from Neanderthal (1856) and that of 1908 from La Chapelle-aux-Saints (**26** on page 29).

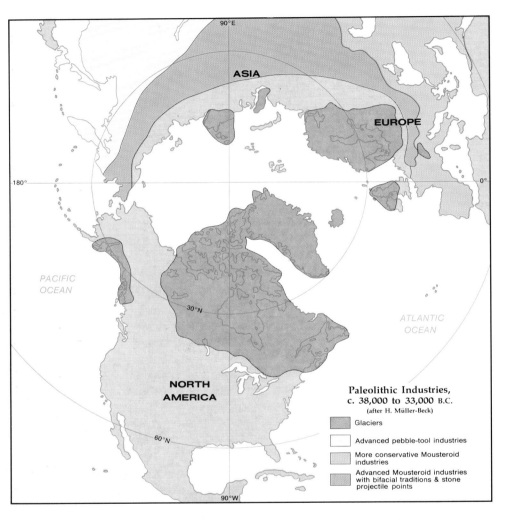

Map 9. Whereas the Eastern peoples held to pebble tools, those in the West advanced to the hand ax. By c. 38,000 B.C., the Mousteroid industry—which had appeared with Neanderthal Man, c. 150,000 B.C.—had been not only enriched and improved, but also carried across the whole of circumpolar Eurasia. When increasing cold once again enlarged the glaciers, impounding water and lowering the sea level to expose the Bering landbridge, a way was opened to the New World.

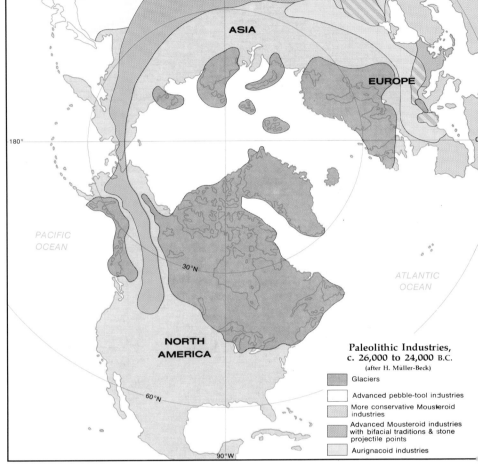

Map 10. Whether archaic *Homo sapiens* entered the Americas is still a question. Since, as geologist William G. Haag notes, animals moved freely across the landbridge during the entire last glaciation, Asiatic man would almost certainly have followed. "Archaeologists need not be too surprised in the future," he suggests, "to discover evidence of man here and there in North America 50,000 years old or even older."[3] The earliest generally recognized possibility is that shown above.

The Americas

The datings of the earliest migrations out of northeast Asia into America roughly match those out of the southeast into Old Melanesia; for, as the ocean levels fell and rose, the landbridges became exposed and submerged. Whereas the stone tools of the southeast were of the old pebble, flake, and chopper types, however, those carried to America were, *first*, of an advanced Mousteroid development and *then*, from c. 8000 B.C., Aurignacoid. Hansjürgen Müller-Beck's schematic maps (above) illustrate the conditions, first, before the appearance of the landbridge;

next, from c. 26,000 to c. 24,000 B.C., when there was an open way across Beringland; third, c. 18,000 B.C., when the open way was closed by advancing ice of the Wisconsin glaciation, after which there developed in isolated America from the given Mousteroid base a number of distinctive "Llano industries" (notably, Sandia, Clovis, and Folsom); and then finally, from 10,000 B.C., when the passage again opened and there entered waves of advanced hunting tribes equipped with Aurignacoid blade tools, burins, and harpoons.

During the late 1960s and early 1970s, Richard S. MacNeish, director of the Robert S. Peabody Foundation for Archaeology, excavating in the large Pikimachay Cave near Ayacucho in highland Peru

(see Map 13, page 37), identified a series of cultural strata going back to at least 20,000 B.C. Pikimachay is a rock shelter more than 50 yards long and 25 yards deep. Beneath its floor the first deposits unearthed were of a ceramic period of c. 1000 B.C., and beneath these were preceramic floors to c. 7000 B.C., overlying an accumulation of rocks about 6 feet deep (some weighing 3 to 4 tons) that had fallen from the cave roof. "The roof fall," states MacNeish, "which was of the consistency of cement, securely sealed off the earlier deposits from any possible later intrusions."[43] And what the earlier deposits disclosed were: first, a level from terminal glacial times; next, two intermediate strata, radiocarbon-dated to between 11,000 and 14,000 B.C.; and finally, four more strata,

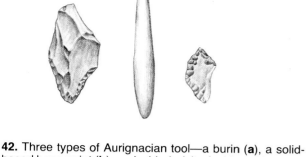

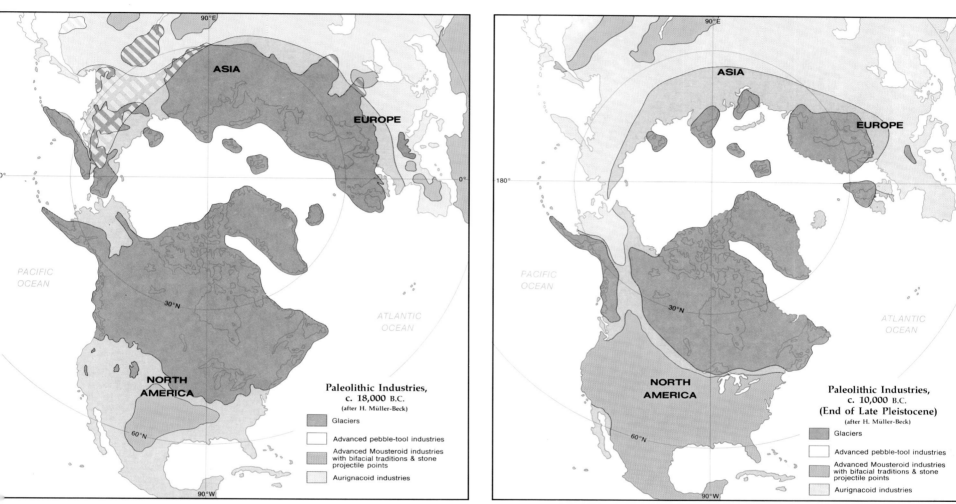

42. Three types of Aurignacian tool—a burin (**a**), a solid-based bone point (**b**), and a blade (**c**)—fashioned by modern *Homo sapiens* in the Old World. **43.** W. K. Gregory's classic reconstruction of Cro-Magnon Man, based on the great skull of the "Old Man of Cro-Magnon," found (1868) near Les Eyzies in the Dordogne: type skull of the Cro-Magnon race, its cranial capacity is ± 1600 cc. **44.** three types of tool of the Llano industry, developed in the New World from an introduced Mousterian base: Sandia (**a**), Clovis (**b**), and Folsom (**c**) points.

Paleolithic Industries,
c. 18,000 B.C.
(after H. Müller-Beck)

- Glaciers
- Advanced pebble-tool industries
- Advanced Mousteroid industries with bifacial traditions & stone projectile points
- Aurignacoid industries

Paleolithic Industries,
c. 10,000 B.C.
(End of Late Pleistocene)
(after H. Müller-Beck)

- Glaciers
- Advanced pebble-tool industries
- Advanced Mousteroid industries with bifacial traditions & stone projectile points
- Aurignacoid industries

Map 11. During the 14,000 years between the time of Map 10 and that of Map 12, western Alaska was culturally a part rather of Asia than of North America. While in the Old World during this season Mousteroid tools were being supplanted by Aurignacoid, in both continents of the New World local refinements were appearing of the inherited Mousteroid tradition. Separated by polar tundra and glacier-covered mountains, the two systems were now developing independently.

Map 12. When the Yukon corridor again became hospitable, the developed Mousteroid tool and weapon systems of the North American Plain spread north to meet the incoming Aurignacoid from Alaska. Then, finally, Beringland dissolved, and there were left what appeared to be two separate hemispheres—still visible to each other across 56 miles of shallow water, with the islands of St. Lawrence, Big and Little Diomede, and a few lesser landing stops between.

representing a still earlier glacial age and containing no less than eighty artifacts mixed with the remains of extinct species of sloth, horse, deer, and giant cats. Radiocarbon datings for this Paccaicasa. Phase range from c. 11,300 to 19,200 B.C., and the artifacts include, in MacNeish's words: "crude large bifacial and slab choppers, cleavers, hammers, scraping planes, and crude concave- and convex-sided unifacial scrapers or spokeshavelike objects, as well as a single pointed flake that could have served on a projectile, and a flake showing blows from a burin. The cave," he adds, "was apparently occupied during brief periods by hunters and their families, who probably attacked the 10- to 15-foot-tall giant sloths in their den and then stayed to butcher and eat the results of their kill."[44]

The most reliable North American find of equivalent antiquity is, in MacNeish's view, that reported in 1958 from a site near Lewisville, Texas (see Map 13, page 37),[45] where a pebble chopper, a stone hammer, and some flakes were discovered in association with hearths and the burned bones of extinct mammals. The hearth charcoals were radiocarbon-dated to c. 38,000 B.C. or earlier. Seven other sites in both North and South America (less securely dated than these, but containing comparable artifacts) have been identified as of the same culture stage: at Alice Boer, in the Rio Claro valley, Brazil,[46] and at Richmond Hill, Belize[47]; in Mexico, at Tequixquiác[48] and San Isidro, Nuevo León[49]; at Calico Hills, California[50]; and in Canada, both at Frazer Canyon

near Yale, British Columbia,[51] and at Fort Liard, Northwest Territories,[52] (see Map 13, page 37, Stage 1).

"We may guess," states MacNeish in summary of the findings not only of these nine very early sites, but also of some sixty-odd others of various later dates, "that migrating bands crossed the Bering Strait landbridge some 70,000 ± 30,000 years ago and subsequently moved southward at a very slow rate. What little evidence we have," he continues, "suggests that these people were also unskilled hunters—almost collectors of big game rather than hunters—like the people of the Lower and Middle Paleolithic of Europe and of the chopper-chopping complexes of the Fen-ho industry and upper cave culture of Choukoutien in

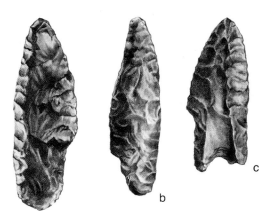

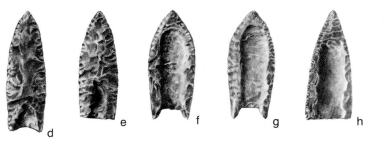

45. Sandia points (**a–b–c**) from the Lucy site, New Mexico, c. 20,000 to 10,000 B.C.; Clovis points (**d–e**) from the Lehner site, Arizona, c. 20,000 to 10,000 B.C.; and Folsom points (**f–g–h**) from the Folsom site, New Mexico, c. 8700 B.C.[4]

46. Projectile point among the ribs of an extinct sub-species of bison. Folsom, New Mexico, c. 8700 B.C.

47. One of three crude sandstone heads from gravel pits near Malakoff, Texas. Associated Pleistocene faunal remains suggest considerable antiquity, possibly c. 40,000 to 30,000 B.C.[5]

China."[53] They were tribes, that is to say, of the earliest *Homo sapiens* stage, which must have crossed the strait on a land-bridge (if this early dating can be sustained) during the Riss glaciation.

A second major stage, of more advanced tool fashioning, which MacNeish compares broadly with the Mousterian of Europe and the so-called Ordos industry of Middle Paleolithic China, is documented by artifacts, not only from the Pikimachay Cave just above the Paccaicasa stratum, but also from some fourteen other well-investigated sites in both American continents. The industries, in MacNeish's view, could have arrived by way of the landbridge, but also might have been developed independently in North America itself. His basic dates for this Stage 2 are, for North America, about 38,000 B.C.; for Central America, about 23,000 B.C.; and for South America, perhaps 14,000 to 10,000 B.C. Compare the datings of the Müller-Beck Maps 9 and 10.

A stage 3 is then represented, in MacNeish's view, by finds of bifacial leaf-points, burins, blades, and endscrapers at about a dozen widely scattered sites from Alaska to Venezuela and Peru; and his suggested dates for these are in the range, for North America, of c. 23,000 to 11,000 B.C., and for Middle and South America, c. 13,000 to 8000 B.C. The tribes, in Mac-Neish's words, were "hunters of big game or herd animals in a wide variety of environments,"[54] and their considerably advanced technology was directly anteced-

ent to the proliferation of expertly fashioned tools of the next development, Stage 4, which he assigns in its beginnings to the end of the last glacial age, c. 11,000 to 8000 B.C. Compare the dating of the Müller-Beck Map 12.

Some twenty or more distinct industries from sites throughout the Americas have been identified as of this complex, and whereas MacNeish believes that these could have been native adaptations and refinements out of the Lower Lithic beginnings of his Stages 1 and 2, Müller-Beck, as we have seen, has interpreted them, rather, as products of the Mousteroid migration represented in his Map 10, with the artifacts of MacNeish's Stage 4 then viewed as local American developments out of the Mousteroid base of Map 10 during the period represented in his Map 11. In Müller-Beck's own words:

"The Llano complex of North America [Clovis, Sandia, Folsom points, among others, of c. 20,000 to 10,000 B.C.] differs from Aurignacoid industries in numerous aspects and cannot be derived from either an early or a late Aurignacoid technological level....Aurignacoid industries were present on the Siberian plains at least 15,000 years ago. It can be assumed that they would have been present in Alaska beginning at about this same time. The

AT THE UTTERMOST PART OF THE EARTH

49. A photograph, taken c. 1899, of a family of the Ona tribe, the tall mountain people of inland Tierra del Fuego. They hunted chiefly guanaco, a species of wild llama, wore robes and head coverings of its fur, and dwelt—in spite of the Fuegian cold—in open wind breaks made of its hide. A second race, the Yahgan (or Yamana), shorter in stature and more squarely built than the Ona, inhabited the southern coasts and the rocky islands southward to Cape Horn. Clothed only in capes of animal hide, these were a beachcombing boat people, living on berries and fungi, birds and shellfish, occasional seals and whales. Their canoes, with sharply raised and pointed ends, carried fireplaces amidships; and it was the nighttime glow of the many little fires on the waters, as well as on land, that suggested to Magellan the name Tierra del Fuego (Land of Fire), when, in 1520 (from October 21 to November 28), he navigated the strait that now bears his name.

48. Lanceolate and fishtail points from Fell's Cave, southern Chile, c. 8700 B.C.[6]

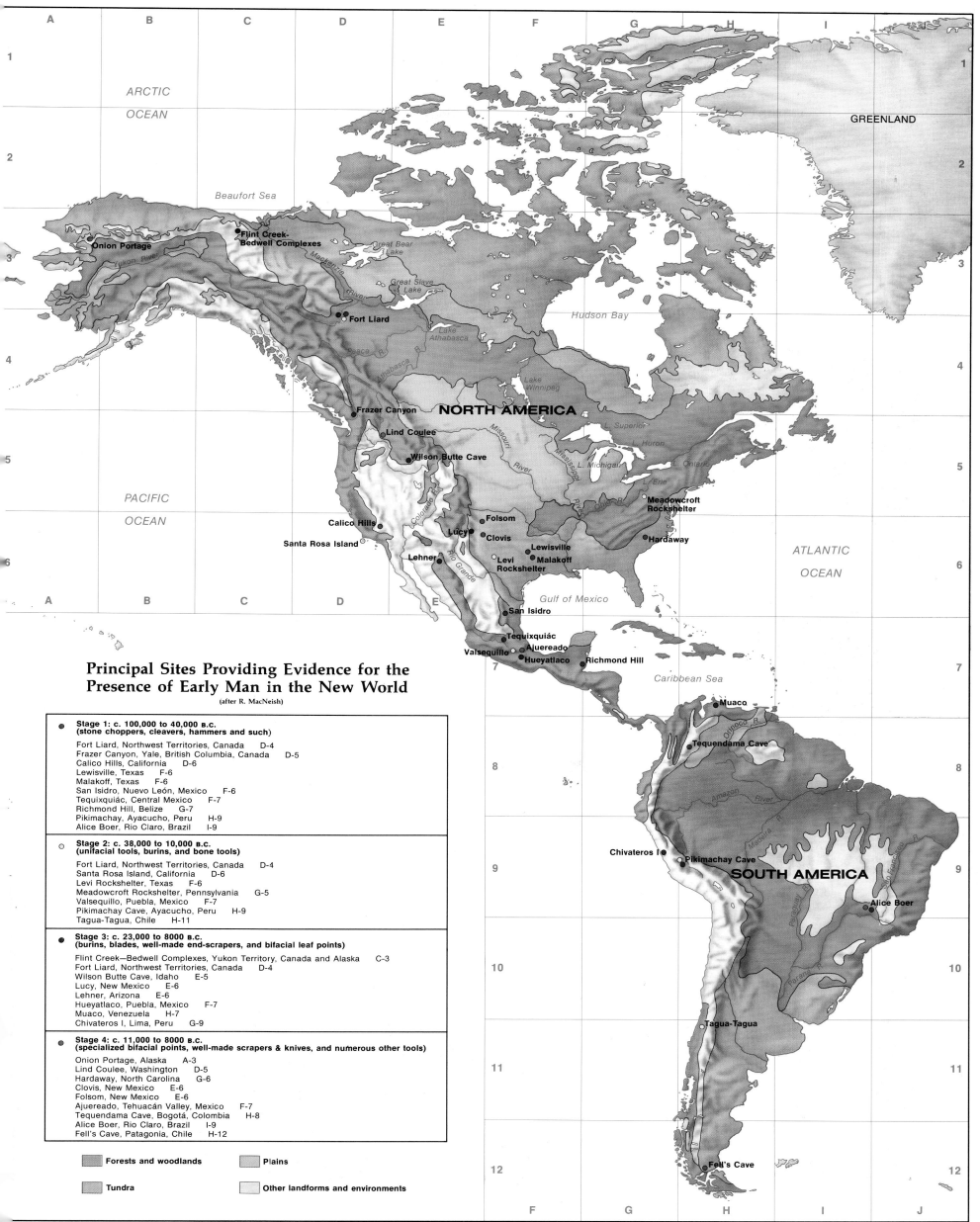

Principal Sites Providing Evidence for the Presence of Early Man in the New World

(after R. MacNeish)

- ● **Stage 1: c. 100,000 to 40,000 B.C.**
  (stone choppers, cleavers, hammers and such)

  Fort Liard, Northwest Territories, Canada   D-4
  Frazer Canyon, Yale, British Columbia, Canada   D-5
  Calico Hills, California   D-6
  Lewisville, Texas   F-6
  Malakoff, Texas   F-6
  San Isidro, Nuevo León, Mexico   F-6
  Tequixquiác, Central Mexico   F-7
  Richmond Hill, Belize   G-7
  Pikimachay, Ayacucho, Peru   H-9
  Alice Boer, Rio Claro, Brazil   I-9

- ○ **Stage 2: c. 38,000 to 10,000 B.C.**
  (unifacial tools, burins, and bone tools)

  Fort Liard, Northwest Territories, Canada   D-4
  Santa Rosa Island, California   D-6
  Levi Rockshelter, Texas   F-6
  Meadowcroft Rockshelter, Pennsylvania   G-5
  Valsequillo, Puebla, Mexico   F-7
  Pikimachay Cave, Ayacucho, Peru   H-9
  Tagua-Tagua, Chile   H-11

- ◑ **Stage 3: c. 23,000 to 8000 B.C.**
  (burins, blades, well-made end-scrapers, and bifacial leaf points)

  Flint Creek—Bedwell Complexes, Yukon Territory, Canada and Alaska   C-3
  Fort Liard, Northwest Territories, Canada   D-4
  Wilson Butte Cave, Idaho   E-5
  Lucy, New Mexico   E-6
  Lehner, Arizona   E-6
  Hueyatlaco, Puebla, Mexico   F-7
  Muaco, Venezuela   H-7
  Chivateros I, Lima, Peru   G-9

- ● **Stage 4: c. 11,000 to 8000 B.C.**
  (specialized bifacial points, well-made scrapers & knives, and numerous other tools)

  Onion Portage, Alaska   A-3
  Lind Coulee, Washington   D-5
  Hardaway, North Carolina   G-6
  Clovis, New Mexico   E-6
  Folsom, New Mexico   E-6
  Ajuereado, Tehuacán Valley, Mexico   F-7
  Tequendama Cave, Bogotá, Colombia   H-8
  Alice Boer, Rio Claro, Brazil   I-9
  Fell's Cave, Patagonia, Chile   H-12

| ▮ Forests and woodlands | ▮ Plains |
| ▮ Tundra | ▯ Other landforms and environments |

50. Chinese mask, bronze, eighth century B.C., use unknown. Compare **54.**

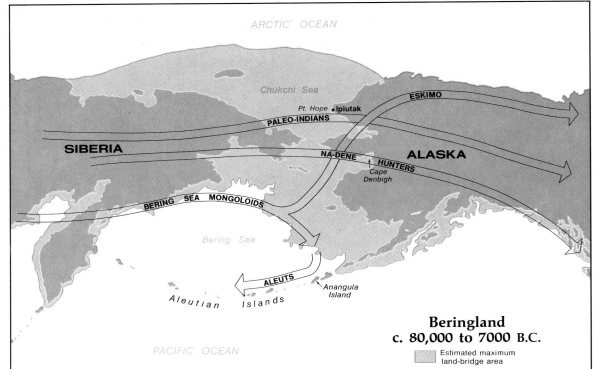

Beringland
c. 80,000 to 7000 B.C.
☐ Estimated maximum land-bridge area

Map 14. Some 1300 miles at its widest, the broad tundra plain of Beringland gradually diminished as the waters rose with the melting of the glaciers. Its seacoasts were thereby lengthened, and along this northern arc of the Pacific, the Bering Sea Mongoloids continued their fishing and sea-mammal hunt- ing, while inland, other Mongoloid hunters, equipped with advanced Aurignacoid and Mesolithic weap- onry, passed—with the opening of the corridors— into the Canadian forests and North American plains, there to become ancestral to the Athapascan, Algonquian, and possibly other Indian tribes.

uninfluenced continuation of the more Mousteroid projectile point tradition rep- resented by the earliest-known Llano in- dustries requires isolation from Late Pleis- tocene technological developments in Eurasia. Isolation from Aurignacoid influ- ence was clearly impossible in Siberia; iso- lation in Alaska is highly unlikely, al- though it cannot be completely ruled out. More probable, however, is an isolation of the ancestors of the Llano complex in interior North America south of the coa- lescing glaciers of the Canadian Shield and the northern Rocky Mountains."[55]

When the passage through the Cana- dian Shield then opened, somewhere c. 10,000 to 9000 B.C., various bearers of Au- rignacoid weapons and tools began mov- ing south, while behind them the once great landbridge that for centuries had been their home was disappearing.

Most of the critical evidence from Ber- ingland itself has, of course, been lost be- neath the waters of what is now a strait. However, on Anangula Island in the Aleutians, which was part of its southern coast, a unifacial core and blade industry has been found, of a date c. 7000 B.C., which was clearly an extension of the ad- vanced Aurignacoid of Japan and interior Siberia, which is known to date from c. 11,000 to 7000 B.C. The Japanese prece- ramic specialist M. Yoshizaki has re- marked that its material could fit easily in a context of that period from Hokkaido.[56]

The Anangula settlement was of fishing folk exploiting the waters of a coastline rich in marine life, and, as W. S. Laughlin has remarked, the inhabitants of that coastline were not forced to abandon their manner of life as the waters gradually rose and the shoreline moved back. "In fact," he points out, "the southern perimeter of the Bering Land Bridge expanded greatly in absolute length as well as in proportion

56/57. Two examples of Scythian goldwork, showing on the animals' shoulders and hips a distinctive pear- shaped boss that is characteristic of this art of the seventh to third centuries B.C. and apparently passed, by way of Mongolia and/or China, to the

to the shrinking land mass." Further- more: "This increase in coastline favored the numerical expansion of the coastal- adapted ancestors of the Bering Sea Mon- goloids—the Aleuts, Eskimos, Chukchi, and Koryak, and possibly some of the Kamchadals."[57]

The hunting peoples of the much colder interior, meanwhile, were being forced to move either eastward or westward as their hunting ground diminished and at last disappeared. These, and not the coastal folk, were then the migrants who would have passed into the American in- terior. The Indians must be descended, therefore, from earlier and later hunting tribes which at one time or another inhab- ited and moved across Beringland, whereas the Aleuts and Eskimo are suc- cessors of the fishing villagers of the coast.

"The Bering Land Bridge," as Laughlin tells, "was an enormous continental area

fishing villages of Alaska. The Scythians were Cen- tral Asian nomads skilled in horsemanship, who founded an empire in southern Russia, north of the Black Sea, and are best known today for the ele- gance of their craftsmanship in gold.

extending nearly 1,500 km from its south- ern extremity, now the eastern Aleutians, to its northern margin in the Arctic Ocean. It was an area that could accom- modate many permanent residents, hu- man and animal, and it endured for a longer time [c. 70,000 years] than that doc- umented for the entire period of human occupancy in America. The southern coastal area was ecologically quite differ- ent from the interior regions and pro- vided the basis for the differentiation of the sea-oriented Mongoloids, ancestors of the Aleuts and Eskimos, and the land-ori- ented big-game hunters of the interior, the ancestors of the American Indians. It is obvious that several generations of oc- cupants, some of them moving slowly eastward and southward, were unaware that most of their territory would eventu- ally be submerged."[58]

The Anangula Island industry of the terminal period of the landbridge, c. 7000

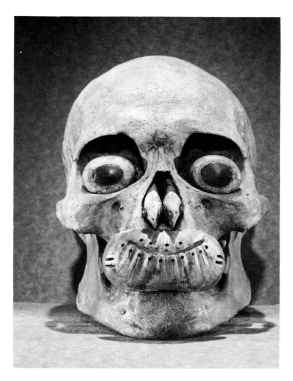

51. Asian influences continued to reach Alaska even after Beringland's disappearance, as is evident both in these microliths of the Denbigh Flint Complex (c. 3000 to 1500 B.C.) and in the remarkable Ipiutak ivories from Point Hope, Alaska, of the second to sixth centuries A.D.

52/53. Ceremonial interment, the burial skull featuring artificial eyes of ivory and jet, an ivory mouth cover, and two nostril plugs, each plug carved to represent the head of some fabulous bird. Skull shown in close-up and in situ. Ipiutak culture, Alaska, probably second to sixth centuries A.D.

54/55. Ivory burial mask. Ipiutak culture, Alaska. Probably second to sixth centuries A.D. Below, the mask in situ, resting partly on the skeleton of a child and partly on the knees of an adult male between whose legs the child was placed. Beneath the mask was a brown paste: the remains of wood in which the ivory sections had apparently been embedded and in which two cheek plugs were embedded still. Two bits of jet (one lost) may have been the pupils of wooden eyes. (Compare the eyes of **53**.)

58. Ivory walrus with exposed ribs and backbone (a shamanic feature). On each hip an imitation Scythian boss (see **56/57**). In an Ipiutak grave it lay at the skeleton's shoulder, where once sewn (as leg and body holes indicate) to the shamanic costume.

59. Ivory polar bear, with exposed ribs and backbone. On each hip is an imitation of the Scythian boss, and along the belly a deep slot for suspension runs from the chin to the tail. Ipiutak culture, Alaska, probably second to sixth centuries A.D.

B.C., was but the earliest of a number of assemblages testifying to the Asian background of the whaling and fishing communities of the North American Arctic. A second site, some 4000 years later, from c. 3000 to 1500 B.C., when the landbridge had long disappeared, tells of the arrival on the Alaskan coast of the people of the Denbigh Flint Complex, from the remains of whose village on the west side of Cape Denbigh on Norton Sound, some 1500 beautifully worked microflints have been recovered (Figure 51).[59] "The delicacy of the flaking," as one scholar has remarked, "is extraordinary. In one case a specimen about an inch and a quarter long bears more than twenty ribbon-like scars on each face."[60] Some of the burins and blades resemble types from the European Upper Paleolithic; others are similar to later forms from post-Paleolithic Siberia; and there are a few fluted points of Folsom character as well, representing an in-

fluence coming north from the Plains as the glaciers retreated and the game animals followed, together with their Indian hunters.

A third site, rich in astonishing signs of both near and remote Asian connections, was discovered and excavated in 1939 on the shore of Point Hope, Alaska, where at some time between the second and sixth centuries A.D. a whale-hunting town, Ipiutak, of no less than 600 semi-subterranean houses arranged in streets along the shore of the Chukchi Sea, had flourished for about a hundred years. As reported by its discoverers, there are "undeniable resemblances," not only between Ipiutak's burial customs and artifacts and those of several cultures of northeast Asia, but also between its ivory death masks and certain works of early Chinese art (Figures 50 and 54).[61] Moreover, signs even of a Scythian influence are evident in the pear-shaped bosses on the haunches of

some of the skillfully carved, ivory and antler animal figurines (see Figures 56 to 59). A bear cult, a ghost cult, and shamanism are suggested. Walrus, seals, and the whale were hunted with toggle-headed harpoons; caribou with the bow and arrow. Thus, influences are apparent, both from a general, Pacific, northern maritime tradition in Ipiutak's seal- and whale-hunting techniques, and from the inland cultures of northeast Asia in its shamanic features. Indeed, even elements from southwest Asia had filtered into its art, so that, evidently, the disappearance of Beringland, c. 7000 B.C., had not dissolved the North American link with Eurasia.

The Five Basic Races

In the light of all these signs of influences moving west to east throughout the Paleolithic with nothing as yet returning, it is evident that the primary creative cultural centers of the period are to be sought neither in America nor in Asia, but in Africa and Europe. Leo Frobenius, in the first years of this century, wrote of the culture-history of those times as marked by a general west-to-east trend,[62] noting further that within the western area itself there were signs of what he thought should be interpreted as an alternation of earlier movements south to north, and then north to south.[63] Subsequent discoveries in Africa of the earliest remains, not only of human life, but also of stone industries that later appeared in Europe, have confirmed this comprehensive insight. But Frobenius had something further to suggest, namely, that the inspiration for the sudden appearance in Europe of those now well-known "Paleolithic Venuses" should perhaps also be attributed to Africa, where the first examples would have been fashioned, not of stone, but of wood.

"Is it not singular," he asks, "that in the Late Paleolithic of Europe, as also in the Neolithic of Egypt, sculptured representations of the human form should have appeared already fully realized and stylistically secure? May it not be that the stone sculpture of the north was born of an art of wood sculpture from the south, and led thereby to a blade culture as well? May it not be that in primeval times the cultural trend was from south to north, as later, from north to south? May the alternation of the west-to-east and then east-to-west pendulations not have had an earlier analogue in movements, south-to-north, and thereafter, north-to-south? It is obvious that everything of wood must have returned, since those times, to the earth, and that only by chance can any specimen have survived—as in arid Egypt. Such disappearances could explain the gap that separates the distributions of southern European and central African assemblages. It is worth keeping this possibility in mind."[64]

The same principle was invoked by William Howells to explain the crudity of the stone tools of Old Melanesia, where again wood must have been the material preferred and most natural. Frobenius described the southern, equatorial, tropical culture, as compared with the northern, temperate culture field, as the realm of the "invisible counterplayers," suggesting that many of the so-called historic developments of the relatively well documented cultures of the north may actually have been, not properly "developments," but responses to undocumented influences coming from the south. In his own words:

"The grandiose high cultures of antiquity occupied, according to our knowledge, no more of the world than a belt reaching from about 20 degrees to about 45 degrees north; that is, they were confined to an area north of the Tropic of Cancer. Over against this demonstration of archaeology, the ethnological branch of our science could not fail forever to recognize that southward of this belt, from West Africa, through India, the Malay Archipelago, and Melanesia, cultures have survived to this day whose traits not only cannot be derived from those of the historical cultures, but also represent a world of their own, which is no less distinct from the other than the plant world from the animal. This domain of *a second kind of culture* is a fact. This second kind is in all and everything so different from the character of the historical cultures that it is not possible to associate it with any historical circumstance; for it offers no external key or clue to its age. Externally regarded, it exhibits only static vistas and perspectives. It appears to have whiled its life away, like the plant world of its homeland, without spring or winter, heights or depths.

Map 15. Expanding influences from centers of the earliest high civilizations progressively drew more and more of the peoples of the earth into the vortex of world history. Pressed to the margins of the continents or into remote jungle retreats were those persisting in the ways of their Paleolithic "fathers and grandfathers." Likewise dwelling in timeless zones were others in whose unmeasured past the step from hunting to primitive planting had been taken and whose ancestors had there rested; while in empty regions of tundra, semidesert, or grass, nomads range, herding reindeer, yaks, sheep, goats, swine, or cattle and, in America, llama and alpaca. New influences from new centers are today reaching even the most secluded of these tribes.

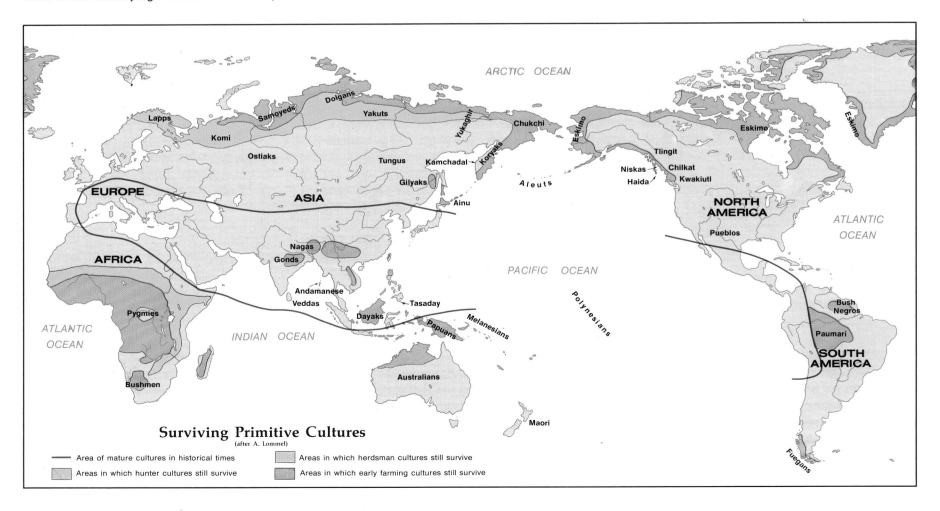

Surviving Primitive Cultures
(after A. Lommel)

— Area of mature cultures in historical times

☐ Areas in which hunter cultures still survive

☐ Areas in which herdsman cultures still survive

☐ Areas in which early farming cultures still survive

"I would term this great group of cultures 'the invisible counterplayers' (*die unsichtbaren Gegenspieler*) in the history of the cultures of mankind.

"And although its existence is seldom attested in historical documents and so can hardly ever be directly demonstrated, nevertheless I have no doubt that it has worked upon the higher cultures, from the south."[65]

Whatever the immediate inspiration may have been, whether out of an impulse from the south, as here suggested, or directly out of a Mousterian base, the emergence in Professor Pilbeam's "Garden of Eden" (see page 29) of the Eurasian Aurignacian complex of c. 35,000 to 20,000 B.C. exactly coincided not only with the appearance on the scene of a race of modern character, Cro-Magnon Man, *Homo sapiens sapiens,* but also with the final retreat of the glaciers.

The climate of Europe at that time was moist and extremely cold. The landscape was of an arctic tundra, and the animals upon it were the musk ox, woolly rhinoceros, reindeer, and woolly mammoth; also, the arctic fox, hare, wolverine, and ptarmigan.[66] However, with the further retreat of the ice the climate, though remaining cold, became dry, and steppe conditions began to preponderate over tundra. This change brought, in addition to the animals just named, great grazing herds of bison, wild cattle, the steppe horse, ibex, and argali sheep; and as a result the conditions of human life greatly altered. In the earlier period of the mammoth, the hunting stations appear to have been widely scattered but comparatively stationary; in this period of the great herds, a shift to a more continuously ranging style of nomadism took place, at least in the European sector. Farther east, in the colder reaches of Russia and Siberia, the mammoth remained, and with it, a continuation of the earlier style as far as to Lake Baikal, and thence onward, as we have seen, into America. The period is known in Europe as the Solutrean: in America it is approximately that of the third map of Müller-Beck's schedule (page 35). Moreover, in Europe there had arrived, following the animals, a new hunting race from the east, the Brünn, whose particular talent was for the fashioning of beautiful spear points.[67] Their period, comparatively short, was from c. 20,000 to 15,000 B.C.—when there followed another cold, wet period, during which the European steppes gave place to forests, and the grazing herds, moving out northeasterly, took with them many of the hunters, some of whose descendants went on to inhabit the landbridge into America. With the forest there had entered Europe, meanwhile, the red deer and the fallow deer, the forest horse and the moose; but the days of the Great Hunt

were no more: people were turning for additional fare to the rivers and the sea. Harpoons were being fashioned for the whale and the seal, while across the arctic north, from Finland to Kamchatka, Alaska, and on across Canada to Greenland, adaptations of the Paleolithic orders were developing that have endured to the present hour.

In North Africa, on the other hand, a new arena of the Great Hunt had meanwhile opened; for, as the European ice

60. Flint working reached a climax in Europe with the arrival of the Solutrean hunters, c. 17,000 B.C. Their characteristic product was the pressure-flaked, bifacial, "laurel leaf" spear-point. This fine example is from the type site of the culture, La Solutré, Dordogne, France.

had been drawing back, the African pluvial line had been moving north, and where now there is desert, there were plains. Moreover, in the rock art of that now-vanished landscape, we see that the bow and arrow had arrived; also, the domesticated dog. The type station is Capsa (Gafsa) in Tunisia, after which the period has been called the Capsian. Its chief art monuments survive in the Sahara Atlas Mountains, the Fezzan, and in southern Spain. The characteristic industry is of microlithic flints, tiny, chiefly trapezoid, rhomboid, and triangular points, with a geographical distribution greatly beyond that of the art—from Morocco to the Vindhya Range of India and from the Cape of Good Hope to the Baltic. We have seen something of its effects in the Denbigh Flints of Alaska (page 39, Figure 51). But of its origins we know practically nothing. It was another undated production of Frobenius's "invisible counterplayers." Its breakthrough into Spain and thence into northern Europe occurred when the glacial retreat was nearly complete, c. 10,000 B.C., and in those parts it has been termed, variously, Final Capsian, Tardenoisian, Microlithic, Mesolithic, proto-Neolithic, epi-Paleolithic, and Azilian.

But then, of course, as formerly in Europe and also now in Africa, the great days were not to last forever. With the continuation of the glacial retreat the pluvial line, too, continued northward, and therewith there ensued, from c. 3000 B.C., a gradual desiccation of the Saharan hunting fields and their transformation into desert. This was answered by a movement southward of both the animals and their hunters, in the way of a north-to-south retreat. So that, just as survivors of the old European epi-Paleolithic hunt carry on to this day along the arctic fringes of Eurasia and North America, so too, in the ultimate refuge zones of Africa, the Kalahari Desert and the deep jungle retreats of the Congo, the Bushmen and the Pygmies continue, as well as they can, as of old.

But the Bushmen, though an African race, are not Negroes. Carleton S. Coon has classified them as one of the five races of modern man, which, in his view, are namely: (1) the Australoid, among whom he reckons "the Australian aborigines, Melanesians, Papuans, some of the tribal folk of India, and the various Negritos of South Asia and Oceania"; (2) the Mongoloid, "most of the East Asiatics, Indonesians, Polynesians, Micronesians, American Indians, and Eskimo"; (3) the Caucasoid, "Europeans and their overseas kinsmen, the Middle Eastern Whites, from Morocco to West Pakistan, and most of the peoples of India, as well as the Ainus of Japan"; (4) the Congoid, "the Negroes and Pygmies of Africa"; and finally, (5) the Capoid, "the Bushmen and Hottentots and other

61. A Pathan from the Indian northwest frontier. Caucasoid race: eyes, blue; grey, green, or hazel to dark brown; hair, wavy to straight; yellow, red, auburn, or brown to black; males heavily bearded; complexions very fair to very dark.

62. A Shilluk from the Sudan. Congoid race (Negroes and African Pygmies): statures range from extremely tall and lanky to sturdy and very short; complexions, black to mahogany; features generally prognathoid; lips everted; frizzly hair.

63. A Taiwan aborigine. Mongoloid race: complexions, light yellow to coppery brown; hair, black, lank, can be very long; little body hair, little beard; face, flat; incisors, large, usually "shoveled"; eyes, wide apart, with heavy upper-eyelid fold.

relic tribes, like the Sandawe of Tanganyika." This fifth group has been named the Capoid, after the Cape of Good Hope, near which they now live. But since they once—that is, in Capsian times—occupied Morocco, "the cape," Coon suggests, "can be thought of as Cape Spartel."[68]

Thus the Bushmen are the last descendants of the tribesmen of the Capsian Great Hunt, pressed southward, first by an expanding northern Caucasoid population, and then, from c. A.D. 500, by the expanding Congoid Bantu, who had recently acquired, not only a knowledge of iron, but also an improved horticulture based on the introduction from Indonesia of the yam, taro, and a superior banana, which had been brought to Madagascar and the Azanian coast by a migrating wave (east to west, now) of Mongoloid Malayo-Polynesians.[69] Stage by stage retiring before *force majeure*, while persisting, like the Tasaday, in the ways of their timeless "fathers and grandfathers," the harassed and harried Capoids, having abandoned to the invading desert their formerly abundant hunting range, are now, ironically, terminating their years, still as hunters, in a second desert, the southern wastes of the Kalahari.

The Congoid Pygmies, who, when the Capoid-Capsian bushmen had been dominant in the plains of the north, had themselves been hunting masters in the Africa south of Sahara, now likewise have retreated to an ultimate sanctuary—and likewise, still as hunters—to survive in scattered vestigial bands through the untamed Congolese jungle, from Gabon and the Cameroons to Uganda and Rwanda-Burundi. As summarized by Basil Davidson:

"By about A.D. 800 . . . the whole of continental Africa had entered a thriving Iron Age but for a few regions in the centre and the south, where Bushmen and their like continued a Late Stone Age kind of life, hunting and gathering food,

64. A Bushman boy from the Kalahari. Capoid race: complexion, apricot yellow; hair, black, in thick, tight clusters ("peppercorn"); both sexes steatopygous; male genitalia, normally semi-erect; female, with extended labia minora (the "Hottentot apron").

65. A Tiwi from Melville Island. Australoid race, three varieties: (1) full-sized with straight or wavy hair (Australoid proper); (2) full-sized with kinky hair (Tasmanian and Papuo-Melanesian); and (3) Pygmy-sized with kinky hair (Negrito).

painting and engraving on rock as the Iron Age Bantu-language peoples seldom or never did: a way of life that has continued, little altered to this day, in remote segments of the Kalahari and among some of the Pygmies of the Congo forestland. Everywhere else populations had greatly multiplied, developed their farming and metal-using technology, worked out their characteristic religions, embarked on new forms of social and political organization ranging from powerful states like ancient Ghana to intricate systems of tribal democracy among a wide range of different peoples, and laid foundations for the growth of their civilization into modern times."[70]

Thus it will have to be among the marginal peoples—mainly at the northernmost and southernmost parts of the continents or in hitherto inaccessible inland forest fastnesses—that we shall have to seek whatever shreds of myth from Paleolithic times may still survive. Whatever their original forms, ritualized applications, and allegorical interpretations may have been, they will have generally, through the centuries, lost much of their mythic force; and yet, like the fragments of ancient marbles found in the flooring of peasant stables or in the walls of medieval churches, they may still speak to those with eyes and ears attuned to the signs and syllables of their gospel. Significant differences will be evident between the primary Paleolithic and recent ethnological materials; also, between the mythologies of hunting, foraging, planting, and herding tribes, no less than between those of nonliterate and literate traditions. Nevertheless, through all these contrasts, to which it will be our first task to give attention, there will be recognizable a constellation of permanent, archetypal themes and motifs, which are as intrinsic to human life and thought as are the ribs, vertebrae, and cranial parts to our anatomies.

SHIFTS OF THE HUMAN SUBSPECIES
FROM PLEISTOCENE TO c. A.D. 1492

Carleton S. Coon has proposed a classification of the living peoples of the
earth into five, originally geographical,
groups: the Capoid, Congoid, Caucasoid, Mongoloid, and Australoid. In the
course of the c. 10,000 years since the
end of the Pleistocene, the distributions
of these five subspecies of *Homo sapiens sapiens* have greatly changed.

Map 16. "Toward the end of the Pleistocene," states Coon, "after all five geographical races of man had become
sapiens . . . each race may have contained nearly equal numbers of individuals."[7] Of the five subspecies, the Congoid was the most isolated, in contact
with only the Capoid, to the north. Most
of Europe and all of the Near East into
India were occupied by Caucasoids. Indonesia and southeast Asia, by Australoids. The Mongoloid hearth was China.

Map 17. With the glacial retreat, the two
northerly groups vastly expanded. Mongoloids occupied the Americas and the
Pacific isles, and pressing southward,
entered areas formerly Australoid. Caucasoids dispossessed the Capoids of
North Africa, who, migrating south, took
possession of the East and South African plains. The Congoid populations
thereby became confined, for a period,
to the Congo Basin and Sudan.

Map 18. The most notable expansion
during the first centuries A.D. was of the
Congoids (specifically, Bantu), following
the introduction from Indonesia of the
banana and the yam. After 1492, both
the Congoid and the Caucasoid expan-
sions were prodigious. The Australoids
are today on the decline except among
the aboriginal tribes of India, and the
Capoids are all but extinct.

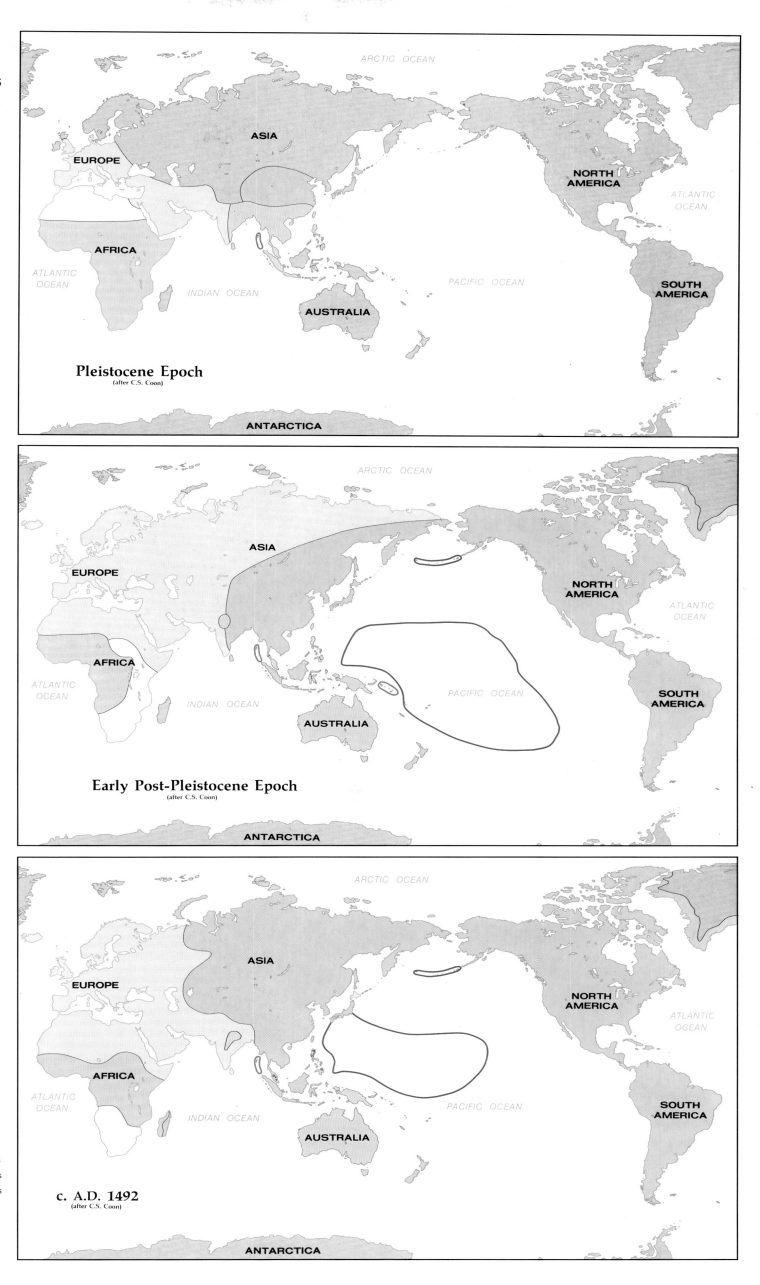

Pleistocene Epoch
(after C.S. Coon)

Early Post-Pleistocene Epoch
(after C.S. Coon)

c. A.D. 1492
(after C.S. Coon)

Australoids
Caucasoids
Mongoloids
Capoids
Congoids

MYTHOLOGIES
OF THE
PRIMITIVE HUNTERS
AND GATHERERS

I term *collective* all psychic contents
that belong not to one individual
but to many, i.e., to a society,
a people, or to mankind in
general. The antithesis
of collective is
individual.

C. G. JUNG, *Psychological Types*

As the infant is linked to its mother in a profound *participation mystique,* even to such a degree that it will absorb, and thus inherit, her tensions and anxieties, so has mankind been linked to the moods and weathers of its mother Earth. And as the infant yet unfolds according to the laws of growth of its nature, so too has this human race evolved in the way of a single unfolding life through its millions of apparently separate individuals in all quarters of the earth and through all weatherings. Nor has there been any period of the long history when the interaction of these two forces—the inward of organic growth and outward of a shaping fosterage—was more evident than during the last of the glacial ages, when the stage of *Homo sapiens sapiens,* modern man, was attained in all quarters simultaneously, while the mothering earth itself was passing through a season of the greatest transformations.

Biologically, in what theologians call our animal nature, we are as deeply grounded as the animals themselves: moved and motivated from within by energies that have been generating, shaping, and destroying living creatures on earth for hundreds of millions of years. The patterns of impulse and response inherent in nerves and protoplasm have thus a long prehuman history, pointing back through many stages of ascent from the earliest beginnings of life in Paleozoic brine to the present chaos of international affairs; and from first to last, the question has not been "To be, or not to be?" but "To eat, or to be eaten?" of which desire and terror are the effects—as represented

66. *Venus of Laussel,* carved limestone block, height 17 inches, from a rock shelter (Laussel) in the Dordogne, France, c. 20,000 to 18,000 B.C.; known also as the *Woman with the Horn* (see pages 66–68). The Paleolithic *Venus of Laussel* (**66**) and the dual-faced ceramic statuette (**67**, on page 49) from the Valley of Mexico are here introduced as the muses, respectively, of this volume and the forthcoming volume II.

in the old creation myth from the *Brihadaranyaka Upanishad* (page 13) of that primordial Being-of-All-Beings who, in the beginning, thought "I" and immediately experienced, first fear, then desire.

The desire in that case was not to eat, however, but to become two, and then to procreate. And in this primal constellation of themes—first, of unity, albeit unconscious; then of a consciousness of selfhood and immediate fear of extinction; next, desire, first for another and then for union with that other—we have a set of "elementary ideas," to use Adolf Bastian's felicitous term (page 9), that has been sounded and inflected, transposed, developed, and sounded again through all the mythologies of mankind through the ages. And as a constant structuring strain underlying the everlasting play of these themes, there is the primal polar tension of a consciousness of duality against an earlier, but lost, knowledge of unity that is pressing still for realization and may indeed break through, under circumstances, in a rapture of self-loss.

Schopenhauer, in his essay "On the Foundation of Morality," asks how it is that one can be so immediately moved by the pain and danger of another that, forgetting one's own well being and safety, one springs to that other's rescue. How is it, he asks, that what has been described as the first law of nature, self-preservation, can be suspended in this way, immediately, spontaneously, and even to the loss of the rescuer's life? To this he replies that this expression of the mystery of compassion is an effect of the experience of an antecedent truth of nature, namely, that "I" and "that other" *are* one. Our sense and experience of separateness is of a secondary order, a mere effect of the way in which lightworld consciousness experiences objects within a conditioning frame of space and time. More deeply, more truly, we are of one life:

which, finally, is but the philosopher's way of stating something that in a biological sense becomes clearly evident when the mind's eye, running back along the time chart of the branching tree of life, comes to its Archeozoic root (pages 18–21).

The two claims, on the one hand, of an individual existence, and on the other, of transpersonal identity, alternate and compete in the lifetimes both of beasts and of men; and whenever the larger force takes over, the individual, forgetting itself in a seizure, acts in manners stereotyped to the species, often with little or no regard for self-preservation. The courtship dances and displays of birds and fish are examples of such performances. Many of the choreographic patterns develop through intermeshing sequences of stereotyped responses to specific signals from the partner, and if any of these fails from either side, the contradance breaks off.

None of the moves in such a display has been learned. All are common to the species, released from within compulsively in response to specific sign stimuli. Among fish, for example (quoting N. Tinbergen in his *Study of Instinct*): "The courting behavior of a male stickleback before a pregnant female is dependent on at least two sign stimuli: the swollen abdomen and the special posturing movement of the female. . . . The female's reaction to the courting male is released by two sign stimuli: the red belly and the male's special movements, the 'zigzag dance'."[1] "As far as available facts go," Tinbergen states, "this dependence on only one or a few sign stimuli seems to be characteristic of innate responses. . . . Conditioned [i.e., learned] reactions are, so far as we know, not usually dependent on a limited set of sign stimuli, but on much more complex stimulus situations."[2] Continuing: "The strict dependence of an innate reaction on a certain set of sign stimuli leads to the conclusion that there must be a special neuro-sensory mechanism that releases the reaction and is responsible for its selective susceptibility to such a very special combination of sign stimuli. This mechanism we will call the Innate Releasing Mechanism (IRM) . . . in general no two reactions of a species have the same IRM.''[3] And finally: "The fact that each reaction has its own releasing mechanism may lead to ambivalent behavior when two sign stimuli belonging to different reactions are present at the same time.''[4]

The question arises: Are there any such innate releasing mechanisms in the human nervous system? To which the answer is, yes, of course!—as anyone whose mouth has ever watered when his hungry nose has caught the odor of a kitchen surely must know. However, IRMs are of two sorts. The first is that already noted in the stickleback, whose stereotyped reactions are released by signs effective for the species. Baby chicks just hatched, with fragments of eggshell still adhering to feathers, scamper for shelter if a hawk flies overhead, but not if the bird is a gull, a heron, or a pigeon. Furthermore, if the wooden model of a hawk be drawn along a wire over their coop, they react as though it were alive—unless it be drawn backward, when there is no response. Here we have an extremely precise image, never seen before, yet recognized with reference not merely to its form but also to its form in motion, and linked, besides, to an immediate, unplanned, unlearned, and even unintended system of appropriate action: flight to cover. The image of the inherited enemy is already sleeping in the nervous system, and along with it the well-proven reaction.

Furthermore, even if all the hawks in the world were to vanish, their image would still sleep in the soul of the chick— never to be roused, however, unless by some accident of art; for example, a repetition of the clever experiment of the wooden hawk on a wire. Can it be that in the central nervous system of the species *Homeo sapiens*, there sleep any number of such archaic sign stimuli, surviving from his centuries of evolution during periods of the woolly mammoth and the cave bear? *"Our Birth,"* wrote the poet Wordsworth:

> *is but a sleep and a forgetting:*
> *The Soul that rises with us, our life's Star,*
> *Hath had elsewhere its setting,*
> *And cometh from afar:*
> *Not in entire forgetfulness,*
> *And not in utter nakedness,*
> *But trailing clouds of glory do we come*
> *From God, who is our home:*
> *Heaven lies about us in our infancy!*[5]

Not only of woolly mammoths, but memories—deeper—of some seat of silence, do seem to sleep profoundly in the nerves, which wake at times with a shudder, mysteriously, to some sound or sign of recollection.

As observed among the apes, the birds, and the fish, the gestalt psychologist Wolfgang Köhler has termed such resonating structures "isomorphs." The animal, directed by innate endowment, comes to terms with its natural environment, not as a consequence of any long slow learning through experience, not through trial and error, but immediately and with the certainty of recognition. The sign stimuli that release the responses are immutable and correspond to the inner readiness of the creature as precisely as key to lock; in fact, they are known as "key-tumbler" structures.

However, there also are systems of animal response that are established by particular experiences. In such, the structure of the IRM is described as "open." It is susceptible to "impression" or "imprint." And where these open structures exist, the first imprint is definitive, requires sometimes less than a minute for its completion, and is irrevocable.

Imprinting is not to be compared with conditioned learning, which is not only slow and often tedious, but also, as Tinbergen points out, usually dependent, not on a limited set of sign stimuli, but on much more complex stimulus situations. An imprint occurs instantaneously, at a moment of ripened readiness when, in a critical period of the animal's growth, the innate disposition intended comes to maturity. Most of the IRMs of the human species are of this kind, "open," open to imprinting; and the imprintings are, of course, culture-bound, specific to the time and place of the individual's birth, earliest impressions, and development. They would not be the same for an American Indian born on the Kansan buffalo plains and the child of a Polynesian fisherman watching for sharks. They would be different again for the son of a Hasidic rabbi in the Bronx. Yet, in spite of the very great differences of the sign stimuli thus offered in the various theaters of human life, the innate energies to be released remain the same throughout the species. They are not of the culture, but of nature: innate, transpersonal, pre-rational, and when alerted, compulsive.

The address of mythological symbols is directly to these centers; and the responses proper to their influence are, consequently, neither rational nor under personal control. They overtake one. The symbols function, that is to say, as energy-releasing and -directing signs; and in traditionally structured cultures, they are deliberately imprinted in vividly impressive (often painful) rites, timed to catch the individual at those moments of ripening readiness when, in the critical periods of our human growth, the intended innate dispositions come to maturity.

In this sense, a mythology in its pedagogical functioning might be defined as a corpus of culturally maintained sign stimuli fostering the development and activation of a specific type, or constellation of types, of human life. Its address is not to rationality but to primal centers of the nervous system, "central excitatory mechanisms" (CEMs) and "innate releasing mechanisms" (IRMs), such as motivate the human animal—which, however, is an animal of a very special sort, with developed zones between the ears that are unmatched in any other beast and are open, not only to extraordinary imprintings, but also to possibilities of intentional learning and performance otherwise unknown to the animal world.

Undoubtedly, the increase in size of the human brain during the course of what we now know to have been some 4 million years of development will have had something to do, not only with our ability to learn, but also with the relative proportion of open to closed structures in our cerebrospinal organization. At what stage, one may ask, however, was the critical threshold crossed? Would the increase from, say, the 500 cc of an australopithecine or gorilla to the 800 cc of the first Turkana skull (Figure 21, page 28) have released the subject from what we have termed earlier the "innocence of nature"? Or would this have occurred, rather, at some point between the 900 cc of Java Man and the 1275 cc of Swanscombe? Today, the norm being about 1450 cc, the force of such biologically inherited stereotypes as the image of the hawk in the nervous system of the chick has been largely supplanted by the more variable forms of culturally conditioned imprints.

An important conditioning factor in the shaping and enforcing of these imprints during the first many thousand years of distribution of our species over the continents was the character of whatever landscape was entered and made its own by any of the tribes; and the landscapes were, in the main, of three contrasting sorts: open animal plains; equatorial rain forests; and marginal coastal regions, from which authority over the sea would be gained. The earliest periods of expansion were of peoples afoot, moving apart and settling in slow stages. And wherever they came, the animals of the area, the plants, and the hills became their neighbors and instructors, recognized as already there from of old: mysterious presences which in some sacred way were to be known as messengers and friends. As the Pawnee chief, Letakots-Lesa, explained: "When a man sought to know how he should live he went into solitude and cried until some animal brought wisdom to him. . . . Thus were the sacred songs and ceremonial dances given the Pawnees through the animals."[6]

In this way, the very mysterious way of the reception of imprintings, there became established between the earliest human communities and their landscapes a profound *participation mystique* which in all truly primitive mythologies comes to expression, whether among peoples of the broad animal plains, the forests, or the seacoasts.

In certain especially favorable regions, then—apparently out of the initiative rather of the females than of the males—from the activity of plant gathering the idea of gardening developed, and along with that, the domestication of animals. The earliest zone of such innovations now seems to have been Southeast Asia, where there was also developed an art of sea voyaging that not only carried such domesticates as the yam, banana, and coconut to great distances, but also inaugurated an epoch when peoples who had long been apart began rediscovering each other: a movement that today has culminated in our recognition of the one family of man of this planet.

Accordingly, the folkways and mythologies to be explored in the first two volumes of the present work are of two orders: (1) of hunting and gathering tribes, and (2) of the earliest planting cultures. The Paleolithic *Venus of Laussel* (Figure 66, page 47), shown elevating in her right hand a bison horn engraved with thirteen vertical strokes, the other hand on her belly, is from a rock shelter in the Dordogne, southern France, of a date c. 20,-000 to 18,000 B.C. She is representative here of the mythologies of the hunt, of which (although no word survives from her time) there is rich evidence in the rock paintings and engravings of a period of magnificent religious art which endured for 300 centuries.

Figure 67, on the other hand, is representative here of the earliest planting culture stage. She is from Tlatilco (a name meaning "where things are hidden"), a village site hardly twenty minutes drive from the heart of Mexico City. There, in the precincts of a brick factory, an astonishing assortment of ceramic figurines came to light during the decade of the 1940s, all from graves of the Mexican Middle Preclassic Period of c. 1200 to 700 B.C. And although nothing is known of the mythologies of that period (for it is still of a preliterate stage of culture), such a figurine as this already suggests a theme well known to the planting cultures of the world, that namely of the dual goddess, the great mothering power of the two worlds: of the dead and of the living, the planted and the sprouting seed.

There is evidence at Tlatilco of influences from the earliest of the native American monumental, high civilizations: the Olmec of Tabasco and Vera Cruz, c. 1500 to 500 B.C. Thus Tlatilco was a village at the threshold of a development beyond the range of these first two volumes. A third is therefore indicated for the history of those literate high cultures and their religions which suddenly first came to manifestation in the temple towers of ancient Sumer and in the pyramid tombs of Egypt, where there was joined to the timeless earlier mysteries of the animal messengers, sacred mountains, and plant spirits, a new and grander mystery of the circling eons of the heavens. The goddess mother of the alternating tides of life and death, who formerly had been chiefly of this earth, became then equally of the cosmic order in its ever-circling rounds of day and night, creation and dissolution; and under innumerable names—as Inanna, Isis, Hathor and Nut, Anahit, Satī, Mary, and Kwan Yin—she receives worship as the supreme personification of that ambiguous mystery, *tremendum et fascinans*, which is of life in death, as of death in life.

67. Dual-faced "Pretty Lady" figurine in terracotta. Tlatilco, Valley of Mexico, Middle Preclassic Period, c. 1200 to 700 B.C. From more than 200 Tlatilcan graves a rich harvest of figurines of clay has been collected, finely modeled, highly polished, in a varied range of styles. Most are of women with long, slanting eyes, small breasts, short arms, slim waists and large, bulbous legs; some are standing, some seated; others carry babies on their hips or caress small dogs held in their arms. Most are naked. Others, however, are stylishly dressed in abbreviated skirts of cloth or of grass; their hair is usually painted red, as though dyed or bleached with lime. A few have two heads; another few, as here, two faces. All are charming, and appropriately, they have been called, as a class, "Pretty Lady" figurines. What, however, was their function? "Beyond the fact," states Miguel Covarrubias, who supervised the excavations, "that these figurines were made to be buried with the dead, their purpose remains a mystery." [1]But not, let us add, an irreducible mystery: being buried with the dead, they serve as an assurance of the maternal power of the seeded earth, there to receive them.

EARLY HUNTERS OF THE OPEN PLAIN

The Recognition of Death

The first law of life in the animal kingdom—"to eat, or to be eaten"—remained for Early Man, the Hunter, the first structuring law of his own address to the world. This was most emphatically so on those vast, northern animal plains of the Upper Paleolithic Great Hunt, onto which Neanderthal Man (**69**) was apparently the first of humankind to venture. To all appearances, the human species, in those terminal glacial millennia, was an unlikely candidate for survival among the mammals then abounding in possession of the earth. Earlier, the great reptiles had reigned, and from those had evolved both the serpents and the birds (**68**). It is remarkable that these two related yet contrary forms—one bound to the earth, the other released to the sky—should have been recognized early in the imagination of humankind as signs of the extremes to which the human spirit itself might turn. Seen as archetypal of the powers beneath and

Through all the remains in stone and bone of the first 4 million years or so of the evolution of our species, the earliest indubitable evidences of ritual, and therewith of mythic inspiration motivating human thought and action, appear toward the close of the Riss-Würm interglacial, in the cave burials of Neanderthal Man, as for example in the burial discovered, in 1908 in France, in the lower grotto of Le Moustier, where the remains of a youth of about sixteen had been left arranged in a sleeping posture, head resting on the right forearm, pillowed on a pile of flints.

70. Dazed and bewildered, a mother chimpanzee holds her new baby, four weeks old, dead of poliomyelitis. Still dazed, she carried it into the wilderness and returned alone to Jane Goodall's research camp.[2]

above, it was between them that the later-evolved mammalian species had appeared, of which the human was the latest to come: still bound to the beasts' order of life, but already aware of ambiguities and inventive of symbolic acts by which to neutralize the mind's anxieties, even while continuing the general, primary battle of life, which lives on life.

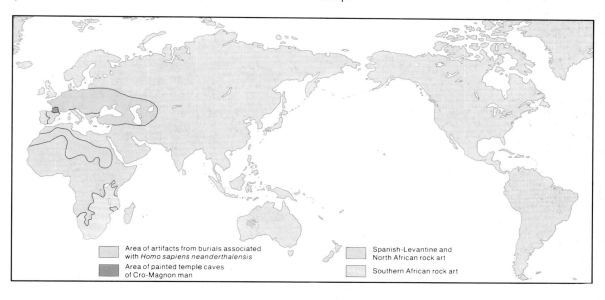

Area of artifacts from burials associated with *Homo sapiens neanderthalensis*
Area of painted temple caves of Cro-Magnon man

Spanish-Levantine and North African rock art
Southern African rock art

At one hand lay an exceptionally fine Late Acheulean hand ax, and round about were the charred split bones of sacrificed wild cattle (Figure 73).[7] A few miles eastward of this site, in the grotto of La Chapelle-aux-Saints, there was also found that year the remarkably well preserved skeleton of a male of about fifty (Figure 26, page 29), carefully laid out in a west-east orientation, surrounded by shells, Mousterian flints, and the remains of reindeer, horse, bison, and a woolly rhinoceros. A hole nearby contained a single bison horn, and there was another in which the large bones of the animal had been stowed.[8] More recently, at Mount Carmel in Israel, a cemetery was excavated of no less than ten Neanderthal burials, where, by the right hand of one of the adult males, the jawbone had been placed of a large wild boar (Figure 71).[9]

Map 19. Primary Burial and Rock Art Horizons. With *Homo sapiens neanderthalensis,* the first of the human species to bury the dead with offerings, the history of mythology begins. With the painted cave temples of Cro-Magnon Man, a second chapter opens with a pictorial tradition, which then, passing—north to south—through Spain to Africa, culminates in the rock art of the Bushmen.

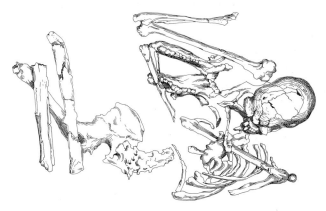

71. The jawbone of a large wild boar is visible at the right shoulder of this skeleton from a Neanderthal cave-burial at Mount Carmel, Israel.

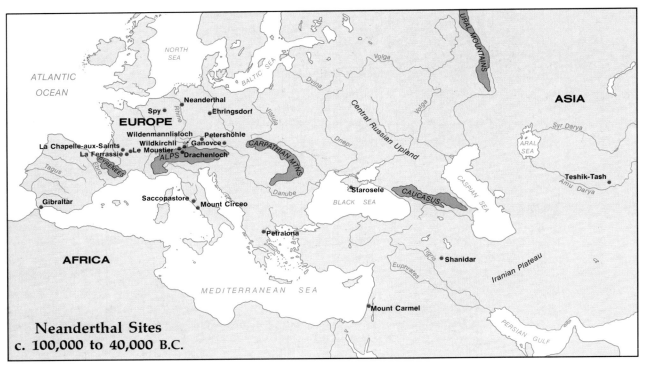

The analogy of death and sleep and the associated thought of a waking are clearly suggested in these finds, while the west-east orientation may have implied some sort of reference to the setting and rising of the sun. The buried bison horn has not been interpreted, nor has the scattering of shells. Neither do we know what, if any, the mythic reference might have been of that jawbone of a boar in the Mount Carmel grave. One thinks of later mythological figures of the Near East, slain by a boar, who yet rose again: Adonis, for example. However, associations of this kind, over a span of 60,000 years or more, are dubious, and not possible either to demonstrate or to refute.

Then again in France, in 1909, in a cave at La Ferrassie, there were found the skeletons of two adults, a male and a female, head to head, together with four children, two of whom were at the female's feet, the others a little apart. The woman had been buried in a shallow depression, arms folded, legs drawn up hard to the belly and bound, apparently with thongs. The male (Figure 74), again with legs hard-flexed, lay on his back, his head and shoulders protected by stone slabs. The children, supine, were in shallow graves, in one of which scraping tools had been laid; and close by was a hole containing the ashes and bones of a wild ox.[10]

Whatever the specific myths may have been that inspired these primeval burials, there is one general idea represented in all: that of a continuation of life beyond death, whether in this world or some other. Oswald Spengler, in *The Decline of the West*, wrote of a "Recognition of Death" (*Blick auf den Tod*)[11] as the initiating moment of every high, mythologically inspired culture style; and here we already have it in the first awakening of consciousness to its powers at the stage of *Homo sapiens*. Some of the higher animals exhibit profound grief when bereaved, but have no way to resolve it (Figure 70). How *Homo erectus* may have dealt with the experience, no one knows. But the earliest answer of *Homo sapiens* comes out clearly in these burial caves: "There is no such thing as death; there is but a passing on."

Furthermore, the confrontation with the mystery has in every case been ritualized in represented analogies of death as a kind of sleep; and in one case, possibly also as comparable with a sunset to be followed by a sunrise. Whether caves were selected to suggest a return to the womb for rebirth is a question that has been argued; so is the question of whether such flexed positions as those at La Ferrassie can have been meant to suggest the fetal posture. A second suggested possibility is that the legs may have been flexed and bound to keep the ghosts from walking and breaking into people's dreams.

One of the largest and most important, as well as surprising, burial chambers of all has been reported from the Zagros Mountains of northern Iraq, at Shanidar, 250 miles north of Baghdad. Here there is a huge cave, 132 feet deep with a mouth 175 feet wide, in which to this day nomadic Kurds winter with their flocks.

Within, excavations have opened a succession of levels to a depth of 45 feet, representing an accumulation of approximately 100,000 years, and at a depth dated c. 8600 B.C. twenty-six skeletons of a proto-Neolithic period were unearthed, beneath which, at various levels, the remains were found of seven Neanderthal burials. That of c. 40,000 B.C. was of a one-armed male, crippled from childhood, whose right arm and shoulder had never developed (Figure 75). He had been about forty years old when killed by a roof-fall in the cave, and at some time in his life the arm below the elbow had been amputated. The fact that he had survived to that age, cared for by his fellows to whom he could hardly have been of much practical help, tells something of Old Stone Age man not formerly suspected.

The most significant find, however, came to light at a level of c. 60,000 B.C. It consisted of the skeleton, with a badly crushed skull, of a male about 5 feet 8 inches tall, which for a Neanderthaler was large. The body had been laid to rest on a litter of evergreen boughs heaped with flowers (Figure 76), of which the surviving pollens have been identified by microscopic analysis. An infant had been placed first in the grave, two women above the infant, and then finally, as Ralph S. Solecki, the excavator, states, "room was made for the male, who was evidently an important man."[12]

The flowers of this burial were of eight species or more, relatives mainly of the grape, hyacinth, bachelor's button, hollyhock, and a yellow-flowering groundsel, seven of the eight being known today in Iraq as medicinal herbs. "These flower pollens," Solecki observes, "were not accidentally introduced into the grave, and hence must represent bouquets or clumps of flowers purposely laid down with the Shanidar IV burial [the technical name for the male skeleton of this quadruple grave]. The hollyhock is especially indicative of this since it grows in separate individual stands, and cannot be grasped in bunches like the others. Some person or persons once ranged the mountainside collecting these flowers one by one."[13]

Specifically, the critical plants of this earliest known (though now invisible) funereal bouquet were (1) a sort of yarrow (Achilles santolina) with insect-repellent properties, whose leaves are useful against intestinal disorders, colic, dysentery, and as a general tonic; (2) a variety of cornflower (Centaurea cyanus), which is now used as a diuretic, an emmenagogue, a tonic, a stimulant, an astringent, a pectoral, a febrifuge, and a collyrium; (3) St. Barnaby's thistle (Centaurea solstitialis), which is collected by the peasants of Iraq today for herbal remedies; (4) a groundsel or ragwort (Senecio vernalis), which possesses diuretic, emetic, and purgative properties; (5) the grape hyacinth (Muscari), of the hiliaceal family, the bulb of which is poisonous, but which also is collected for its stimulant and diuretic properties; (6) a variety of woody horsetail (Ephedra altissima), which is a cardiac stimulant and may be used as a cure for asthma and epidemic dropsy; and finally (7) the hollyhock, or Althaea (which name is from the Greek αλθαινω, "to heal"), from the roots, leaves, flowers, and seeds of which a variety of medicines of a great many uses can be made. "It may be simply coincidence," Solecki concedes, "that the flowers have medicinal or economic value (at least in our present knowledge), but the coincidence does raise speculation about the extent of human spirit in Neanderthals. . . . One may speculate," he continues, "that Shanidar IV was not only a very important man, a leader, but also may have been a kind of medicine man or shaman in his group."[14]

One is moved to wonder, also, about

A recognition of the mystery of death, and therewith, of life, marks the spiritual separation of man from the beasts.

72. The entrance to the grotto of La Chapelle-aux-Saints where the skeleton of a mature Neanderthaler lay surrounded by grave offerings (see 26 on page 29).

73. Artist's reconstruction of the burial at Le Moustier (see page 51).

74. This skeleton lying on its back with its legs flexed is the male in the multiple burial at La Ferrassie.

75. From the great Shanidar cave in Iraq, this one-armed male known as Shanidar I was apparently killed by a rock-fall c. 40,000 B.C.

76. The now-famous flower burial known as Shanidar IV, of c. 60,000 B.C. The body was placed on its left side, head to the south, facing west.[3]

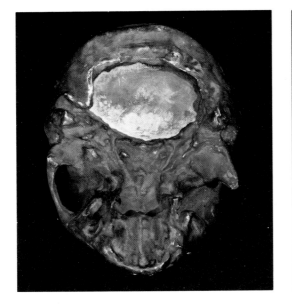

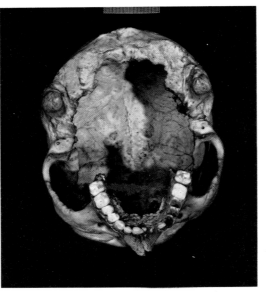

the multiple burial at La Ferrassie; for, as observed by the nineteenth-century master anthropologist, Edward Tylor: "Men do not stop short at the persuasion that death releases the soul to a free and active existence, but they quite logically proceed to assist nature, by slaying men in order to liberate their souls for ghostly uses. Thus there arises one of the most widespread, distinct, and intelligible rites of animistic religion—that of funeral human sacrifice for the service of the dead. When a man of rank dies and his soul departs to its own place, wherever and whatever that place may be, it is a rational inference of early philosophy that the souls of attendants, slaves, and wives, put to death at his funeral, will make the same journey and continue their service in the next life, and the argument is frequently stretched further, to include the souls of new victims sacrificed in order that they may enter upon the same ghostly servitude."[15]

In a five-chambered grotto on the Italian coast at Monte Circeo, some 80 miles southeast of Rome, a single Neanderthal skull, set in the midst of a roughly circular heap of stones, has been found. Receptacles round about contained the remains of sacrificed animals, and the skull itself was broken open at the base (Figure 77), as were all of those of Solo Man discovered at Ngandong (Figure 31). The headhunters of Borneo still open skulls that way in order to eat the brains, and there were a number similarly opened in the caves of Peking Man. Jane Goodall has told of one of her chimpanzees enjoying the brains of a young baboon from its freshly taken head, broken open at the crown (Figure 79).[16] Apparently, primates like the taste of each other's brains. However, the formal arrangements of the Solo skulls, and the way in which that of Monte Circeo had been set upon its pile of stones, suggest not simply cannibalism, but a ritual communion of some kind.

Of interest is the fact that on the summit of Monte Circeo the ruins stand of a Roman temple dedicated to the nymph Circe, who introduced Odysseus to the

Two skulls broken open to facilitate the eating of the brains: **77.** An opened Neanderthal skull from Monte Circeo, Italy. **78.** A skull from Melanesia.

79. A chimpanzee uses a leaf sponge to wipe the remnants of brain from the skull of a baboon.[4]

entrance to the Land of the Dead. In the folk tradition, this headland with its many caves, nearly surrounded by the wine-dark sea, has long been identified as Circe's Isle.

80. Profile of the excavation at Drachenloch based on a sketch by the excavator, Emil Bächler, September, 1920.

The Master Bear

A second body of evidence testifying to the force of the mythic imagination in the ordering of life in Neanderthal times came to light in the first decades of the present century, when a series of high mountain grottoes was discovered within which cave-bear skulls had been stored: Wild-kirchli, Drachenloch, and Wildenmann-lisloch in Switzerland, and in Germany, Petershöhle in Middle Franconia, near Velden (Map 20). All were at least 7000 feet above sea level, Drachenloch nearly 8000. Hence, none could have been entered during the period of the glaciers, and their remains have been judged, consequently, to belong to the late Riss-Würm interglacial. This estimate is supported not only by the early and pre-Mousterian tools found within them, but also by the faunal remains, which include three large interglacial species: the cave panther, cave lion, and huge cave bear, the principal animal hunted in that time and accordingly revered. For it has been observed that in hunting societies, generally, the principal food animal is the normal pivotal figure of the religious cult.

In Drachenloch, the Dragon's Den, high on a peak overlooking the village of Vättis (Map 20, and Figure 81), Emil Bächler in the spring of 1917 commenced excavations which he continued into 1922; and what he uncovered and charted were seven distinct layers, dating back to interglacial times. The first two were relatively recent and of no archeological interest, but at Level 3, cave-bear remains appeared with Paleolithic artifacts. At Level 4, there

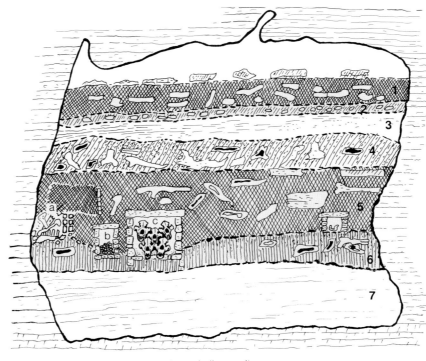

Cave rock

Cave interior

1. Dark gray upper layer

2. White sinter, sterile

CAVE BEAR REMAINS AND ARTIFICATS

3. Threefold culture level,
4. bright red to dark brown,
5. sinterlike, earthy, loamy

STONE CABINETS

6. White loam, compact, sterile

7. Bedrock

a. bone storage bin c. stone skull-repository
b. fire hearth

DRACHENBERG - OSTSEITE MIT DRACHENLOCH-HÖHLE (2427m)
NACH EINER FLUGAUFNAHME VON WALTER MITTELHOLZER 1918   TONI NIGG 1977

81. Eastern slope of the Drachenberg (Dragon Mount) in the Engadine, from an air photo made in 1918; height, 2427 meters (7963 feet). Drachenloch (the Dragon's Den), within which in 1917 the remains were found of a cave-bear-skull sanctuary, can be seen high upper left.

82. A cave-bear skull from a stone tabernacle in Drachenloch, with a longbone (its own?) placed in its mouth as though in offering, "himself to Himself." Compare the Ainu bear sacrifice, I.2: 150–152.

83. In Wildkirchli (the Wilderness Chapel), another Alpine sanctuary dedicated to rituals associated with the hunt, these stone worktables and benches were the furniture of a workshop for the fashioning chiefly of handaxes, but also of implements of bone.

it seems we may be confronting here what is truly a First, in the elder Paleolithic: the original offering cult, namely, of mankind."[17]

Doubts concerning this interpretation have been expressed by the distinguished French authority André Leroi-Gourhan, who suggests that the reported arrangements may have been the work, not of Neanderthalers, but of the later Magdalenians, who ranked the bear, along with the rhinoceros and large felines (lions, leopards, and panthers), high among the symbolic beasts of their mythological cycles. The cave bear no longer existed in their time, yet they might have recognized the large skulls and bones as representing gigantic members of the species, and, in reverence, then have arranged and stored them as they were found. Or some of the reported dispositions might even have been the work simply of chance, when bears, on entering the caves to hibernate, nuzzled and nestled among the bones of earlier members of their kind that had died there.[18]

It is not easy to imagine, however, how the people of the postglacial Magdalenian period could have set up storage bins, worktables, and other equipment in strata three to four and five levels below the earth floors of their day. And with respect to the movements of hibernating bears: Drachenloch and Wildenmannlisloch were, in Bächler's words, "never the resorts and deathbeds of cave bears, but the dwellings of the cave bear hunters."[19]

"At the excavations in Drachenloch and Wildenmannlisloch," he continues, "those parts of the caves nearest the entrances proved to be all but barren of both animal and prehistoric remains. One could speak

were massive accumulations of cave-bear remains, again associated with artifacts; and at Level 5, stone cabinets made of slabs were found, containing cave-bear skulls, remarkably well preserved. Some years earlier, from 1903 to 1908, at Wildkirchli, the Wilderness Chapel, Bächler had conducted a similar operation, and there had unearthed an actual Paleolithic workshop with stone tables and benches (Map 20, and Figure 83). Large quartzite nuggets lay about, brought in to be fashioned into tools, while a superior hand ax and a scattering of implements, both of stone and of bone, gave evidence of the craftsmanship of the shop. And then from 1923 to 1927, in Wildenmannlisloch, the Wild Man's Den (Map 20), Bächler completed his investigations, and in 1940 wrote, in summary:

"The purposeful collection and arranged preservation of the cave-bear skulls and long bones behind dry walls (*Trockenmauern*) set up along the sides of the caves; and more especially, the hermetic sealing away of the skulls, either in crudely built stone cabinets, protected by slab coverings, or in repositories walled with flagging, allow for no other conclusion, after the realistic consideration of every possibility, but that we have here to do with some sort of Bear Cult, specifically a Bone-offering Cult, inspired by the mystical thoughts and feelings of an Old Paleolithic population; thoughts involving transcendental, super-sensual ideas. Many ethnological parallels testify to a broad distribution of bone-offering cults in the historic period, especially among the hunting peoples of the north. And so,

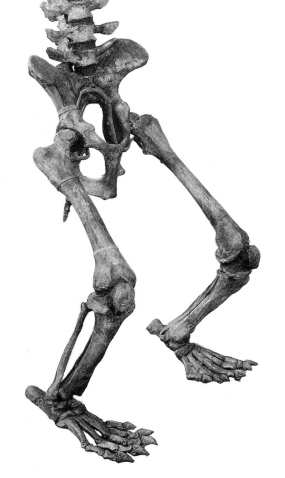

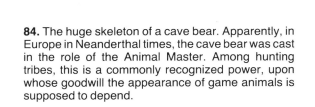

84. The huge skeleton of a cave bear. Apparently, in Europe in Neanderthal times, the cave bear was cast in the role of the Animal Master. Among hunting tribes, this is a commonly recognized power, upon whose goodwill the appearance of game animals is supposed to depend.

kind for the preservation of the skulls, some of which were even found in what appeared to be intentionally symbolic arrangements. For example, there was one surrounded by a circle of small stones; another had had the long bones of a bear (possibly its own) placed beneath its snout (Figure 82); and a third had had similar long bones thrust through its eyes. In the German cave of Petershöhle, which had been excavated by Konrad Hörmann during the same years that Emil Bächler was working in Drachenloch, five skulls were found arranged neatly in recesses in the walls.

There can be no doubt that we have here the evidence of a cult of some kind in veneration of the cave bear, and unless the excavators have greatly misread their evidence, the cult was of the same period as that of the earliest known human burials. This is to say, the interpretation of death as but a passing had been applied, not only to the subject, man, but also to the objects of his hunting, and, lest resentment on their part should follow upon a good hunting day and so perhaps spoil the next, rites of gratitude, praise, and appeasement were enacted. For hunters, the two orders of ritual, burial and animal worship, were complementary, the metaphysical reasons for the first directly implying a need for the second. And that the two were finally grounded in one system of propositions would seem to be evident in the comparable handlings of the human skull at Monte Circeo and the bear skulls of these mountain caves.

The Sentiment of Wonder

We may seem, at this point, to be close to answering the old question, beloved of theologians and formerly also of anthropologists, of the origins of religion; but in fact, we are not. For, when viewed in relation to the finds from 4 million years ago at Olduvai and Lake Turkana, these earliest, mythically inspired rites of burial and

cabinet containing skulls which occupied more than half the width of the chamber [Figure 85], provided evidence enough for the significance, both of this area, and of the backmost portion of the cave: the most important place for safe keeping, in the deepest darkness of the cavern depth . . . 'where not everyone might enter.' "[20]

"What these finds reveal to us," he declares again, "is a picture of the completely *pious* treatment of the largest, handsomest bones of spoils of the hunt, establishing this third section of the cave as a *sanctuary*, shut off by a 'tabu'. In any case, they have nothing to do with the usual hoarding of bones of the hunt; the picture would then have been of a totally different kind. And it was finally impossible to withhold oneself from this increasing realization, when, at the end of our excavations in Grotto III, at the back of its rocky wall, we broke, once again, upon a formal funereal row of nine skulls, which had been protected from all damage by slabs of stone laid slant against the rock wall."[21]

In sum: There were found in these caves, in strata bearing the remains of interglacial fauna, evidences, on one hand, of workshops for the fashioning of tools and weapons associated with the bear hunt, and on the other hand, of sanctuaries for the worship of the bears that were killed. There were fire hearths in the caves, stone worktables and benches, flagstone floorings, and bins of various

only of 'scatterings.' But the picture immediately changed the moment one entered Grotto II of a cave and came to those parts that had served its human inhabitants as dwelling, work, and sleeping quarters—made evident not only by the masses of animal bones but also by the worktools bearing witness to the labors of the one-time occupants. . . .

"The striking, intentionally arranged, partial shutting off of Grotto III at Drachenloch by a screened fire hearth beneath the entrance, as well as by a large stone

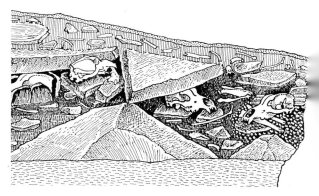

85. In Drachenloch, Grotto III, a stone cabinet occupying more than half the width of the chamber and containing cave-bear skulls protected by a covering of large stone slabs. These preserved skulls are clearly the relics of a cult.

worship, dating from no more than 70,000 years past, are practically of the present. The antecedent 4 million years of nothing but skull fragments, long bones, flints, and scatterings of teeth tell us nothing of what thinking may have inhabited those skulls, what prostrations moved the bones, or what communion meals graced the teeth. Amplifications of skull capacities have been registered, from the cubic content of a gorilla's brain of about 500 cc, upward and onward to the 1600 cc of Neanderthal and then downward to the 1500 cc or so of mankind today. At which stage, however, did human thinking ever open to a larger field than that of animal economics: nutrition, reproduction, self- and species-preservation, the building and defense of nests, leisure-time entertainment, and the comforting of wounds? When did the earth and skies open to wonder and the mind respond with an exaltation to which everything else thereafter might become subordinate?

"We observe," wrote Giambattista Vico in *The New Science* (1730), "that all nations, barbarous as well as civilized, though separately founded because remote from each other in time and space, keep the following human customs: all have some religion, all contract solemn marriages, all bury their dead. And in no nation, however savage and crude, are any human actions performed with more elaborate ceremonies and more sacred solemnity than those of religion, marriage, and burial. For, by the axiom that 'uniform ideas, born among peoples unknown to each other, must have a common ground of truth,' it must have been dictated to all nations that from these three institutions humanity began among them all, so that the world should not become again a bestial wilderness."[22]

This eighteenth-century statement that "uniform ideas, born among peoples unknown to each other, must have a common ground of truth," or, in twentieth-century terms, "a common ground in the psyche," defines a principle tacitly taken for granted in all psychological approaches to the interpretation of myths. Frazer, in *The Golden Bough*, thought to explain the observed resemblances as "the effect of similar causes acting alike on the similar constitution of the human mind in different countries and under different skies";[23] and C. G. Jung, in his subsequent exploration of the mind that Frazer had thus recognized, used the term "archetypes of the collective unconscious" to designate those structures grounded in the general anatomy of our species, to which the observed resemblances might be referred. "Although tradition and transmission by migration certainly play a part," he conceded, "there are very many cases that cannot be accounted for in this way and drive us to the

Two objects from a Neanderthal site in Tata, Hungary, that may reflect the awakening of a sense of wonder:

86. A shaped piece of mammoth ivory, suggesting an Australian *tjurunga*.

87. A nummulite (an Eocene formaniniferal fossil) engraved with a cross.

hypothesis of 'autochthonous revival.' These cases are so numerous that we are obliged to assume the existence of a collective psychic substratum. I have called this the *collective unconscious*."[24]

Adolf Bastian, as already remarked (page 9), employed the term "elementary ideas" (*Elementargedanken*) with reference to the products of this universally human ground, while in his second term, "ethnic ideas" (*Völkergedanken*), he recognized the differences of their appearances among the greatly differing cultures. Vico's institution of "burial," for example, as exemplified among the Vedic Aryans, modern Hindus, or Buddhists,

would have to be described rather as "cremation" than as "burial." And his institution of "marriage" likewise exhibits variations. The Muslim authorization of four wives, along with a dozen or so—or even a hundred or more—concubines, is not readily brought under one rubric with Roman Catholic monogamy; nor would it seem quite to serve the Viconian function of "moderating the passions." Nevertheless in a general way, the elementary idea can be recognized of an institution (to quote an applicable dictionary definition) "whereby men and women are joined in a special kind of social and legal dependence, for the purpose of founding and maintaining a family."[25] Marriage, so defined, appears to be already indicated in our finds from Neanderthal times: in the cave of La Ferrassie, for example, with its skeletons of two adults, head to head, and four children; or in the cave at Shanidar, with the male body heaped with flowers, beneath which two women and an infant had been buried. What the forms or form of marriage in that primordial era may have been, we do not know; nor can we tell whether ceremonial manners of disposal of the dead other than burial may have been observed. However, it does look very much as though Vico's three elementary institutions of religion, marriage, and burial may have come simultaneously to manifestation in that period when, in the course of the evolution of life, the first degree had been attained of the "sapient" mind.

The evidence for burial in that distant era is secure, that for marriage, circumstantial, while that for religion asks for a much more generous definition of the term than the famous one of Parson Thwackum in Henry Fielding's *Tom Jones:* "When I mention religion I mean the Christian religion; and not only the Christian religion but the Protestant religion, and not only the Protestant religion, but the Church of England." James G. Frazer, in *The Golden Bough*, greatly (and yet not sufficiently) enlarged this insular view when he wrote:

"By religion then, I understand a propitiation or conciliation of powers superior to man which are believed to direct and control the course of nature and of human life. Thus defined, religion consists of two elements, a theoretical and a practical, namely, a belief in powers higher than man and an attempt to propitiate and please them. Of the two, belief clearly comes first, since we must believe in the existence of a divine being before we can attempt to please him. But unless the belief leads to a corresponding practice, it is not a religion but merely a theology; in the language of St. James, 'faith, if it hath not works, is dead, being alone.' In other words, no man is religious who does not govern his conduct in some measure by the fear or love of God. On the other hand, mere practice, divested of all religious belief, is also not religion."[26]

The anthropologist has here fallen—not as dramatically as Fielding's Parson Thwackum, yet no less inextricably—into a specifically Christian manner of speech. Interpreting in his sense the evidence of the cave-bear shrines as the earliest known prehistoric signs of "a propitiation or conciliation of powers superior to man," one would have to ask, and leave open, the question as to what kind of "powers superior to man," or what God, the cave bears and their relics were supposed to represent or to be. Can the huge beast have been revered as "God" in any such sense as that implied by Frazer's capitalization of the term? Or was it even equivalent to Letakots-Lesa's concept of an animal sent by the One Above as a messenger? Indeed, was there any One Above at all in that period; or were the bears revered, among other creatures and objects, simply in and for and as themselves?

André Leroi-Gourhan has found in the evidences of Neanderthal times suggestions for a definition of religion that point beyond these unanswerable rationalistic questions to a certain state, mode, or quality of consciousness that is specific to religion, basic and antecedent to all the historic orders of polytheism, monotheism, pantheism, atheism, fetishism, animism, henotheism, and the rest. As one of the most scrupulous authorities in this field of scholarship, he has refused either to accept as proven any evidence that is uncertain, or to interpret imaginatively even evidence that he accepts. The Neanderthal bear cult, for example, he has seriously questioned. The burials he recognizes but refuses to interpret. Yet, he has remarked a number of other, more modest witnesses to what he describes as an order of interests on the part of Neanderthal Man (whom he does not regard, by the way, as of *sapiens* rank) that are "not confined to eating and drinking": little clumps and deposits of red ocher, assembled shells, collected fossils, piles of spheroid stones, and a number of curious limestone slabs on which little cup marks appear. "That the extraordinary should have been explicitly perceived," he remarks, "warrants a strong presumption in favor of an intuition of the supernatural, though probably not in the sense in which we have conceived of it for some millenniums. . . . Certain facts sufficiently well authenticated suffice to show that practices not related to techniques of the material life existed before the period of *Homo sapiens*; we may call them religious, because they testify to interests beyond those of the vegetative life."[27]

The perception of the extraordinary is, of course, something known already to the animal kingdom. The Chinese have a saying: "One dog barks at a shadow, and four hundred dogs make it a fact." But, in the sense in which Leroi-Gourhan has written of the perception of the extraordinary as an opening of the mind to a dimension of religious awe, it is also something else. To quote Vico again: "Wonder is the daughter of ignorance; and the greater the object of wonder, the more the wonder grows."[28] Whether it be a cockleshell or the mystery of death, the *mysterium fascinans* or *mysterium tremendum*, this wonder is that of which Goethe wrote in those lines of his *Faust*:

> *Das Schaudern ist der Menschheit bestes*
>   *Teil.*
> *Wie auch die Welt ihm das Gefühl*
>   *verteuere,*
> *Ergriffen fühlt er tief das Ungeheuere.*[29]

The history of our subject, then, is of the progressive enlargement of man's knowledge of the magnitude of his own ignorance and the expansion thereby of his wonder—and religion.

The Temple Caves

To stand, even today, in the Rotunda of Lascaux is a profound experience. The mind, flung back through millennia, scans a landscape hung between day and night, underground yet overhead, of immortal herds of woolly ponies, immense bulls of a species now extinct yet here alive, beautiful stags with luxuriously branching antlers; and among all these, the arresting, very curious form of an animal such as cannot have lived in this world even in the Paleolithic age (Figure 90). Two long, straight horns point directly forward from its head, like the antennae of an insect or a pair of poised banderillas; and the gravid belly hangs nearly to the ground. This surely is a wizard beast, and the most mysterious presence of the whole magnificent vision.

To the right, below this enigmatic form, an opening in the craggy wall leads to a pictured rock-corridor known to science as the Axial Gallery (Figure 93), where, as we enter, our eyes are greeted by another animal array: at the right, a black stag; to the left, a large galloping bull; and beyond, the whole tunnel is spectacular, even to the ceiling, with its herds, again, of trotting ponies, cows, and at the far end, a pair of ibexes. Here and there we discover what appear to be flying darts; and there are four cryptic quadrangular

88. Pech Merle, one of the greatest of the painted temple caves: its stalagmites and stalactites, when struck, resound like gongs.

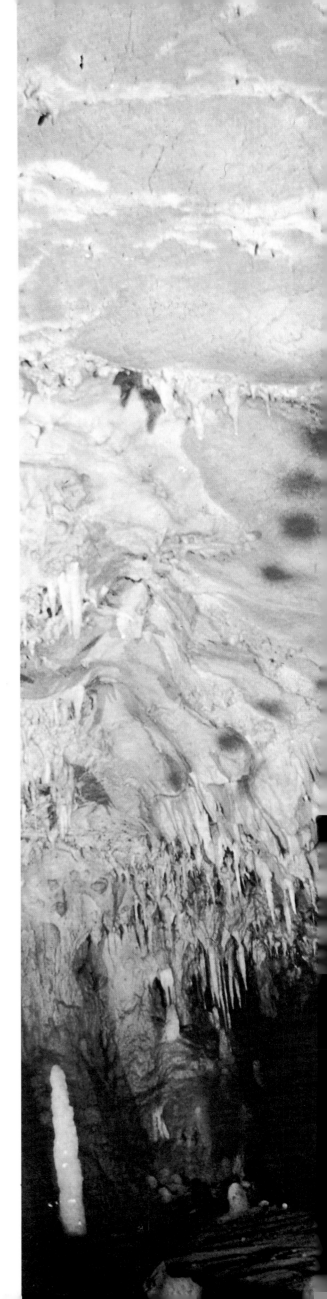

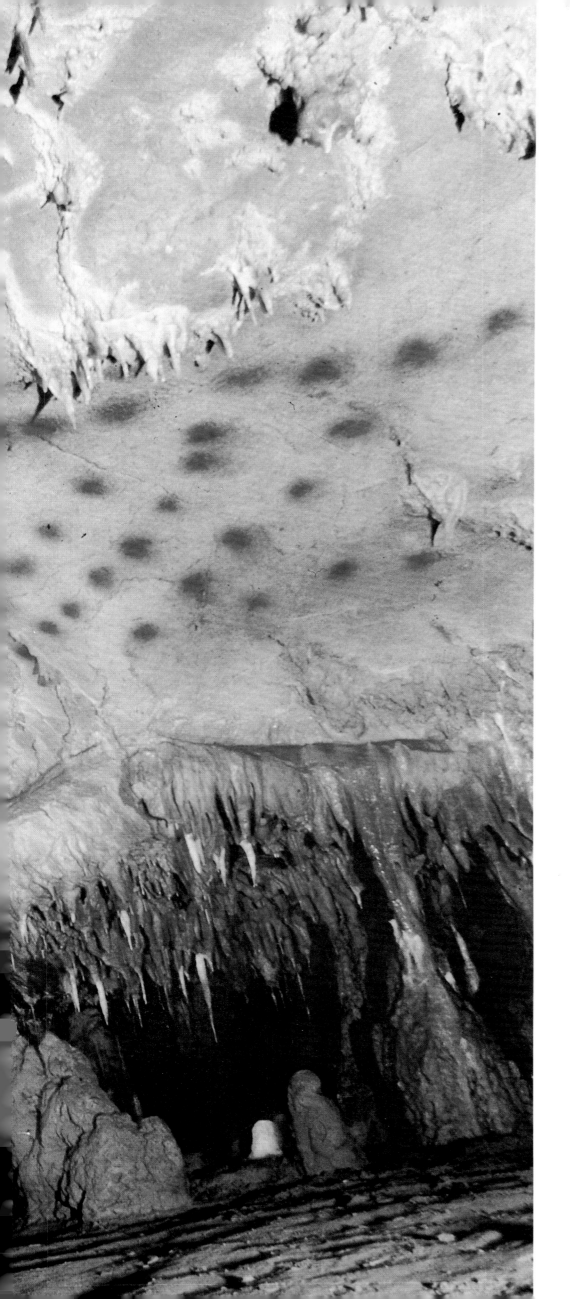

signs, each set, as André Leroi-Gourhan has remarked, in a different section of the composition.[30] Beneath the first black stag, furthermore, and out before him runs a long, curving row of large black dots.

The prehistorians have been hard put to interpret these Paleolithic signs, of which there are many throughout the subterranean galleries. Leroi-Gourhan has proposed what is perhaps a clue, namely, a complementarity of female and male signs: the female, variously represented as triangles, ovals, rectangles, and claviforms; the male, as barbed strokes, short lines, and dots.[31] Moreover, in the assignment of such symbols to various parts of the great caverns, this scholar has recognized an apparent consistency. "The male signs are found almost exclusively," he

The idea of a temple as distinguished from a chapel or shrine—namely, of an enclosed area in which all the forms beheld are of vision—was conceived and first realized in the great painted caves of southwestern France and northern Spain, and most marvelously in those termed by the Abbé Breuil the "Six Giants": Altamira, Font-de-Gaume, Les Combarelles, Lascaux, Les Trois Frères, and Niaux. As in Chartres Cathedral the mystery of the hidden history of the universe is revealed through the imagery of an anthropomorphic pantheon, so here, in these temple caves, the same mystery is made known through animal forms that are at once in movement and at rest. These forms are magical: midway, as it were, between the living species of the hunting plains and the universal ground of night, out of which the animals come, back into which they return, and which is the very substance of these caves.

91/92. The ceiling of the Rotunda at Lascaux. Today it is impossible to imagine the mood of mystery and awe that the illumination of this great Rotunda of Lascaux must have evoked in those here participating in the men's rites. Impossible, also, to imagine by what miracle of inspiration this vision of an everlasting hunting ground was conceived, and by what art realized! The wizard beast, upper left, dominates the composition. The bulls are its glory. The opening in the wall, lower center, is the entrance to the Axial Gallery. That to the right is the beginning of the Passageway to the Crypt and Nave.

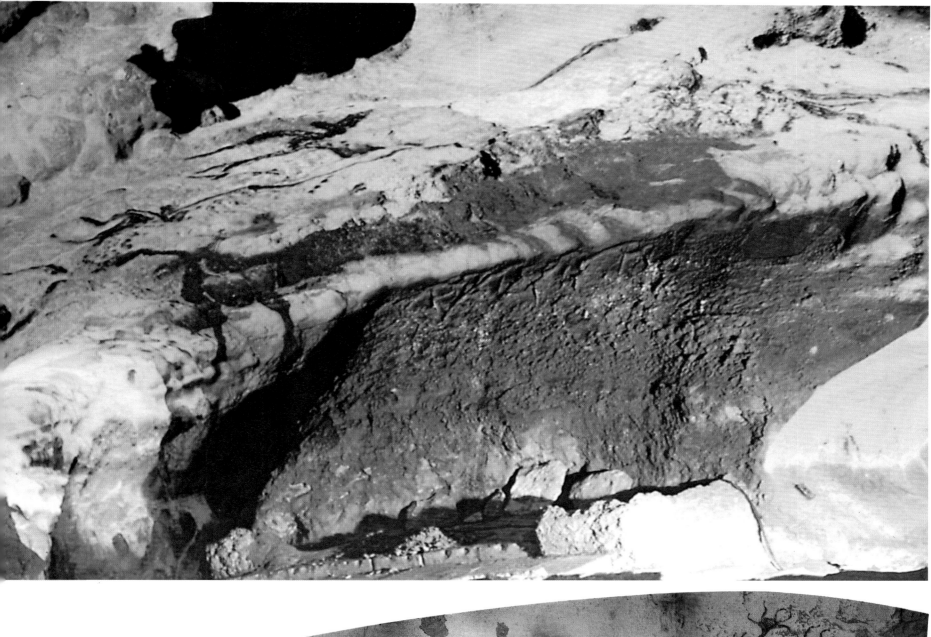

93. The entire right-hand wall of the Axial Gallery. What the function of this corridor may have been is unknown. It is craggy, narrow, yet pictured to the ceiling. As we enter, the black stag with antlers branching is to our right. To our left is a galloping black bull. The rectangular forms and arrowlike strokes distributed among the animals have been variously interpreted. Some regard them as traps and arrows. André Leroi-Gourhan reads them as female and male symbolic signs, relevant to an underlying mythology of polarized forces, which, in his view, was the informing inspiration of all the religious sanctuaries of this Paleolithic era.

writes, "at the point where the sanctuary begins and in the remotest parts of the caves; they also appear in the transitions leading from one central composition to another. Within the central compositions, on the other hand, female signs are normally associated with signs of the male set."[32] A computerized count of the animal species also led to a recognition of pairings. "Certain animals turned up next to each other too often," this interpreter found, "for such associations to be explained only as chance."[33] Oxen or bisons would be found next to horses, for example, or bisons next to mammoths. "The fundamental principle," he concluded, "is that of pairing: let us not say 'coupling,' for there are no scenes of copulation in Paleolithic art. The idea of reproduction perhaps underlies the representation of paired figures but what we shall see subsequently does not absolutely establish this. Starting with the earliest figures, one has the impression of being faced with a system polished in the course of time—not unlike the older religions of our world, wherein there are male and female divinities whose actions do not overtly allude to sexual reproduction, but whose male and female qualities are indispensably complementary."[34]

Or we may think of the old Chinese yang/yin, light/dark, hot/cold, dry/moist, male/female, polarity. In the caves, on the yin, or female, side are the ox, bison, and hind; on the yang, or male, are the horse, stag, and ibex. At Arcy-sur-Cure and Pech Merle the mammoth appears with the bison, whereas at Baume Latrone its companions are the feline and the horse; in certain other cases, mammoths are complementary to bovid/horse arrangements. "The role of the mammoth," Leroi-Gourhan concedes, "is hard to unravel." Nor, indeed, have more than a few of the numerous riddles of these caves been solved.

The recognition of a consistent *architectural* order in the distribution of the symbolic beasts and signs is another important clue to the mythology of these subterranean temples.

"What constituted for Paleolithic men the special heart and core of the caves," this author declares, "is clearly the panels in the central part, dominated by animals from the female category and female signs, supplemented by animals from the male category and male signs. The entrance to the sanctuary, usually a narrow part of the cave, is decorated with male symbols, either animals or signs; the back of the cave, often a narrow tunnel, is decorated with the same signs, reinforced by horned men and the rarer animals (cave lion or rhinoceros). Although crowded with images this framework is quite simple; it leaves us completely in the dark

94. Deep in a cavern at Montespan is this roughly molded, headless model of a bear. When discovered, a bear's skull lay on the ground before it. Following a ritual of some kind, a bear's pelt with the head still attached had been left draped over this form.

concerning what we should like to know about the rites, and, let us say, about an underlying metaphysics. However, it rules out any simplistic idea concerning the religious system of Paleolithic men."[35]

A third point—of obscure yet indubitable significance—appears when the animals chosen for representation are classified and numbered. "First of all," states Leroi-Gourhan, "it must be said that, statistically speaking, the number of species represented is much lower than the number of species known to have existed at the time. Paleolithic artists did not portray just any animal but animals of certain species, and these did not necessarily play an important part in their daily life. . . . The main actors," he reports further, "are the horse and the bison, the animals next in importance being the hinds, the mammoths, the oxen, the ibexes, and the stags. . . . Bears, lions, and rhinoceroses play an important part, but as a rule there is only one representation of each per cave, and they are by no means represented in every cave."[36]

With respect to the importance of the bear and of bear worship in this period, an extraordinarily interesting discovery was made in 1923 by the Count Bégouën and Norbert Casteret in a cave about a mile and a half long and extremely difficult of access, at Montespan (Haute-Garonne). In the middle of a chamber, toward the end of one of the convoluted passages, the light of their lamps fell upon a heap of clay, crudely shaped to suggest a bear couchant, but with no head. The stump of the neck was smooth and at a slant, and on the ground before it, be-

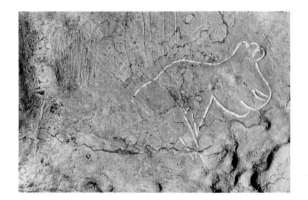

95. Very different in feeling from the other galleries is the Chamber of Felines with its engraved, unpainted lions, the only carnivores among these abounding herds.

tween the effigy's paws, lay the actual skull of a bear cub. The clay body, punctured with a number of holes, had been covered, apparently as a mere support, with the hide of the beast for a ceremony of some sort, during which the image was dealt sharp blows.[37] We have no idea of how many years, centuries, or perhaps millennia this bearskin rack may have served; what the prayers or ritual acts may have been that accompanied its service; or when the last fresh pelt was laid on its back, to be abandoned at the end of an age, left alone in the silence, rotting, and at some point in time releasing its skull—until struck by the light of an electric flash, some fifteen millennia later.

The general message, however, is obvious; namely, of a Paleolithic hunting ceremonial performed among flickering torches in this deep, dark womb of the earth. For these great painted grottoes, chill, dangerous, and labyrinthine, wherein all orientation to the quarters of the sky is lost, and time stops—or rather, continues without punctuation of day and night—were never dwelling places, but temples beyond the tick of time, preserved to us in the depths, so to say, of the historical unconscious of our species. Their herds are the herds, not of time, but of eternity, out of which the animals of the light-world come, and back to which they return for renewal. Some of the bulls in the animal frieze of the Lascaux Rotunda are more than 17 feet long, rendered with a fluency and grace of line, as alive as life itself.

At the end of the Axial Gallery there is a sharp turn to the left; the tunnel narrows, and, continuing on, we find a bison/horse group completely cut off from the rest of the composition. "Further on," as Leroi-Gourhan tells, "the passage becomes a constricted tunnel where we find

LASCAUX: GENERAL FLOOR PLAN

Each gallery has its fascination. The very different groupings of the various animal messengers appeal to us aesthetically, and we feel joined in a kinship of experience with the artists who produced them. However, to the special mystical function that each of these galleries served—for millennia—we have no clue. Entering the cave today, one confronts directly the breathtaking spectacle of the Rotunda (see **91/92**). Above are the great bulls and woolly ponies; and to the left, as though herding them, is the "wizard beast" with its "pointing horns" (**90**). There is a sense here of a presence inhabiting these forms.

100. In the Lascaux Shaft, or Crypt, about 16 feet below the general level of the cavern floor, is the most crucial scene in the whole sanctuary: an eviscerated bison bull, a masked shaman lying before him, and a rhinoceros walking by with lifted tail (**105**).

THE SHAFT

THE APSE

THE ROTUNDA

THE NAVE

THE PASSAGEWAY

THE AXIAL GALLERY

96. The grace and rhythm of this beautiful run of swimming stags immediately enchant the eye at the entrance to the Nave.

97. Among the animals of the Nave, some way along the left wall, two back-to-back bison are outstanding.

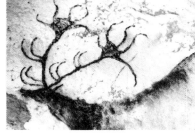

98. This extraordinarily beautiful stag (to the right as we enter the Axial Gallery) matches in position the swimming stags of the Nave.

101. Not the least of the wonders of the art of the cave is the vitality of the prodigious bulls: their graceful ease of line.

99. Among the many unforgettable sights of this subterranean, painted labyrinth is the whole right wall of the Axial Gallery (**93**) with its herd of woolly arctic ponies and this glorious leaping cow.

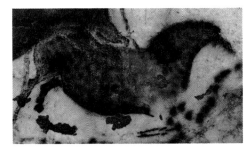

102. One of the ponies among the animals on the Axial Gallery's left wall: very like the woolly ponies to be seen today grazing and trotting about throughout Iceland.

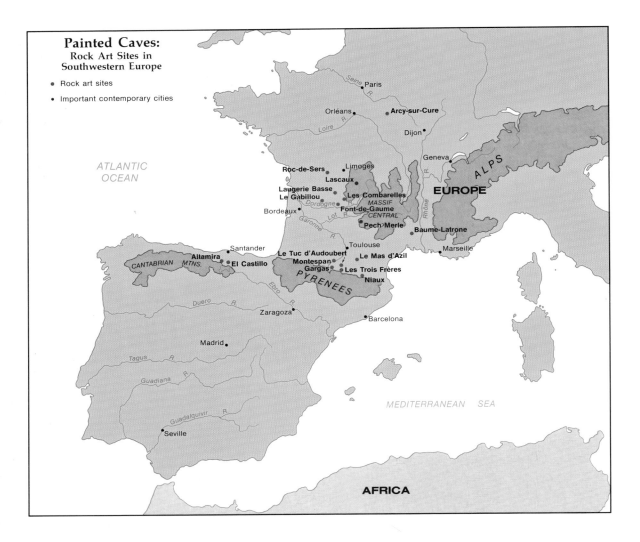

Map 21. The principal locations of the temple caves are shown on this map. Far to the east, in the southern Urals on the south bend of the Belaya River, paintings in a related style have lately been found in the Kapovaya cave. There may be other undiscovered sites. The nuclear area of the development of this earliest of mankind's art traditions, however, was undoubtedly that of southwestern France, the Cantabrian hills, and the Pyrenees.

a few engraved horses and, at the very end, the red markings that so often indicate the end of the decorated parts of the caves. The Axial Gallery as a whole, then," he concludes, "consists of two alternating groups: cow/rectangles/horses, and bull/barbed sign/cows, both groups flanked by stags; there are complementary ibexes, and an isolated bison/horse composition."[38]

We return to the Rotunda and proceed from the Axial Gallery into an opposite opening in the almost circular wall leading to the ample Passageway in which the figures are extremely faint. In Leroi-Gourhan's opinion, this chamber is probably the oldest of the grotto, with a decoration based, in his words, "upon a large ox/horse + ibex group, with at least one bison/horse composition." Continuing, we enter the sharply narrowing Nave, and there, directly before us, to the right, is that beautiful, now famous frieze of the heads of five stags, apparently swimming. To the left is a bison/horse + ibex group, with associated rectangular and barbed signs, along with an ox/horse composition which also includes female and male signals. These are followed by two

magnificent bison, back to back, after which the tunnel again sharply narrows to a long, undecorated corridor, ending in the Chamber of Felines. Some thirty animal figures are to be seen here, as well as a great number of signs, distributed among three bell-shaped subchambers, each about 3 feet in diameter. In the first two are six uncolored engravings of felines, among horses, ibexes, a bull, and a number of male and female signs. The last composition comprises horses, painted strokes and other signs, stags, bison, and a rhinoceros, beyond which, at the rear of the chamber, there appears again only such a series of red dots as we found at the end of the Axial Gallery.

Evidently, this whole, really glorious, subterranean temple compound was conceived, either by someone or by some original master group, as an ordered whole. But to what end, we cannot say. No crude anthropological theory of "primitive magic" suffices to explain its extraordinary beauty, the aesthetics of its organization, or the magnificence of its forms. Why, precisely, a cluster of felines here, bulls and horses there, ibexes at the ends of compositions, red dots, quadrangles and black dots, various pairings, postures, and arrangements? As the meticu-

103. From Double Hand Shelter, Queensland, Australia.

104. From a Paleolithic cave in France.

What is the meaning of such hand prints left on the walls of sacred places throughout the world? They are testimonials to participation in a mystery.

lous studies of Leroi-Gourhan have demonstrated, there was some sort of mythological implication in all this iconography, which is evidently represented, furthermore, throughout the entire great series of these French and Spanish Paleolithic grottoes.

The enigma deepens when, on returning from the Chamber of Felines through the long and narrow Nave back to the Passageway, we turn there to the left, through the circular Apse, and descend gingerly, by means of a modern wooden ladder, into the Shaft, which is about 16 feet deep. On the way down, we note the painting of a small, black horse's head, and on turning, confront an amazing composition which has baffled even the most learned and intuitive of the many great students of this art. On the left is a rhinoceros, apparently walking away, under whose tail there is an arrangement of six black dots.."The rhinoceros," states Leroi-Gourhan, "is a back-cave or marginal animal . . . : to find it at the bottom of the Shaft, accompanied by aligned dots, is perfectly normal."[39] So far, so good. But now, behind this beast, to our right, there lies, supine with outflung arms, a man (comparatively crudely

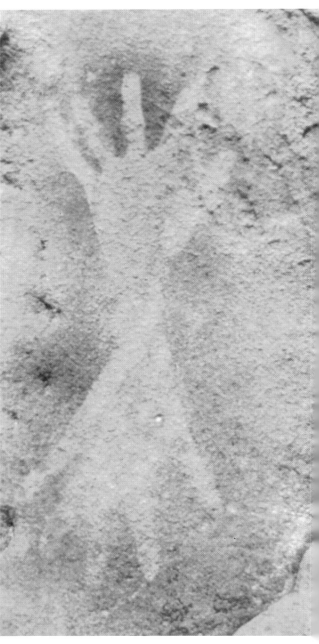

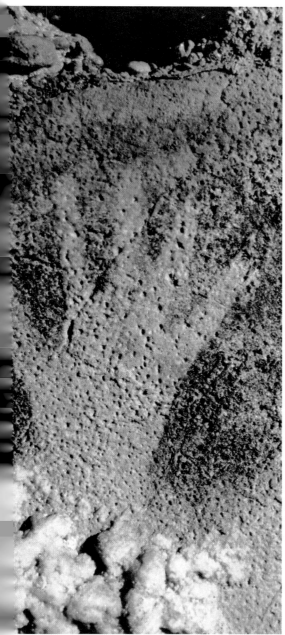

drawn) with erect phallus and what would appear to be a bird's head—or perhaps he is wearing a mask. His hands also are birdlike, and there is the figure of a bird perched upon a vertical staff at his right. "Birds are rare," remarks Leroi-Gourhan, "both in cave art and in decorated objects, and their position in symbolism is uncertain. About all we can say is that the lower part of the sign painted here resembles a male sign."[40] But birds, on the other hand, are, in later, shamanistic contexts, the normal vehicles of wizard-flights in ecstasy, whether to the underworld, to the heavens, or to those realms beyond the horizon from which shamanic powers derive. Bird-decorated costumes and staves, as well as bird transformations, are the rule in shamanistic contexts. Hence, it seems to me entirely possible that the prostrate figure in this crypt, or holy of holies of the cathedral of Lascaux, is not at all a hunter slain by a bull and here memorialized, as the Abbé Breuil suggested in his interpretation of the scene,[41] but a shaman, rapt in trance. Before him is a great bison bull, eviscerated apparently by a spear that is represented as though resting aslant against the beast's flank, but was meant to be seen, almost certainly, as having transfixed its anus and emerged through its sexual organ. There is no one behind the bull from whose hand the lance might have been thrown. However, at the man's feet there is a kind of barbed stick, which the Abbé Breuil interpreted as a spear thrower, an atlatl. Leroi-Gourhan rejects this sugges-

105. This scene of mystery in the Shaft, or Crypt, the "holy of holies" of the Lascaux temple cave, may represent an episode from a legend of that era. Three other, possibly related, man/bull confrontations have been identified in art works of the period, c. 17,000 to 12,000 B.C.: one, an engraving on reindeer horn from a rock shelter, Laugerie Basse, in the neighborhood of Lascaux; another, a painting deep in the temple cave, also nearby, at Villars; and the third (some 5000 years earlier), a sculptured block in a rock shelter, Le Roc de Sers, in Charcute, dated c. 17,000 B.C.

tion, reading the stick as a male sign, complemented by the falling entrails of the wounded beast, which descend in four concentric ovals. These he interprets as a female sign, suggesting that what we may have here is "a variant form of the assimilation of phallus-to-spear and vulva-to-wound." "Does the male sign," he asks, "imply an assimilation of phallus-to-spear-thrower?"[42]

The question remains open. But a telling point is made when this author calls attention to an engraved reindeer horn from a dwelling site not far from Lascaux, known as Laugerie Basse, which, in his words, "has on one side a bison marked with one stroke and an ithyphallic man with outstretched arms, on the other side a horse." In the Lascaux Shaft, as we have seen, there is an incompletely rendered horse, constituting, together with the bison, a standard bovine/horse composition. "The same scene, with the same protagonists, turns up," Leroi-Gourhan continues, "in sculptured form at Le Roc de Sers and in painted form at Villars."[43]

That is to say, it is evidently the illustration of a crucial scene from some essential legend of the period; a legend, furthermore, that must have enjoyed a long career, since the sculpture of Le Roc de Sers is of the Solutrean Age, c. 17,000 B.C.,[44] a good 5000 years earlier than the period of the painting at Lascaux.

This legend, then, we can register as a component of our first known (yet unknown) documented mythology, having flourished, one way or another, from c. 17,000 to 12,000 B.C. Moreover, from the position of its illustration in the most inaccessible holy of holies of the magnificent great sanctuary—this Sistine Chapel of the Paleolithic, as it has been called—we may judge it to have been, very probably, the inspiring legend of the entire grotto, with the wizard beast in the Rotunda representing a projection of the power of the shaman in the crypt, the magic of its pointing horns corresponding to that of his pointing phallus.

By analogy, there is still practiced in Australia a lethal phallic rite of magic known as the "pointing bone," one variety of which has been described thus by Geza Róheim:

"Black or hostile magic is predominantly phallic in Australia. . . . If a man has been 'boned', his dream will show it. First he sees a crack, an opening in the ground, and then two or three men walking toward him within the opening. When they are near they draw a bone out of their own body. It comes from the flesh between the scrotum and the rectum. The sorcerer, before he actually 'bones' his victim, makes him fall asleep by strewing in the air some semen or excrement which he has taken from his own penis or rectum. The man who uses the bone holds it

under his penis, as if a second penis were protruding from him.

"The Pindupi refer to black magic in general as *erati,* and a special type is described as *kujur-punganyi* ('bad-make'). Several men hold a string or pointing bone with both hands and, bending down, point backward, passing the magical bone just beside the penis. The victim is asleep, and the bone goes straight into his scrotum."[45]

Strictly thinking, it is improper to make comparisons of this kind, jumping centuries and culture provinces. However, as we have already seen (page 32), the Australian natives have had spear-throwers for some 7000 years, and so too had the people of Lascaux, 10,000 to 20,000 years earlier. Stenciled hands appear in Australia on the rock walls of the Tombs Shelter and Kenniff Cave; so also at El Castillo, Gargas, Pech Merle, and many more of the great European grottoes. Furthermore, we have learned something of the perdurability of Old Stone Age forms and principles; and where the idea of a spear-thrower can have been handed on, so too can that of a pointing bone. The curious horns of the Lascaux wizard beast are remarkably similar in form to the "pointing sticks" worn by performers in ceremonies of the Australian men's dancing ground; and further, the position of the lance, piercing the anus of the Lascaux bull and emerging at the penis, spills the bowels from the area between, which is exactly the spot affected by the pointing bone of the Australians. Finally, there is in Róheim's account of the Australian rite a plausible suggestion for an interpretation (in Stone Age terms) of the force, not only of the pointing penis of the shaman of Lascaux, but also of those six black dots beneath the passing rhino's tail, as representing the lethal magic of its dung. For, if originally a feature of the legend of the pictured bison scene, this formidable beast may well have played the mythic role of the shaman's trance-vehicle or familiar. Where so many extraordinary features fall so neatly into place, it is difficult not to suspect a connection.

106/107. Between the art of the temple caves and the rituals of Australia, there are many suggestive analogies. A clue to the strange horns of the wizard beast of the Lascaux Rotunda may be seen in the lethal "pointing sticks" of Australian magic, as here worn by two performers in an Aranda initiation ceremonial.[5]

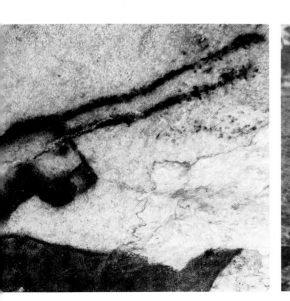

Symbols of the Female Power

In a posture and with a gesture eloquent of some legend, the knowledge of which has been lost, the *Venus of Laussel* (Figure 109; also, Figure 66, page 46) stands before us like the figment of a dream, of which we dimly know but cannot bring to mind the meaning. The mythology of which she is the messenger remains in absolute silence behind her, like the rock out of which she is hewn. As reviewed by the art historian Sigfried Giedion: "The figure and the block are inseparably interlocked. In the position selected by the artist for this relief, the block had a slight overhang, so that the figure swelled forward gently. When seen from the side, the curve appears as taut as a strung bow. It swells up to the supreme point, the maternal belly, then falls away at either end and sinks slowly into the rock, in which the feet seem to melt. The upper part of the body curves gently backward, and the head, resting between two rock projections, seems to be reclining, as though on a cushion."[46] The piece, in Giedion's words, is "the most vigorously sculptured representation of the human body in the whole of primeval art."[47] And the miracle is that it was fashioned with chisels of flint.

Discovered in 1911 by a physician, J.G. Lalanne,[48] this impressive piece, no more than 17 inches high, was only one of a number found preserved in a long ledge situated only a few miles from Lascaux (Figure 108). "The limestone overhang which shelters the dwelling site," states Giedion, "is here particularly beautiful, and the dwelling place itself was on a terrace, over one hundred meters long, above a drop down to the foot of the valley. It was, in every respect, an exceptionally protected shelter, and at its end stood the sanctuary in which the Venus block was found, the figure facing outward towards the shelter."[49] The other pieces include two reliefs of females holding unidentified objects, and a third female with what appear to be the head and shoulders of a male upside down beneath her (Figure 110), in such a position as to have suggested a birth scene to Lalanne, but to others the earliest known representation of coitus; further, a few slabs and blocks incised with female genital symbols; and finally, a fragment bearing the figure of a male, head and arms gone, but in an attitude suggesting a javelin thrower. The site was inhabited from Mousterian times, with the period of these sculptures falling somewhere c. 20,000 to 18,000 B.C.[50]

For millennia, apparently, the dominant presence in this shelter was the *Woman with the Horn*. Alexander Marshack, in his volume *The Roots of Civilization*, has observed that the horn is marked with thirteen lines. "The count of thirteen," he adds, "is the number of crescent 'horns' that may make up an observational lunar year; it is also the number of days from the birth of the first crescent to just before the days of the mature full moon."[51] The figure must have represented some mythic personage so well known to the period that the reference of the elevated horn would have been as readily understood as, say, in India, a lotus in the hand of the goddess Shrī Lakshmī, or, in the West, a child at the breast of the Virgin. The left hand laid on

108. The rock shelter of Laussel, site of the images shown below. On a terrace more than 300 yards long, fronting a drop to the valley floor, this limestone overhang served, not only as a dwelling site, but also, apparently, as a ceremonial center to the mystery of generation.

109/110. Whereas the art of the painted caves was of animal forms with occasional male magicians among them, that of such dwelling sites as the rock shelter of Laussel (**108**) was mainly of the human female. These two images from that long-inhabited sanctuary evidently represent some mythology of the mysteries of the womb, the lunar cycle, and the generation of life. For, although Leroi-Gourhan has declared that "there are no scenes of copulation in Paleolithic art" (see page 62), it is difficult to see anything else in **110**, where beneath the female is evidently a bearded male. In Egyptian art the sky-goddess Nut overarches the earth-god Geb, her spouse.

Two Triple Goddess monuments separated by 10,000 years:

111. Within a shallow Paleolithic cave at Angles-sur-Anglin (Vienne), three powerful female presences made manifest above the head of a bull (lower right). Date, 13,000 to 11,000 B.C.

112. On a Gallo-Roman altar, formerly on the site in Paris now occupied by the Cathedral of Notre Dame, the image of a bull beneath a tree upon which there perch three cranes symbolic of the Celtic Triple Goddess. Inscription: *Tarvos Trigaranus*, "The Bull with Three Cranes." Date, probably first to third centuries A.D.

the belly may have been significant of the womb as the vessel of birth and rebirth, which in its monthly mystery is matched by the measures of the moon. Indeed, if this were a goddess of the Neolithic age, we should have no doubt of her meaning. However, she is of a hunting age and people, and the elevated horn is specifically of a bison—possibly the same legendary beast that we have seen disemboweled in the crypt of the nearby grotto of Lascaux.

Leroi-Gourhan, it is recalled, proposed that the legend illustrated in that scene was one well known to the period, with a history of some 5000 years or more. There was a legend, known to a number of the bison-hunting tribes of the North American plains, of the woman who married a bison and through her life-restoring magic became the institutor of those hunting rites by which the lives were restored of the slaughtered beasts (page 234). Such rites are known to hunting peoples everywhere. There is no reason to believe that the races of the Paleolithic knew nothing of such things. Leroi-Gourhan points out,

further, that on the ceiling above the entrance to the Lascaux Shaft there is a "compartmented rectangular sign," and on its stone rim a cluster of "claviforms."[52] These are both, in his classification, "feminine" signs, and as such, must have suggested to those descending into the sanctuary that its mystery was to be of the womb, giving and renewing life. This is the mystery symbolized as well in the *Venus of Laussel*, by her left hand over the pregnant womb and the horn of the waxing moon elevated in her right.

The evidence of these two neighboring monuments, then, is of a common Upper Paleolithic mythology whose legends have not reached us, but whose imagery is familiar. For the phases of the moon were the same for Old Stone Age man as they are for us; so also were the processes of the womb. It may therefore be that the initial observation which gave birth in the mind of man to a mythology of one mystery informing earthly and celestial things was the recognition of an accord between these two "time-factored" orders: the celestial order of the waxing moon and the

earthly order of the womb. The annual disappearances and reappearances of the birds and beasts must also have contributed to this sense of a general time-factored mystery. For, once again, as we have heard from the Pawnee chieftain Letakots-Lesa: "Tirawa, the One Above, . . . sent certain animals to tell men that he showed himself through the beasts, and that from them, and from the stars and the sun and the moon, man should learn."[53]

The paintings of the caves were inspired by the teachings of the beasts. The figurines, on the other hand, and such rock-carved reliefs as those of the Sanctuary of Laussel, took their inspiration, rather, from the mysteries of the female body. And the qualities of the art of the known sanctuaries of this second kind differ greatly from anything found in the painted caves.

For example, at the Abri du Roc aux Sorciers, at Angles-sur-Anglin (Vienne), there was brought to light in 1948 an astonishing wall bearing a large relief of three colossal female presences (Figure

111): the loins, legs, and bellies, with accented sexual parts, the heads and upper torsos lost to view above, in the primal substance of the mother rock.[54] One thinks of the triple-goddess clusters of later European mythologies: the Graces Three, Fates, Furies, Norns, and the great triad of the Judgment of Paris, Aphrodite, Hera, and Athene. The Paleolithic triad is standing on a bison, so that, as in the Sanctuary of Laussel, there is again an explicit association of the female with this beast. The date at Laussel was c. 20,000 B.C.; that of this shrine, nearly a hundred centuries later, is c. 13,000 to 11,000 B.C. Roughly another hundred centuries, and there is the carved square block of a Celtic, Gallo-Roman altar, excavated from the site of the Paris Cathedral of Notre Dame (Figure 112), on one face of which there is standing a large bull beneath a tree with three cranes perched upon its head and back and with the words *Tarvos Trigaranus* (The Bull with Three Cranes) engraved above. In Celtic mythologies the great Triple Goddess repeatedly appears in the form of a crane.

A third significant site of this order has been lately identified some 50 miles south of Lascaux, at La Madeleine (Tarn), where, on the rocks at either side of the entrance to a shallow cave, there is a re-

clining female figure carved in a style unique in Old Stone Age art (Figure 113). In Giedion's description, "The figures lie, light as a breath, upon the rock face. They are so delicately modeled that they lay unnoticed by the generations of prehistorians who excavated at the entrance to the cavern. A classic Magdalenian engraving of a horse is situated immediately above the excavated area, but it was only in 1952 that the female reliefs were discovered by the keen eyes of an engineer who had been building roads in the Sahara Desert for more than twenty years. H. Bessac first recognized the left-hand figure, then the right. What first caught his eye was the deeply cut, geometrically formed sexual triangle of the left-hand figure; after this he was able to follow her outlines, and then see the companion figure on the right-hand wall . . . .

"What seems so strange about these figures is their unusual pose, which is very unlike an idol's. Both figures lie stretched out in positions of utter repose, one arm bent and supporting the head. They arise from the rock as 'foam-born' Aphrodite arose from the sea . . . .

"Both forms were exposed from the beginning to the direct effects of the open air and variations of temperature, and have suffered severely from the weathering of

the rock wall. But their grace could not entirely be obliterated. . . . An unexpected delicacy of line and an elasticity in handling the surface of the skin are expressed, which are otherwise quite unknown in primeval art. . . .

"A new ideal of the human figure was here announced: a long-legged, slender figure with smaller breasts. It can only have persisted for a short hour. Development followed a radically different direction. But, as in nature, art has sometimes put forth strangely premature blossoms which are condemned to perish."[55]

The period of this shallow cave ("Some flickers of daylight," according to Giedion, "penetrate even into the farthest recesses") is the same as that of the triad of Angles-sur-Anglin, c. 13,000 to 11,000 B.C. Below the figure on the left there is a bison; to the right of the other, a large horse. That is to say, the classic formula of a Magdalenian bison/horse composition is here displayed; and, as Leroi-Gourhan has observed: "All that is missing to complete the composition is an ibex and a

113. Almost effaced by 15,000 years of weathering these two reclining female forms flank the entrance to La Madeleine, a cave in the Aveyron valley (Tarn). They are astonishingly graceful, yet, like most female figures of their period, without faces.

114. This tiny ivory head, 1⅜ inches high, from Brassempouy (Landes) is unusual. It hints of the female (or possibly a specific woman) seen, not simply in relation to reproduction, but as a muse.

115. A mammoth-ivory disk, from a grave at Brno, Moravia, possibly symbolizing the vulva of rebirth.

116. Mammoth-ivory "buttocks image" from Perkana, Moravia.

117. Headless "buttocks profiles" from La Roche (Dordogne).

small male head. The attitude of the women," he adds, "is unique in Paleolithic art, reflecting a nonchalant freedom of which we know no other example."[56]

Approximately a hundred centuries earlier—roughly contemporary with the Laussel relief of the *Woman with the Horn*, i.e., c. 20,000 to 18,000 B.C.—there had appeared over a large part of Europe the earliest of those female statuettes, no more than 3 to 6 inches high, of which Figure 118, the *Venus of Willendorf* (Austria), is the classic representative, and Figure 119, the *Venus of Lespugue*, from the foothills of the Pyrenees (Haute-

Garonne), the undoubted masterpiece. Fashioned of mammoth ivory, 5½ inches high, this exquisite little thing, made, it would seem, to be held and admired in the hand, translates the most typical features of its genre into a boldly styled aesthetic statement of extraordinary charm. All such images are without feet and the heads are featureless, the accent falling on the breasts, sexual triangle, and buttocks—which in the elegant little figure from Lespugue have all been constellated in such a symbolic arrangement as Mother Nature could never have brought forth. For this definitely is *not* a work of natural-

istic art, but a conceived abstraction, delivering a symbolic statement. The somewhat smaller *Venus of Willendorf* is similarly symbolic, as are all the other figures of this series. Only one example, that from Dolni Věstonice in Moravia (Czechoslovakia) (Figure 120), is exceptional in that, despite the realism of the torso, the sexual triangle is missing. On the other hand, four holes in the top of the head suggest that flowers, leaves, or feathers may have been inserted there to signify the power of the goddess to foster seasonal growth.

From European Russia many notable finds have come, mainly from stations of

118. *Venus of Willendorf* (Austria); limestone; height, 4 inches. The legs without feet, when implanted in the soil of a shrine, would support the image upright.

119. *Venus of Lespugue* (Haute-Garonne, Pyrenees) marks a climax in the development of this genre. Seen here both in profile and in rear view, it gives evidence of a distinctive (almost modern) aesthetic interest in the styling of a work of art.

120. From Dolni Věstonice, Moravia, this enigmatic figure of clay and pulverized bone lacks genitalia, and its crude face has no mouth. In the crown of the head are four holes.

the Late Paleolithic mammoth hunt, which continued in that region, when in the west, the great pachyderms had been replaced by reindeer herds and all but forgotten.[57] At Yeliseevici (a dwelling site between Bryansk and Mglin on the right bank of the river Desna), an accumulation of mammoth skulls arranged in a circle was uncovered with a Venus statuette among them as a goddess-patroness, evidently, of the hunt. At Kostienki on the right bank of the Don, where a number of images have been found, three were discovered in a special rounded niche in the wall of one of the huts, about 6 feet from the hearth. One, of mammoth ivory, was without its head; another, of limestone, about a foot tall (the largest yet found anywhere), had been broken in four pieces and thrown back into the niche; the third was an ill-made specimen of mammoth tusk or of bone. Other signs here, and at certain other mammoth hunters' settlements along the Don, show that in that distant day a disaster of some kind overtook these people and that it was thought important by those responsible that the powers, not only of the people themselves but also of their statuettes, should be broken.

121. *La Polichinelle*, a tiny figurine (only 1¾ inches high) made of vitreous rock and found at Grimaldi on the Riviera.

122. Hematite torso from Ostrava-Petrkovice, Moravia.

123. A torso of mammoth ivory found in the wall niche of a hut in Yeliseevici on the Desna.

124. Mammoth-bone figure from Kostienki on the Don; its form suggests the *Venus of Lespugue* (**119**).

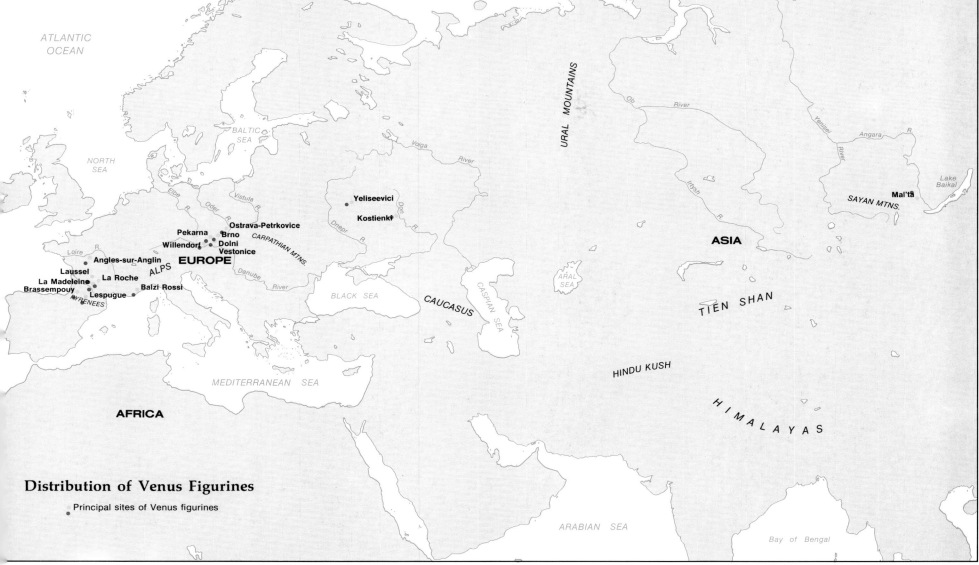

Distribution of Venus Figurines

• Principal sites of Venus figurines

Map 22.

71

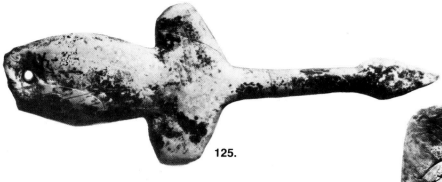

125.

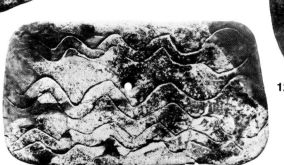

127.

At Mal'ta, near Lake Baikal in Siberia, a cache of twenty symbolic items, dating c. 16,000 to 13,000 B.C., has been discovered, associated with the ceremonial burial of a child (**126**). These items, all of mammoth ivory, included: (**125**) six flying geese, one of which is pictured here; (**127**) a buckle engraved on both sides; (**128**) six figurines, one of which is here pictured and all of which—like their distant sisters in Austria and the Pyrenees—are without feet; (**129**) a staff or wand; (**130**) a necklace; and a fish (not shown) bearing a stippled labyrinth.

The most interesting Russian discovery of all, however, has been made far eastward, at Mal'ta in Siberia, about 55 miles northwest of Irkutsk. Here were unearthed no less than twenty female statuettes of mammoth ivory, from 1¼ to 5¼ inches tall, one represented as though clothed in a cave lion's skin, the others nude (Figure 128). Some fourteen animal burials were also found: six of the arctic fox, six of deer, in each case with the antlers and hindquarters missing (suggesting that the animals were flayed before burial, possibly to furnish shamanistic attire). There was one curious burial of the head and neck of a large bird, and one of the foot of a mammoth. Six flying birds and one swimming, of mammoth ivory—all representing either geese or ducks—were found (Figure 125), along with an ivory fish with a spiral labyrinth stippled upon its side; an ivory

128.

129.

baton, suggesting a shaman's staff (Figure 129); and finally, and most remarkably, the skeleton of a rickety four-year-old child with a copious accompaniment of mammoth-ivory ornamentation (Figure 126).

The little skeleton was found lying on its back in the crouch or fetus posture, but with its head turned to the left and facing east, the direction of the rebirth and rising of the sun. Over the grave was curved a large mammoth tusk, and within were many signs of a highly ceremonious burial. There was a great deal of red coloring matter in the grave—a common finding in Paleolithic sites—and encircling the head was a delicate crown or forehead band of mammoth ivory. The child had worn a bracelet of the same material and a fine necklace of six octagonal and 120 flat ivory beads, from which a birdlike ornamental pendant hung (Figure 130). A second pendant, likewise in the form of a flying bird, as well as two decorated medallions, lay in the grave. One of the latter seems to have served as a buckle; the other, somewhat larger (Figure 127), showed on one side, scratched or engraved, three cobralike wavy serpents, and on the other, a stippled design showing a spiral of seven turns with S-forms enclosing it—the earliest spirals known in the history of art.[58]

126.

130.

The probable dating of this important Siberian site is c. 16,000 to 13,000 B.C.[59] That of the *Venus of Laussel*, it is recalled, was c. 20,000 to 18,000 B.C., and that of the two extraordinary caves at La Madeleine and Angles-sur-Anglin (of the two reclining female forms and the colossal Triple Goddess), c. 13,000 to 11,000 B.C. The numerous female figurines distributed over the whole of the European Upper Paleolithic field were also of these datings. So, from the Pyrenees to Lake Baikal, the evidence now is before us of a Late Stone Age mythology in which the outstanding single figure was the Naked Goddess. And she can already be recognized in a number of her best-known later roles: as Lady of the Wild Things, Protectress of the Hearth, Consort of the Moon-bull, who dies to be resurrected—with herself thereby a personification of the mystery of the moon, which has the power to shed its shadow (as the serpent sloughs its skin) to appear reborn. Not a few of her images suggest pregnancy: she was almost certainly a patroness of childbirth and fecundity. In that Paleolithic age she was specifically a goddess of the hunt, but also, apparently, of vegetation—if we may so interpret the Dolní Věstonice figurine. Another association with the little Mal'ta burial suggests that it was she who received the dead and delivered their souls to rebirth.

The material culture of the Mal'ta settlement was of an Aurignacoid character, evidently brought from the South Russian plains by competent hunters of the reindeer, rhinoceros, and mammoth. Their semisubterranean dwellings (uncovered in an excavated area of some 600 square meters) had had roofs incorporating layers of interlaced reindeer antlers supported by large animal bones. The excavator, M. M. Gerasimov, recognized, in the abundant remains of the interiors,[60] evidence of a clear division between the men's and the women's activities, such as has been normal in hunting cultures everywhere. And, if we may judge from the evidences of their numerous bone figurines and the contents of the little grave, in their mythology the goddess was associated with an imagery of water birds and serpents, to which something strongly suggestive of Ariadne's labyrinth may have been joined. The serpents are cobras, and they are three, as the female forms in the cave at Angles-sur-Anglin are three. Six of the birds have the look of flying geese. We know that in Siberia, shamans, whose spirits are believed to fly, wear bird costumes. We have remarked the bird mask and the bird-on-a-staff of the shamanistic figure of Lascaux. There was also in the Mal'ta grave a little mammoth-ivory staff or wand (Figure 129). In India the wild gander (*hamsa*) is symbolic, not only of the flight of a spirit,

but also of the universal spirit itself. Hence a term of honor addressed to the master yogi is *Paramahamsa*: "paramount" or "supreme" (*parama*) "wild gander" (*hamsa*). There the cobra is a figure profoundly revered, as well as feared. The earth is supported by a cobra's head, directly beneath that Immovable Spot where the Buddha sat when he achieved Enlightenment; and when a storm arose, the earth-supporting cobra, Muchalinda, left his post and, encircling the Buddha's body while sheltering his head with his hood, protected the entranced one there seated in spiritual flight. The central serpent of the Mal'ta plaque has a larger hood than the other two and may represent a male flanked by females. And I find it difficult to interpret as mere chance the fact that the reverse of the plaque shows a vortex spiraling to a center.

This is not to suggest that some school of Upper Paleolithic hunters may have anticipated the Buddha, but to point out that in the iconographies of both the early shamanistic and much later Buddhist trance traditions, there can be recognized the same constellation of myth motifs or elementary ideas. Indeed, there is a native recognition of a significant relationship already indicated in the word "shaman" itself, which is derived from the Tungusic *saman*; this, in turn, being derived from the Sanskrit *śramana*, meaning "Buddhist monk."[61] The bird on the prostrate shaman's staff at Lascaux is not a waterfowl, not a goose; nor do we find cobras in the West. Like the labyrinth (or spiral), these specifications of the bird and serpent forms first appear in this Siberian Mal'ta site. They are not of European but of Asian origin. The question that remains is whether we are to think, with some authorities, of a plant-oriented people from the south that moved up into a difficult but rewarding northern terrain of the hunt, or vice versa, of a northern hunting race, some of whose shamanic symbols were later to penetrate the south, there to become incorporated in legends of the Indian Paramahamsas.

The Shamans of the Caves

The animal envoys of the Unseen Power no longer serve, as in primeval times, to teach and to guide mankind. Bears, lions, elephants, ibexes, and gazelles are in cages in our zoos. Man is no longer the newcomer in a world of unexplored plains and forests, and our immediate neighbors are not wild beasts but other human beings, contending for goods and space on a planet that is whirling without

end around the fireball of a star. Neither in body nor in mind do we inhabit the world of those hunting races of the Paleolithic millennia, to whose lives and life ways we nevertheless owe the very forms of our bodies and structures of our minds. Memories of their animal envoys still must sleep, somehow, within us; for they wake a little and stir when we venture into wilderness. They wake in terror to thunder. And again they wake, with a sense of recognition, when we enter any one of those great painted caves. Whatever the inward darkness may have been to which the shamans of those caves descended in their trances, the same must lie within ourselves, nightly visited in sleep. Moreover, in parts of the world marginal to contemporary civilization, the beat of the shaman's drum may still be heard, transporting spirits in flight to regions known to our own visionaries and to men and women gone mad. Did the shamans of those caves interpret their visionary voyages as shamans do today— shamans whom we can visit and with whom many of us have conversed? Our only evidence is the pictorial script in the labyrinthine secrecy of the silent caves themselves. Why so deeply hidden and in parts so difficult of access?

"Some caves with animal art," as Alexander Marshack has remarked, "are so difficult to get into and their painted and engraved chambers are so deep that hours were spent climbing inside, time was spent in engraving, painting, and ceremony, and more time was spent coming out. This would be a tiring and uneconomic activity for a hunter performing hunting magic! In true hunting magic, one can draw the animal in the sand or scratch it on an open rock surface and perform the rite of magic killing quickly."[62]

Herbert Kühn has described his own visit to the great bell-shaped main chamber, with its overhanging rocks and fissures, of the cave known as Les Trois Frères at Montesquieu-Aventès (Ariège) in the Pyrenees:

"The ground is damp and slimy, we have to be very careful not to slip off the rocky way. It goes up and down, then comes a very narrow passage about ten yards long through which you have to creep on all fours. And then again there come great halls and more narrow passages. In one large gallery are a lot of red and black dots, just those dots.

"How magnificent the stalactites are! The soft drop of the water can be heard, dripping from the ceiling. There is no other sound and nothing moves . . . . The silence is eerie . . . . The gallery is large and long and then there comes a very low tunnel. We placed our lamp on the ground and pushed it into the hole. Louis [the Count Bégouën's eldest son, who, with his father and two brothers,

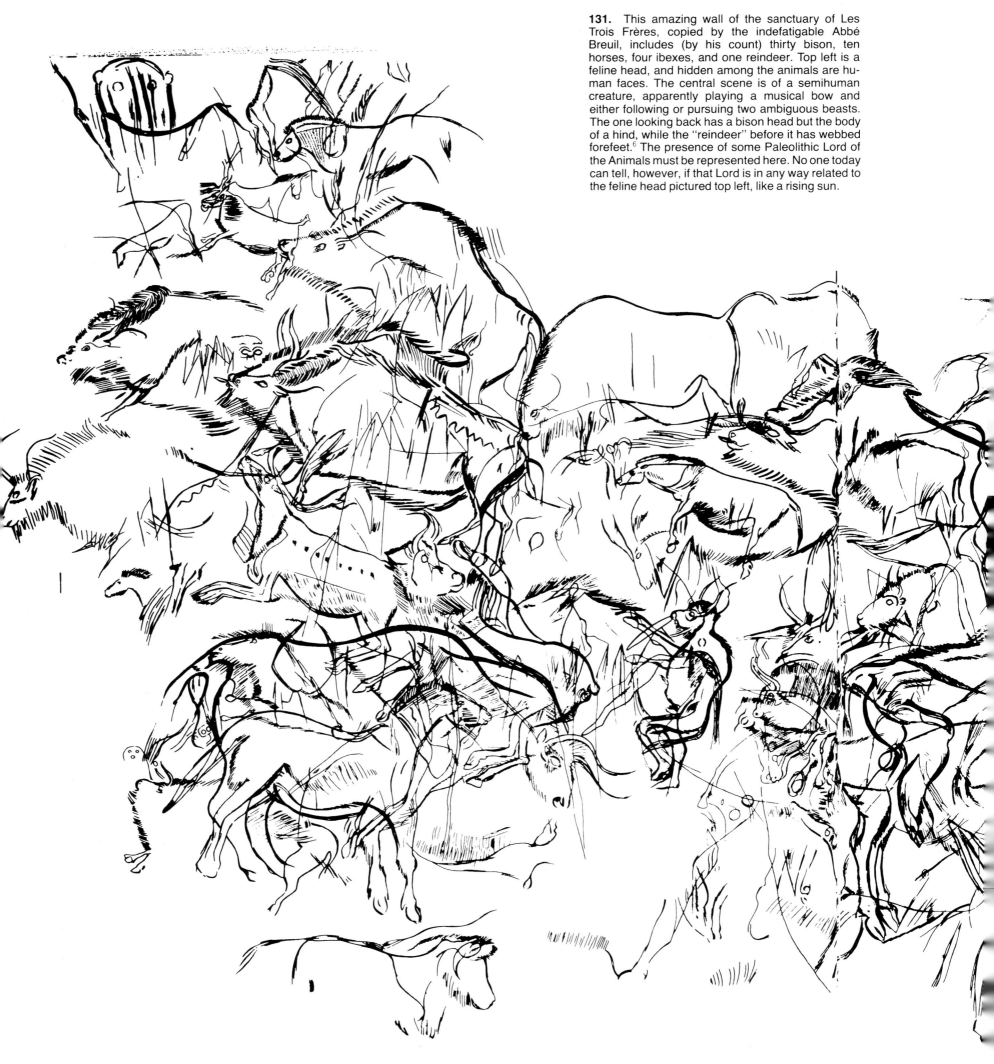

131. This amazing wall of the sanctuary of Les Trois Frères, copied by the indefatigable Abbé Breuil, includes (by his count) thirty bison, ten horses, four ibexes, and one reindeer. Top left is a feline head, and hidden among the animals are human faces. The central scene is of a semihuman creature, apparently playing a musical bow and either following or pursuing two ambiguous beasts. The one looking back has a bison head but the body of a hind, while the "reindeer" before it has webbed forefeet.[6] The presence of some Paleolithic Lord of the Animals must be represented here. No one today can tell, however, if that Lord is in any way related to the feline head pictured top left, like a rising sun.

had discovered and explored the vast cavern just eight days before the outbreak of the First World War] went ahead, then Professor van Giffen [of Gröningen, Holland], next Rita [Mrs. Kühn], and finally myself. The tunnel is not much broader than my shoulders, nor higher. I can hear the others before me groaning and see how very slowly their lamps push on. With our arms pressed close to our sides, we wriggle forward on our stomachs, like snakes. The passage, in places, is hardly a foot high, so that you have to lay your face right on the earth. I felt as though I were creeping through a coffin. You cannot lift your head; you cannot breathe. And then, finally, the burrow becomes slightly higher. One can at last rest on one's forearms. But not for long; the way again grows narrow. And so, yard by yard, one struggles on: some forty-odd yards in all. Nobody talks. The lamps are inched along and we push after. I hear the others groaning, my own heart is pounding, and it is difficult to breathe. It is terrible to have the roof so close to one's head. And the roof is very hard: I bump it, time and again. Will this thing never end? Then, suddenly, we are through, and everybody breathes. It is like a redemption.

"The hall in which we are now standing is gigantic. We let the light of the lamps run along the ceiling and walls; a majestic room—and there, finally, are the pictures. From top to bottom a whole wall is covered with engravings. The surface has been worked with tools of stone, and there we see marshaled the beasts that lived at that time in southern France: the mammoth, rhinoceros, bison, wild horse, bear, wild ass, reindeer, wolverine, musk ox; also, the smaller animals appear: snowy owls, hares, and fish. And one sees darts everywhere, flying at the game. Several pictures of bears attract us in particular [Figure 133]; for they have holes where the images were struck and blood is shown spouting from their mouths. Truly a picture of the hunt; the picture of the magic of the hunt."[63]

The Abbé Breuil has published a magnificent series of tracings and photographs of the walls of this imposing Sanctuary. The style is everywhere firm and full of life, not in paint, but engraved, fixing forever the momentary turns, leaps, and flashes of the animal kingdom in a teeming tumult of everlasting life. And above them all, predominant—at the opposite end of the Sanctuary to the hole through which we have emerged, some 15 feet above the level of the floor, in a craggy apse—watching, staring at the arrival with unflinching eyes, is the now famous *Sorcerer of Les Trois Frères* (Figure 132), the Animal Master presiding over the animals there assembled. He is poised in profile in a dancing posture, but the

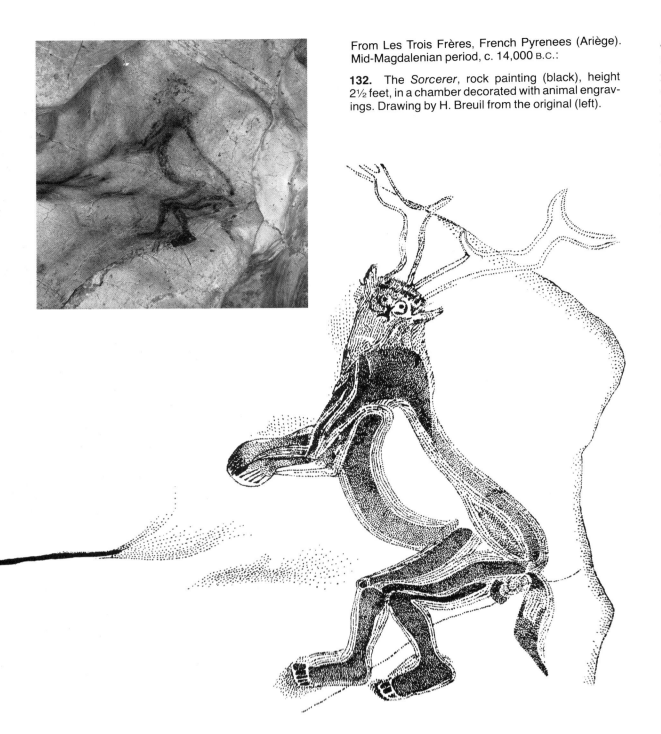

132. The *Sorcerer*, rock painting (black), height 2½ feet, in a chamber decorated with animal engravings. Drawing by H. Breuil from the original (left).

and spouting blood of the engraved bear (Figure 133, like the punctured clay mold in the bear sanctuary at Montespan, Figure 94 on page 62) do indeed suggest a hunting magic, it would have to have been a magic (given the scene of its accomplishment) associated for the hunter himself with an antecedent transformation of his own consciousness, effected in a sacred place, at a sacred time, and enacted in a sacred manner: the magic, that is to say, of a sacrament comparable in its way with the Christian celebration of the sacrificed Savior, or with the Mithraic, of the sacrificed Cosmic Ox.

In such a context, the hunter and the hunted beast—in ritual terms, the priest and his sacrifice—would have to have been experienced in some psychological dimension as one and the same—even as the mixed form of the presiding presence of the Sanctuary, the semihuman, semianimal, dancing Animal Master, already suggests. The beast to be slaughtered is interpreted as a willing victim, or rather, as a knowing participant in a covenanted sacred act wherein the mystery of life, which lives on life, is comprehended in its celebration. And the essential effect of all this upon the young boys who were to be turned by the rites of this sacred place into initiated hunters would have consisted, finally, in the opening of their minds to such an experience of the secondary nature of the passing forms of time that they should become capable of expressing a reverence for life in the act of taking it. As Eugen Herrigel states in *Zen in the Art of Archery*, "the contest consists in the archer aiming at himself—yet not at himself, in hitting himself—and yet not himself, and thus becoming simultaneously, the aimer and the aim, the hitter and the hit."[65]

But are we justified in alluding to any such (for us) recondite Oriental idea, in discussing the imagery of the sacred space of a Paleolithic sanctuary?

antlered head is turned to face the hall. The pricked ears might be those of a stag; the round eyes suggest an owl; the full beard descending to the deep animal chest is of a man, as are the dancing legs; the tail is of a wolf or wild horse, and the position of the prominent sexual organ, placed beneath the tail, is of the feline species, perhaps a lion. The hands are the paws of a lion and the great chest and torso might also be of this beast. The figure is 2½ feet high, 15 inches across. "An eerie, thrilling picture," wrote Kühn.[64] Moreover, it is the only picture in the whole gallery rendered in paint—black paint—which gives it an accent stronger than the rest.

But who or what is this man—if man he be—whose image is now impressed upon us in a way that we shall not forget?

The passage through that tunnel was surely an ordeal more like the experience of a psychologically intended initiation than anything of mere magic: almost literally a reliving of one's birth. And, although the numerous flying darts(if that is what they are) and the punctured hide

133. Punctured by many weapons, this engraving of a dying bear appears among the animals directly beneath the *Sorcerer*. Since the others are not wounded, this bear is evidently in a special symbolic role. Compare the punctured bear at Montespan (**94**) and the wounded bison of Lascaux (**105**).

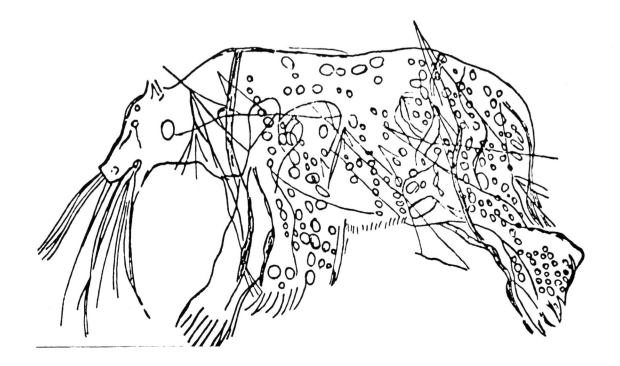

We in the enlightened West no longer have any truly sacred spaces wherein the Aristotelian laws of a rational logic in secular space and measured time are suspended and a mystical logic, resembling that of dream, comes into play—where the dreamer and his dream, though apparently two, as subject and object, are actually one and the same. The Orient to this day, on the other hand, has many such sacred spaces, wherein life itself is to be experienced and known as a dream dreamed by a single dreamer in which all the dream characters dream too, so that everything interlocks with everything else. And how should it then be thought scientifically proper to admit only the application of our own rationalistic laws of thought to the interpretation of forms within the sacred space of a Paleolithic temple cave?

As Ananda K. Coomaraswamy once asked: "If we cannot assume that a language is not understood by those who speak it, we must assume that a doctrine is coeval with the symbolic formulae in which it is expressed."[66] The symbolic formulae here to be noted are: (1) a departure from the light-world of time-factored knowledge and relationships, through a subterranean opening, into darkness; (2) a difficult, dangerous, frightening struggle there through a narrow, tubelike passage; (3) a releasing entry into a vast chamber, torchlit, where (4) a semihuman, semianimal form presides above an everlasting Happy Hunting Ground. Discoverable among the bewildering tangle of beasts is a little human figure with the head, or head-mask, of a bison. There is also a bison with human hindquarters and legs. There are bears, punctured as by the points of darts, with blood spouting from their mouths (Figure 133). And, as though guarding the way to the main sanctuary, there are, in a chapel just before it, two enormous lion heads with bodies in profile, but with faces and eyes turned upon the entering initiate.

The description of this hunters' Sanctuary and of the whole labyrinthine cave by the Abbé Henri Breuil, to whose hand we owe the incredible tracings of its tangled art,[67] gives the hint of its likely function. In his words: "All these complicated hidden passages lent themselves to extraordinary effects which would be inexplicable to uninitiated novices, who must have been deeply impressed. . . . The effect of songs, cries, or other noises, or mysterious objects thrown from no one knows where, was easy to arrange in such a place."[68]

The Sanctuary, as he tells, is an apse with a floor sloping steeply toward the back, the walls converging at the end, where, at the right, there is a deep, twofold recess, and on the left, two or three more recesses. One of these conducts the

visitor to a sunken corridor, where a narrow passage leads, through turns, to a small rotunda ending in a well, and this again, through turnings, winds to a point where, at a height of about 13 feet, there is an opening, a sort of window, beyond which looms the *Sorcerer*. "How the artist who drew it," the Abbé Breuil remarks, "could have worked 4 meters above the floor was a problem which I had to solve myself and without a ladder. Under the window there is a small projecting rock where one's right foot can rest; then taking a firm hold to the right of the window and making a complete half turn, it is possible to sit quite comfortably on the uneven surface, near the right hand entrance to which is the figure we called at first the 'Sorcerer', but which is really the 'God of Les Trois Frères.'"[69] It would have been from here, in the Abbe's view, and from the labyrinth of tunnels and wells beneath (all of which were marvelously decorated), that the company of initiators would have worked their effects.

Meanwhile, in the immediately neighboring cave, the Tuc d'Audoubert (which seems to have been, at one time, part of the system of Les Trois Frères, separated later by 10 yards or so of roof-fall), there is a magnificent succession of immense chambers that can be entered only by way of a very small opening. The sons of the Count Bégouën, who discovered this opening, named it the "cat's hole" (and in first going through it, the count, their father, got stuck and had to forfeit both his shirt and his trousers). Having negotiated this "narrow gate," one passes, as

134. In a tiny chamber within the vast cavern Tuc d'Audoubert (French Pyrenees, Ariège), these two clay bison, a male and a female, apparently represent the primal generating couple. Mid-Magdalenian period, c. 14,000 B.C.

the Abbé tells, through a succession of "wide halls adorned with the most beautiful stalagmitic decorations . . . vast galleries with fairy-like decorations. . . . But all this," he continues, "was nothing in comparison to what was awaiting the visitors at the end of the gallery, where it formed a rather low room.

"Two Bison carefully modeled in clay against a projecting rock, towards the center of this rotunda, were there [Figure 134]; another, much smaller, 13 cm long [5¹/₈ inches], was on the floor in front of the two great statues, a male following a female, their respective lengths being 63 and 61 cm [2 feet ³/₄ inch and 2 feet]. These statues are about 700 meters from the entrance of the cavern. Although they have a slight lateral flattening, they are magnificently made; they no doubt represent fertility rites, destined to obtain multiplication of the species.

"Were these the only ones? On the right, downwards under a low vault, there is a roof of clay slightly goffered by a stalagmitic skin. Here there are several heaps of clay, now formless, probably all that remains of other models, reduced to clay pulp by the greater damp in that corner. In a neighboring recess, there are clay puddings kneaded into phallus form and, on the smooth surface of the clay pool, fifty small-sized heel prints of a young human being, who could not have been

135. *The Dancer of Le Gabillou*, like the *Sorcerer* of Les Trois Frères, suggests something of the rituals of these sanctuaries. A music must have once sounded in their chambers.

more than fifteen years old, can be seen."[70]

Why only the heels? And why only fifty steps? Was this the buffalo dance of some young initiate? There has been discussion, but no conclusion. The antlered figure in the other sanctuary is a dancer. So too is the figure of a man with a bison's head and tail that is to be seen in the Dordogne in the cave of Le Gabillou (Figure 135), which is in the form of a long,

low, narrow corridor, comprising twenty little chambers, in the last of which is the engraving of this dancing shaman.

It begins to look very much as though these caves were the Paleolithic counterparts of the men's dancing grounds or secret-society lodges of the African, Australian, Melanesian, Indonesian, Polynesian, and pre-Columbian American aborigines. The dancing masked figures and the one shown (apparently in trance) before the wounded bison at the bottom of the Lascaux Shaft would then have represented characters from the origin legends of the pictured caves themselves. The episode of the Lascaux Shaft, as we have seen, was from a cycle of myth known for millennia. We can only guess at its theme; but if it was linked in any way to that of the elevated horn in the hand of the nearby *Venus of Laussel,* it must have had something to do with the mystery signified in the cycles of the moon, some myth of eternal return.

And what, then, of the dancer of Les Trois Frères?

The Count Bégouën and the Abbé Breuil first thought of this figure as a Medicine Man or Sorcerer, and *Sorcerer* is the name by which it has been known since. Later, however, as the Abbé has told, he revised his thought and wrote of the figure as a god, the "god of the cave."[71] Herbert Kühn has suggested the artist-magician himself;[72] but this, of course, is little different from the first thought of Bégouën and Breuil. Leroi-Gourhan states simply that "this personage combines all the male symbols then at the disposal of the artist who executed it: his horns and ears are those of a reindeer, his body is that of a man, his tail that of a horse, and his penis, though human, is placed where a feline's would be. It is not surprising to find so hyper-

symbolic a figure at the highest and innermost point of a chamber that is decorated with hundreds of figures, in the arrangement of which Magdalenian symbolism is displayed with a richness unattained elsewhere."[73]

Leo Frobenius, however, has suggested a rather different approach and has looked at the figure with different eyes, eyes trained in the deserts and jungles of Africa, and a mind filled with recollections of images and symbolic forms from many parts of the world.

First, he points out that the explorer of the tunnels of this cave, in his approach to the culminating chamber, passes through a chapel-like alcove that is decorated with representations of animals of the cat family; principally, two large lion heads, the appearance of which amazed the Count Bégouën when he first beheld them. "These are represented," Frobenius reminds us, " 'en face,' the outlines of their bodies being in profile. The male has a mane; its great round eyes fix the beholder [Figure 137]. They seem to be guarding the entrance to the final, most significant chamber of the cave." And when one enters this chamber, Frobenius next points out, there are those innumerable animals all about, and above them, as culmination of the whole, the famous *Sorcerer:* "a being," as Frobenius recalls, "which Bégouën and other pre-historians have regarded as a masked man," whereas, to Frobenius's eyes only the legs and feet are human. The body, in fact, is not of a man at all, but of a lion, *en face,*

136. Painted ceiling of a low-vaulted chamber in the Altamira cave near Santander in northern Spain. Magdalenian period. Discovered in 1879 by the five-year-old daughter of Count Marselino de Sautuola, this was the first masterpiece of Paleolithic art to be exposed to modern eyes. In situ, it is an amazing, spell-binding revelation of the mentality of Paleolithic Man.

137/138. In both the lion (left) from Les Trois Frères, and that (above) from North Africa, the important feature is the magic of the eyes.

with round, staring eyes, exactly like those of the lions in the earlier chapel. The beard can now be seen as part of a lion's mane, and the antlers and tail now look like additions. Moreover, on a face of rock in northwest Africa, in the Sahara-Atlas Mountains, high above a series of engravings of elephants and giraffes, an antelope, and a buffalo—all represented in profile—there is to be seen, exactly where the first rays of the sun should fall upon it, the engraved outline of an *en face* lion (Figure 138), in a pose and position very like that of the *Sorcerer of Les Trois Frères.*[74]

Now the lion, as we all well know, is the King of Beasts—above all other creatures. And in the Sahara-Atlas engraving, he is visibly in this position, as he is, also, in the organization of figures in the cavern of Les Trois Frères (Figure 131, upper left). These two works are of the last millennia of Paleolithic art: the *Sorcerer,* c. 12,000 B.C., and the lion of the Atlas range, c. 7000 B.C. The lion, furthermore, in its mythic role is traditionally the solar beast. At the sound of its roar, the grazing herds of the plain take flight, as do the stars of the sky at sunrise. And the position of the Sahara-Atlas lion, daily touched by the first rays of the sun, illustrates this theme.

In the Spanish grotto of Altamira—which is about contemporary with that of Les Trois Frères—the beautiful bulls are painted, significantly, on the ceiling. Leaning back to view them, one might be gazing at the pictured constellations of the night sky. And in a sanctuary at the back of the cave there is a very strange, featureless, masklike head of rock, showing large, round solar eyes (Figure 139). Very generally among hunting tribes (and in the chapters of this *Atlas* that treat of these there is ample evidence), the sun is the guardian model and patron of the hunter and of his life-sustaining sacred art, the sun's rays being then equivalent to his darts, and the night stars to the beasts to be slain.

So, if we now once again review the symbolic stages of the journey into the cave and to the Sanctuary of Les Trois Frères, something of the sense of its initiatory force will, I think, become evident. Namely, there will have been (1) a departure from the light-world of secular, dualistic experiences (I against Thee, Thou against Me: to devour or to be devoured) followed by (2) a difficult, dangerous, frightening struggle through a birth canal into (3) an earth womb filled with the archetypes of all those animal envoys of the Unseen Power that are born to die in the

139. From the deepest recess of Spanish Altamira, the eyes of this apparition send a mystic influence radiating through the cavern.

upper light-world; here residing, however, in the timeless dark, where (4) above them all there is a lionlike form, *en face,* with great round eyes.

In the light of what we know of the mythological world of shamanism—especially as carried forward in the trance-visions and ecstatic rites of the Ostyaks, Buriats, Voguls, Yukaghir, Tungus, and other shaman-guided peoples of Siberia—the high deity of their pantheons is typically the Sun; and in the folk legends of those areas, as well as in those of the tribes of North America, the testing father, master of all the trials and terrors to which young heros are subjected, is again the Sun. The Sun, then, is both the testing father and the model of the hunter's, as also of the warrior's, given task. His solar rays are his darts and spears. By simultaneous submission to, and identification with, his will, beyond pity and fear when accomplishing the essential act of living—which is killing—the hunter would know himself to be thereby at one with the order of his own animal nature. This then would be the fruit of the realization of these initiations.

Such an ultimately mystical manner of thought is fundamental to the hunter's way, as it is also to the warrior's (as, for example, in the *Bhagavad Gītā*). The sun-lion as their mythic model is therefore the usual emblem of kings—as is also the Solar Eagle, the lion's counterpart among birds. And not only of kings, but also of conquerors in the spirit! The Buddha's throne is represented as a Lion Throne; his Word of Truth, dispelling delusion as the rising sun dispels the shades of night, has been called his Lion Roar; and finally, his transhistorical, transcendental, eternal, so-called Law-Body (*Dharmakāya*) is known as the Great Sun Buddha (*Mahā Vairochana*).

And so, in a startling way, this whole context of sun-lion symbolism has held together through millennia, which is not to say (let us again remark) that the shamans of the painted caves were already realized Buddhas. Acorns are not oak trees. But, on the other hand, no one who has ever entered any one of those six great underground temples that the Abbé Breuil has called "the Six Giants"—Altamira, Lascaux, Les Trois Frères, Font de Gaume, Les Combarelles, and Niaux—and has let the sheer wonder of their masterworks of art deliver to his mind their silent message, will ever doubt that revelations of that order can have come only from artists already great in that transcendent wisdom which has been the secret of the supreme artists of all time. And where there was an art of such majesty, there was, also, an insight into the nature not only of the phenomenal world, but also of the eye, the solar eye, that both regards and shapes phenomena.

Advent of the Bow and Arrow

As a natural bridge between Europe and northwest Africa, Spain throughout its history has been a region of contrary tides, flowing now north to south, now south to north; and already in its monuments of Paleolithic art this ebb and flow is documented in two contrary styles: that in the north, of the Cantabrian mountains—El Castillo, Altamira, and the rest (Map 23, Area 1)—which is of a kind with the French cavern art of the Pyrenees and Dordogne; and that of the eastern hills of Valencia, Catalonia, and Aragón (Map 23, Area 2)—which in both form and content suggests the rock paintings rather of Africa than of Europe.

In the so-called Franco-Cantabrian art of the north it is animal forms that predominate. The human are not only much less numerous, but also very much less faithfully rendered. In the Spanish-Levantine paintings, on the other hand, as also in most of those of both North and South Africa, human figures not only predominate but are shown in vividly active festival scenes or encounters. All of the Spanish figures are small; many, hardly larger than a man's hand; and an animal over 2 feet long is exceptional. The paintings are in earthy reds, browns, and black, and on the walls either of rock shelters or of shallow caves; so that instead of a subterranean, timeless world of archetypal herds, what we here behold in broad daylight are fascinating village, hunting, and battle scenes.

We do not know, of course, what tales or legends these little paintings may have illustrated, but of how the people dressed and lived they tell a great deal. The bow and arrow and domesticated dog have arrived, for example, which of itself indicates that this is an art of a later period than that of the Franco-Cantabrian north: 10,000 B.C., possibly, to perhaps 3000 B.C. The dating has not been even approximately determined. Nor is it known what the relationship (if any) may have been between the people here represented and those of the possibly related African styles. Curiously, the resemblances are even closer to some of the southern African forms than to any of the northern; so that, as Hans-Georg Bandi has remarked, "It is not easy to answer the question whether the style of eastern Spanish rock pictures developed on the spot or whether it can be traced back to African impulses. Indeed, it is just as feasible that the influence radiated from the Iberian peninsula to Africa as from south to north."[75]

These paintings appear on rock surfaces open to the light, under ledges, or in shallow shelters. The lively style, known as Spanish-Levantine, contrasts radically with that of the earlier, Franco-Cantabrian caves and suggests, rather, the North African rock arts of Tassili (pages 82–87) or the South African of the Bushmen (pages 90–101). We note that the bow and arrow have arrived along with this art, apparently from the south. The human figures—in red, brown, or black silhouette—are generally no more than 4 to 8 or 9 inches tall.

Three Mesolithic rock paintings from Eastern Spain, province of Castellon, vaguely dated from c. 10,000 to c. 3000 B.C.:

140.   Battle scene, from Morella la Vella.

141.   Ibex hunt, from the Gasulla Gorge.

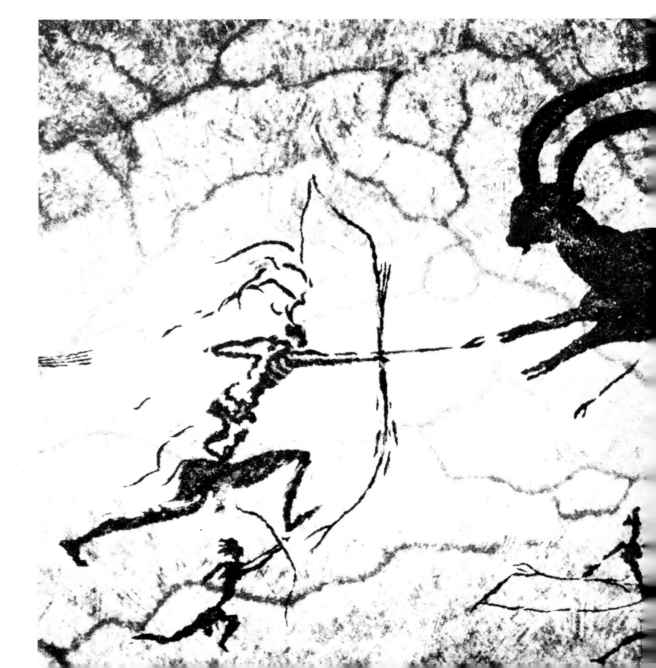

142. Three women, from the Valltorta Gorge.

Culture Tides in a Verdant Sahara

During the early glacial ages, the Sahara, now a desert, was substantially populated. Hand axes of Acheulean type are found everywhere: in the sands, about the rock-strewn wastes, and on the valley floors of the great mountain massifs. The later flake tools of Mousterian type associated with Neanderthal Man are less abundant, however, and confined, furthermore, to the north; while the blade tools and points of Upper Paleolithic manufacture, though known from other parts of North Africa, are missing in the Sahara. Then, suddenly, the whole region between the Atlas range and Niger river becomes repopulated. Neolithic polished axes, pottery shards, and arrowheads are everywhere. And the earliest African rock engravings also appear at this time, marking the opening of a succession of epochs of early Neolithic, as well as of terminal Paleolithic, art. Henri Lhote, to whose Tassili expedition of 1956–57 we owe our knowledge of this history, distinguishes six intermeshing periods and traditions.

Map 23. Five areas of Europe and North Africa in which Paleolithic and post-Paleolithic rock engravings and paintings are preserved.

1. *Franco-Cantabrian province:* c. 35,000 to 8,000 B.C., region of the temple caves (pages 58–79).

2. *Spanish-Levantine province:* c. 10,000 to 3000 B.C. (illustrated on this page).

3. *Northwest African province:* c. 7000 to 4500 B.C. distinguished by majestic engravings of the Bubalus (page 82, Figure 143).

4. *Central Saharan province* (including Tassili and the Fezzan), representing 5 distinct traditions: a)

Bubalus-style engravings, from c. 7000 B.C. b) paintings in the so-called Round-Heads style, from c. 6000 B.C. (see page 83); c) pastoral scenes of a cattle-herding "Bovidian" culture, from c. 4000 B.C., into which late Egyptian influences enter, c. 1570 B.C. (see pages 84–85); d) paintings from an age of invading chariot fighters from the Aegean, c. 1200 B.C. (see pages 86–87); and e) crude engravings showing camel riders (Arabs), some dating perhaps as late as c. A.D. 1200.

5. *Northeast African province:* more examples of the Bovidian style of c. 4000 to 3000 B.C.

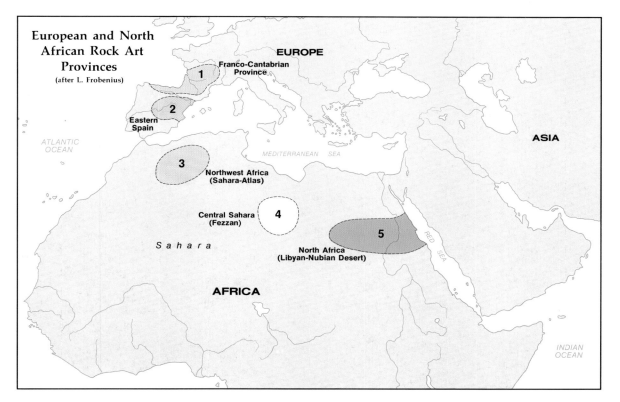

European and North African Rock Art Provinces
(after L. Frobenius)

EUROPE
Franco-Cantabrian Province
1
2
Eastern Spain
ATLANTIC OCEAN
MEDITERRANEAN SEA
ASIA
3
Northwest Africa (Sahara-Atlas)
Central Sahara (Fezzan)
4
5
North Africa (Libyan-Nubian Desert)
RED SEA
Sahara
AFRICA
INDIAN OCEAN

143. Open rock engraving of two Bubalus bulls and an ibis, at Ksar-Amar, Sahara-Atlas range, Algeria. Height (from tip of left horn to rear foot of main bull), 5 feet 4 inches. The massive majesty of these animal forms suggests a connection of some kind with the art of the Franco-Cantabrian caves. The engravings are not in caves, however, but on open rock surfaces, and their period, c. 7000 to 4500 B.C., is already of the Neolithic.

The Bubalus Period, c. 7000 to 4500 B.C.

The characteristic subject, after which this period is named, is a large buffalo of a species now extinct *(Bubalus antiquus)*, before which there may be shown a human figure standing in worship, with any number of other beasts haphazardly round about, such as elephants, rhinoceroses, giraffes, hippopotamuses, ostriches, and large antelopes (Figure 143). Like the bison of Lascaux, this North African buffalo was evidently a "master animal" upon whose will the appearances of the wild herds of the hunt were thought to depend[76]. Only one other beast is shown so venerated in these engravings, a ram with a sun-disk on its head (Figure 144).[77] The

144. Rock engraving at Djebel Bes Seba, Sahara-Atlas range, Algeria (Map 23, Area 3). Bubalus style and period, c. 7000 to 4500 B.C. Ram, crowned with the solar disk, wearing a decorated neck band, confronted by a man in the posture of worship. Below is a smaller ram, also crowned and with a neck decoration. The symbolism of the curious dual figure encircled by what appears to be its own tail remains unexplained.[7]

North African *en face* lion that Frobenius compared with the *Sorcerer of Les Trois Frères* (Figure 132, page 76) was in this style, which, in Lhote's view, was of an early preceramic Neolithic era that commenced c. 7000 B.C.: a product of "the Capsian civilization that sprang up," as he declares, "on the plateau land of western Algeria and Tunisia, among men related in type to Cro-Magnon Man."[78]

There are three major centers in which engravings of this art period and style have been found: the Sahara-Atlas Mountains (Area 3 on Map 23), the Tassili, and

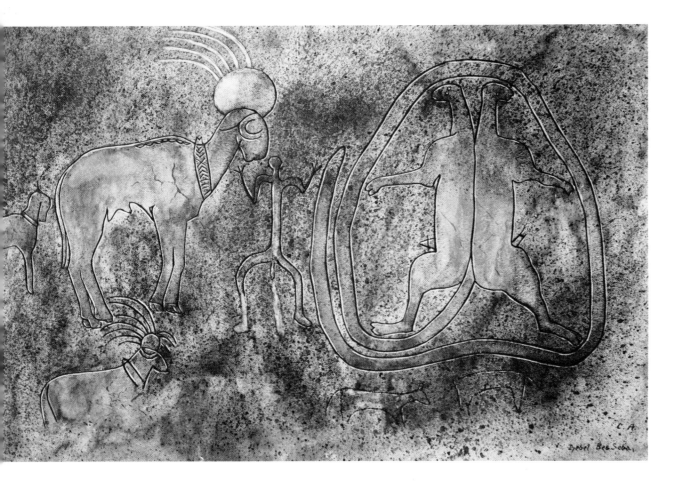

the Fezzan (Area 4). And, as in the European painted caves, so here, the main subjects are the larger animals of the chase, with only occasional human figures, very much less accurately rendered than the animals. In Lhote's opinion, the Bubalus engravings "have no demonstrable affinities with the engraved or painted rock pictures of Europe," the analogies, in his view, being "probably only accidental."[79] Frobenius, on the other hand, saw these engravings as representing an influence from Europe that had come, north to south, through Spain, and in Africa then turned, west to east, toward Egypt—to be met, in return, by a series of waves of more advanced cultural influences from Asia, flowing east to west.

Frobenius notes, for example, that the ram with the sun-disk on its head suggests the sun-ram of the great Egyptian god Amon of Thebes, who was a divinity first venerated in the Libyan Siwa Oasis, his cult then passing in predynastic times into Egypt. There is a Kabyle legend that associates this animal with the introduction of agriculture: it makes feasts and festivals possible and is consulted about sowing and harvest.[80] Thus the two venerated beasts, the bubalus and the ram, are of two distinct traditions: an earlier, from the west, of a late Paleolithic hunting mythology related to that of the French and North-Spanish caves; and a later, from the east, of an agricultural and stock-breeding tradition stemming ultimately from Southwest Asia, where, as early as c. 9000 B.C., the sheep (the ram) is attested as the earliest animal domesticate.[81] In the life and art of North Africa, these two traditions met in mid-Sahara, in the neighborhood of Tassili and Fezzan (Area 4), c. 4500 to 3500 B.C.

Period of the Round-Heads, from c. 6000 B.C.

Among the numerous rock shelters of the eastern Tassili, thousands of paintings in a distinctive style have been discovered, characterized by human figures with round, featureless heads. "It seems" states Lhote in discussion of these finds, "as though we are confronted with the earliest works of negro art—indeed, one is tempted to say, with its origin."[82] Small to start with, the forms gradually increased to extraordinary dimensions: human figures over 16 feet tall, and cattle of natural size. The final works reveal an Egyptian influence, possibly of the Eighteenth Dynasty—which suggests for this art a history of some 4000 to 5000 years. Its most enigmatic forms are immense spirit figures; its most beautiful, some of the masterworks of the period of Egyptian influence; and there are masks represented that strongly suggest some of those of the present-day Ivory Coast.

146.

145. Plumed Bowman, followed by a woman bearing dotted markings that may represent scarifications. From Tassili Jabbaren, where hundreds of paintings in various styles decorate the rock walls. Period of the Round Heads, from c. 6000 B.C.

146. At Tassili Auanrhet, a towering massif within sight of Jabbaren, this masked apparition in the Round-Head style covers an earlier, white, female form. Decorated with checkerwork and with plants issuing from arms and thighs, the figure lacks hands and feet. Lhote was struck by the horned head's resemblance to African masks in the Musée de l'Homme.

147. At Tassili Sefar, where the mountain mass breaks into vast amphitheaters with cathedral-like formations, a dance of men and women who are linked, apparently, by a cord. Evolved Round-Head style with Egyptian influence.

145.
147.

*The Bovidian or Pastoral Period,
c. 4000 to 1800 B.C.*

These rock paintings stand apart in that they are without apparent symbolic function, but of a masterly naturalism and, as their discoverer has suggested, may represent the world's earliest school of "art for art's sake." Figures rendered singly are exceptional; the interest is in compositions. The artists were of the race that introduced sheep and cattle raising to West Africa, and they almost certainly brought with them a knowledge of agriculture. Neither Negroid nor European, they were of an East African Hamitic stock, with copper skin and long straight hair. Henri Lhote sees their descendants in the Fulani of today.

A Post-Bovidian Period of Egyptian Influences

The original pastoralists can have entered the Sahara only from the Nile Valley. Although there is evidence of occupations of that area throughout the Paleolithic, next to nothing is known of the transition period, c. 10,000 to 4000 B.C., when food crops (wheat and barley) and animal domesticates (sheep, goats, pigs, and later, cattle) were introduced from Asia.[83] The first movement from Egypt westward appears to have been that documented in the Bovidian scenes on the Tassili rocks, from c. 4000 B.C. Centuries later, there followed a second movement, about the period, apparently, of the Egyptian Eighteenth Dynasty (1570 to 1432 B.C.). By whom and how this influence was carried is unknown, but it touched the arts of both the Round-Heads and the Pastoralists with a new and lovely grace.

148. *The Horned Goddess*, Tassili Aouarhet, evolved Round-Head style with Egyptian influences.

149. Cattle herd from Tassili Jabbaren. At the right, one of the animals is being sacrificed. Bovidian or Pastoral Period, after c. 4000 B.C.

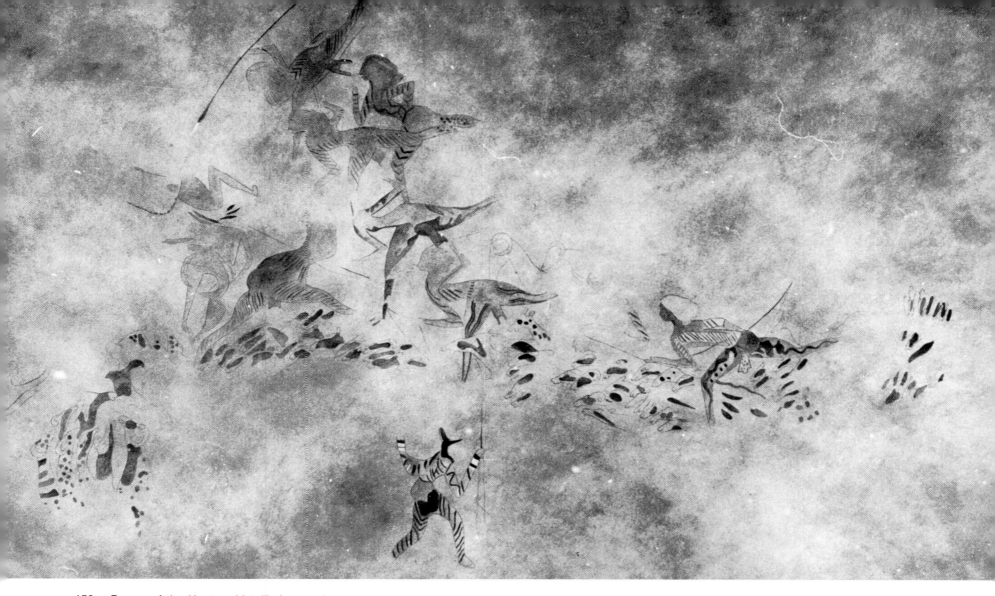

150. *Fresco of the Hunters* (detail), from a deep shelter at Tassili Tamrit, where the green foliage of immense cypresses against the dull red of surrounding rocks, an eighteen-hundred-foot waterfall, and a scattering of little lakes still suggest a landscape of forest glades, grassy vales, and abundant game. The hunters, armed with javelins and bows, have designs painted on their bodies. The game is represented by animals' heads. Early Bovidian Period.

151. From I-n-Itinen, a huge masked man, wearing a helmet and holding what is—apparently—a smaller mask, or head. The painting, in a poor state of preservation, is of the Post-Bovidian Period with Egyptian influence.

152. *The Dancers,* from Ti-n-Tazarift, an immense natural amphitheater. The bodies' forms and garb are of the evolved Round-Head style of **148.** Post-Bovidian Period of Egyptian influences.

152.

151.

The Chariot and Equestrian Periods, from c. 1200 B.C.

About 1200 B.C., the exact period of the Trojan War, a large company of invaders from Mycenaean Crete put to shore in Cyrenaica with the object of conquering Egypt, where they were known as the Peoples of the Sea. The campaign failed and, retiring to the Sahara, they became assimilated there with their Libyan allies. Henri Lhote discovered, not only in the Tassili, but also at stations along an ancient trans-Saharan caravan route from Tripoli (Oea) on the Mediterranean coast (Odysseus's Land of the Lotus Eaters) to

Map 24. The trans-Sahara Chariot Road with its rock-art sites showing chariots drawn by steeds at "flying gallop." From c. 1200 B.C.

153. Fresco in three styles from a rock shelter at Tassili Adjefou. The "flying gallop" chariots (1) are earlier than (2) the file of "bi-triangular" warriors and (3) the pastoral scene (coarser in style than the earlier "Bovidian"). The two warriors with bow and shield (lower right) and the horseman (lower left) are of the Chariot Period, while the negress in white who is conversing with companions is apparently of the "bi-triangular" context. Note the dog confronting the ram and (below) the mother and child.

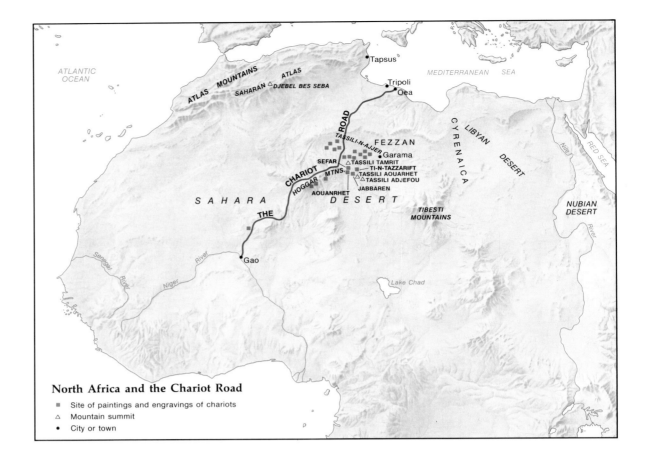

North Africa and the Chariot Road
■ Site of paintings and engravings of chariots
△ Mountain summit
● City or town

Gao on the river Niger, rock paintings of war chariots, the geographical disposition of which "shows," as he has stated, "that the horse-riding populations, descended from the 'Peoples of the Sea' and the Libyans, must have reached the Niger by almost as early as 1000 B.C."[84] (Map 24). Five centuries later, Herodotus (d. 425 B.C.) wrote of the Garamantians of Libya, who drove four-horse chariots in which they pursued the cave-dwelling Ethiopians.[85] Finally, in A.D. 19, the legate Cornelius Balbus returned from Africa to Rome in triumph, having subjugated Cyrenaica, the Fezzan, and every city along the old chariot road to the Niger.[86]

The Camel Period, from c. 100 B.C. (?)

With the arrival from Arabia of the camel, after the green Sahara had become desert, the rock art of the region declined to the level of crude pecked-out engravings. The earliest historical notice of the camel in North Africa is in a Latin account of the battle of Tapsus (46 B.C.), where twenty-two of the animals were taken by Julius Caesar as booty from the Numidian King Juba I. A more likely dating for the petroglyphs, however, would be from the rise of Islam (seventh century A.D.) to the present. They are found throughout the Sahara.

154. Hunting scene along the Chariot Road at Ala-n-Edoument. To the left of the driven chariot are the wheels of a second outfit. "Flying-Gallop" Chariot Period, after c. 1200 B.C.

155. From Wadi Djerat, Tassil, rock-doodlings of the Camel Period. Inscriptions are in Tifinagh, a Libyan alphabet derived from the Punic (Carthaginian) cursive script still used by Tuaregs. After c. A.D. 650.

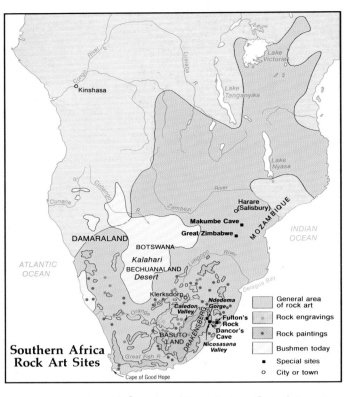

Map 25. The rock arts (in various styles) and most recent rock artists (the Bushmen) of Southern Africa.

South African Painted Rock Shrines

South Africa, from the river Zambezi to the Cape and from Damaraland to Mozambique is strewn with rock paintings and engravings. The earliest European settlers in the region, noticing that the native Bushmen were still producing paintings of the kind, attributed everything to them, and the works became generally known, accordingly, as Bushman paintings. The earliest scientific survey of the field was conducted in 1928 to 1930, by the members of the Ninth German Inner-African Research Expedition under Leo Frobenius, and their immediate discovery was that there were at least three distinct categories of South African rock art: (1) engravings; (2) polychrome paintings in various styles, found mainly in the deepest south, but recognizable also in the earlier layers of Transvaal and Rhodesia; and (3) monochrome paintings executed in a characteristic "wedge" style, which, having originated in Rhodesia, had spread as an influence southward and westward.[87]

The paintings in this wedge style were of especial interest to the expedition, since the area of its origin was that of the ruins of Great Zimbabwe, and the most typical of its scenes and motifs were of royal burials and installations. Such could not have been produced by primitive hunters and gatherers like the Bushmen. Moreover, the appearance of plants, ponds, and rock formations in many of

156. Rock painting in classic Rhodesian "wedge" style, documenting a tradition of ritual regicide. Diana Vow Farm, Rusapi District, Zimbabwe. Picture about one-tenth actual size. The body of the recumbent masked figure spilling its seed is tightly swathed. A little bird perches on the lifted knee, and the object in the lifted hand may be a horn symbolic of the moon, which dies to be resurrected. The smaller recumbent form below is the entombed sacrifice, of which the larger, floating, mythic figure personifies the released life-generating spiritual energy. A ceremony is in progress. The collection of humans, animals, and offerings separated by watery lines from the rest (lower right) is in the mythic other world, under waves, known in this tradition as *Dsivoa*.[8] The art style is classified on page 89 as item 6.

the wedge-style compositions was unique in prehistoric art. Relevant themes in the myths collected by members of the Expedition from the Wahungwe, Wateve, Batonga, Waremba, and other Shona and Sotho (Bantu) tribes in the general neighborhood of Zimbabwe contributed to the interpretation of the monuments. Their affiliations were neither with the Old nor with the New Stone Age, but with an early high-culture mythology grounded in a custom of ritual regicide, of which James G. Frazer had produced the classic study in *The Golden Bough*.

The engravings and polychrome paintings, on the other hand, were indeed Stone Age in character, and of the two, the earlier were evidently the engravings. These were not found on rock walls, but on rock fragments lying about, the finest and apparently oldest being of single animals, pecked out on hard diorite and basalt in a style resembling that of some of the later North African works and often of an astonishing naturalism. Their dating has not been determined, but at Klerksdorp and along the Orange River examples have been found associated with

157. Pecked-out engraving on an upright diabase cone. Date undetermined. Height of giraffe, approximately 2 ft. 3 in. Western Transvaal.

artifacts of a typical Capsian kind. (Figure 157).[88]

The dating of the paintings also is uncertain, but in the Makumbe Cave in the Chinamhora Reserve, Zimbabwe, there is a mural in which fourteen superpositions have been counted by a recent investigation, and these suggest a series of styles from perhaps the first centuries A.D. to the early nineteenth, the period of King Shaka's wars and the decadent years thereafter (Figure 159). These styles are as follows:

158. Rock painting in the classic Rhodesian wedge style showing a scene of human sacrifice (below) with a goddess among clouds (above). Spiritual messengers gather and ascend a heaven ladder, which breaks in a lightning flash that becomes transformed into a rain serpent. Marandelles District, South Rhodesia.[9]

1. The large elephants, in a dark purplish brown, now very pale
2. The smaller elephant and some finely drawn antelopes, in a similar but darker color and in the best animal style
3. Animals of a deep, reddish color
4. Animals of inferior quality, in a pale red
5. *A new people arrive:* animals in yellow or yellow-brown; some sensitively drawn, others lacking finer details
6. Human figures in Frobenius's wedge style; for example, the standing male, upper center, and the "mourner," lower right; both in a dark Indian red
7. The rhinoceros (an important recurrence of a larger animal), body in outline, filled in with a pale yellow
8. A thin man, a thin tree, and two baboons, all in brown
9. A row of men and women dancing (lower left): full of life, but the end of the fine style (Frobenius's polychrome style), c. A.D. 1820, the time of King Shaka's wars
10. Yellow ovals
11. A leaf motif, dark brown
12. Human figures in a crude style, carelessly done
13. A medley of fairly bright red lines, angular and geometric (not included in the section of mural shown here)
14. Massive, crude white animals and occasionally humans and angular forms [89] (also not here reproduced)

159. Rock wall bearing paintings in fourteen distinct styles (see text above). Makumbe Cave, Chinamhora Reserve, Zimbabwe.

Style 6 is of the context associated with Zimbabwe and probably of a date, accordingly, between A.D. 600 and 1500. How much of the rest should be attributed to Bushmen is unknown. These little people had been for millennia the sole inhabitants of the hunting plains of inland East and South Africa, while along the whole Azanian coast to as far south as Deagoa Bay, there had been running since ancient times a sea-traffic of merchantmen from Egypt and Phoenicia, Greece, Rome, Arabia, Persia, India, Indonesia, and even China. The gold, tin, and copper mines in the neighborhood of Zimbabwe had been worked for this trade from as early, certainly, as the seventh century A.D.; yet, in the underdeveloped interior there had been only primitive Bushmen until, from the sixth century onward, the Bantu tribes that now inhabit the region began pouring in from the northwest.

Carleton Coon interprets the Bushmen as having been originally one of the North African, Capsian hunting races, forced southward, first by Caucasoid and then by Congoid (that is, Negro) pressures (pages 42–43). George Murdock views them, on the contrary, as of South and East African origin. Either way, they were not finally driven from the Drakensberg and other last-holding grounds of the best known and best recorded of their polychrome works of art until the late nineteenth and early twentieth centuries.

The earliest Congoids to cross the Drakensberg range into the Caledon Valley were a Bantu people, the Sotho, c. A.D. 1600. Retiring under pressure from other advancing Bantu tribes from the north, notably the Shona, they had arrived peacefully, even intermarrying with the local Bushmen; and one of the high periods of recorded Bushman polychrome art (Style 9 of the above listing) is of the following two centuries in this region, c. 1620 to 1830. The end came only when a later Bantu tide of Nguni tribesmen, in flight from the expanding Zulu conquest state set up in Natal by the chieftain Shaka c. 1818, crossed the whole region, heading northward, ravaging and plundering as they passed.

Meanwhile, the Europeans, who had long been established in South Africa, were also expanding into Bushman territories. The Portuguese Henry the Navigator, in the fifteenth century, had marked the uninhabited Cape of Good Hope as a suitable stopping station for ships under weigh to the Indies. The Dutch colony was established there in 1652; and it was not until c. 1770 that their first encounters with the ever-advancing Bantu occurred in the valley of the Great Fish River. By then the invincible British had entered the scene who, after a series of political exchanges, took control of the Cape in 1814, after which, in 1835, the "Great Trek"

northeastward began of hundreds of disaffected Boers and their families (in ox wagons and with vast herds of cattle and sheep) into regions already in danger from the depredations of tribes scattering from the war machine of King Shaka.

The Bushmen, in the midst of all this turmoil, had become accomplished horse thieves and cattle rustlers, to the exasperation of both their white and their black encroaching neighbors. In the rock murals of their final period, we see them victoriously riding at a "flying gallop," driving off herds of the newcomers' stock.

The Bushman Trance Dance and Its Mythic Ground

In a detailed study of 8478 polychrome rock paintings in the Drakensberg area, Patricia Vinnicombe found that the number of animal species depicted did not match those of the Bushman diet. "Of the animals portrayed," she reports, "antelope are the main focus of interest, yet paradoxically, available archaeological evidence from excavated living sites indicates a preponderance of smaller animals

160/161. The eland, the outstanding Master Animal of this mythology, is to be killed in a special, sacred way, whether with a spear or with a bow and arrow. The hunter identifies himself with the animal struck by his poisoned dart and, during the painful hours of its dying, observes food and behavior taboos thought to advance the poison by virtue of this mystic identification.

rather than antelope in everyday diet."[90] Nor do the paintings present a fair sample of the species of the region. They are, as Vinnicombe declares, neither a menu nor a checklist, but the illustrations of a Late Stone Age mythology, in which the most prominent figure is the eland. (Compare Leroi-Gourhan's finding in relation to the number of species represented in the paintings of the great caves, page 62).

In keeping with this finding, the folktales of living Bushmen represent the eland as the first and favorite creation of their principal divinity: a god variously named, in the various Bushmen areas, as Gauwa, Hishe, Kaggen, Dxui, Gao na, and so on. *Kaggen* means "mantis," and it is in this character that the god commonly appears—not exactly as an insect, but as an ambiguous, manlike figure in the Mythological Age of the Beginning.

It is told, for example, that during that period when all things acquired the forms that must be theirs, now and forever:

Kaggen, at a place where reeds stood, soaked his son-in-law's shoe in the water, returning daily to watch it grow into an eland; and when the animal then approached from the reeds, he would fondle it, rub its sides with honey, and give it honey to eat. But his grandson, Ni, the ichneumon, spied on him one day and, discovering where all the honey was going, reported to his father. Presently Kaggen went away, hunting three days for more honey, and when every comb that he found was dry, he took this for a warning. Returning to the reeds, he called, but his eland did not come. He looked for its spoor, found blood, and following its trail, discovered Ni and his father butchering the beast.

Kaggen aimed an arrow at them, but it returned so close to his head that he narrowly missed shooting himself. Then he attacked with a club; but the others, overpowering him, made him carry wood for their fire until, discovering his slain eland's gallbladder in a bush, he pricked it. This covered him with darkness and he escaped. However, he was himself now unable to see. So he threw his own shoe high into the sky, where it became the moon, shedding light.[91]

162. A Kung dancer entering trance.

The Bushmen's gods, seriously regarded, are very different from this folktale character. Lorna Marshall found that the Kung of Botswana were afraid even to utter their gods' names. "We were aware," she tells, "of their unwillingness to speak of religious matters early in our work and therefore waited until our relations were well established before questioning them . . . . Sometimes we talked literally in whispers and usually at least in low voices, saying 'the one in the east,' 'the one in the west.'. . . The woman who first told me the name of the wife of the great god put her lips to my ear and whispered, barely audibly, 'Huwedi!' Next day, unfortunately, she had a high fever. She recovered, but the episode put an end to my trying to learn from her about the wives of the gods."[92]

According to this authority, the Kung today have two gods: one, the great, in the east, where the sun rises; one, the lesser, in the west, where it sets. Both have wives and are attended by the spirits of the dead. The great god created first himself, then the lesser god, then their wives, each of whom bore three girls and three boys. He also created the earth, its people, and all things. To praise himself, the great god named himself, saying, "I am Hishe. I am unknown, a stranger. No one can command me." He praised himself with a number of names: Gara, for example, when he did things hurtful to people. "He causes death among us," the people then would say. "He causes rain to thunder." Or, again he would declare: "I am Gaishi gai, a bad thing. I take my own way. No one can advise me."[93] To the lesser god he gave all of his own names but one, the

163. Rock painting of a Bushman dance, Dancor's Cave, Nicosasana Valley in the Drakensberg, South Africa. To the clapping of the women, some with babies on their backs, the men dance, led by a figure wearing rattles on his calves who is either masked or undergoing transformation into an antelope.

164. Trance dance of the Kung. During the course of the night, the men, circling to the women's clapping, collapse into states of visionary flight.

165. Rock painting, Rainbow Shelter, Ndedema Gorge in the Drakensberg, South Africa. A range of eland heads above a rainbow, with human legs below, representing, in Harald Pager's view, "a transformation from human to antelope form or vice versa."[10] This suggestion is supported by the presence, lower left, of an *ales*, or "flying buck," the image of a human spirit transformed in flight. (See pages 98–99.)

The degree to which primitive hunters can become identified with the symbolic animal upon whose good will the well-being of the tribe is imagined to depend is illustrated, not only in the myths and rituals of the Bushmen, but also in their hunting practices and in the imagery of their visions. The eland, which in their mythology occupies the high symbolic place, is not a necessary contributor to their diet. Subsistence is based on some thirty-odd plant species gathered by the women, who range daily with their digging sticks within a few miles of the camps collecting birds' eggs, turtles, lizards, and other small game. The men hunt over much larger ranges, and the animals of their encounters hold in their minds a high position, both as challengers to their skills and as presences of occult import. When the Bushman dies he is himself transformed into an eland.

166. Antelope men with an *ales* hovering above. Detail from a panel at Procession Shelter.

167. The main hunting weapon of the Bushmen of the Kalahari is a light bow, with a range of no more than 25 yards, that shoots unfeathered, poisoned arrows. Compare the magnificent weapons of the forest-dwelling Andamanese (pages 118–119).

168/169. Great skill is required to stalk an alert animal to within range of these flimsy but lethal arrows. As revealed in the two photographs below, the first requirement in this game of death is intense identification with the target.

oldest, the human name, with which he appears in the folktales: Gao na, "Old Gao." And to the wives he gave all of his divine names in their feminine forms: Hishedi, Gaishi gaidi, and so on, but each also had her own human name, which can be pronounced aloud without fear.[94]

As Old Gao, the great god is at once himself and not himself, and the people tell his old tales without restraint. They say his name aloud and even howl and roll on the ground with laughter at his humiliations. "Like men," states Lorna

Marshall, "he was subject to passions, hungers, sins, stupidities, failures, frustrations and humiliations, but men imagine his to have been on a larger scale and more grotesque than their own. Like Bushmen of today, his great concerns were hunger and sex. To the Kung the two worst sins, the unthinkable, unspeakable sins, are cannibalism and incest. Old Gao committed both these sins unconcernedly. He ate his older brother-in-law and his younger brother-in-law, and he raped his son's wife."[95]

In the Cape Bushman legend of Kaggen and the first eland, the same duplexity is evident as in the Kung tales of Old Gao. The narratives carry, behind a protective screen of radically reductive metaphor, reflexes of the greatest mysteries. It has been noticed, for example,[96] that the shoe can be understood as symbolic of the vagina, and honey, as of semen. The shoe of Kaggen's son-in-law, then, would have been the organ of Kaggen's daughter, and the honey fed it as an eland, his own procreative seed. In another version:

Kaggen's wife bore the first eland and Kaggen tried to kill it by throwing sharpened sticks, but he missed. Then he left (again for three days) to fetch arrow poison, and while he was gone, his sons discovered and killed the eland. Returning, he rebuked them furiously. But then he and his wife mixed fat from the animal's heart in a pot, together with some of its blood, and churned. The drops became, first, eland bulls, then cows, which spread over the earth. Whereupon Kaggen sent his sons out to hunt them. And that day, game were given to men to eat.[97]

From the moment the eland is struck, the successful bowman is bound to a sympathetic routine of magical observances, to be followed throughout the period of the stricken animal's dying, often a day or more.

Intentional identification with the animal whose occult power is to be invoked through the exercise of a ceremonial is commonly achieved by masquerade; for the energy of which the animal is the vehicle or agent is conducted through some critical aspect of its form. The masks that in our demythologized time are lightly assumed for the entertainments of a costume ball or Mardigras—and may actually, on such occasions, release us to activities and experiences which might otherwise have been tabooed—are vestigial of an earlier magic, in which the powers to be invoked were not simply psychological, but cosmic. For the appearances of the natural order, which are separate from each other in time and space, are in fact the manifestations of energies that inform all things and can be summoned to focus at will. The mythological association of the eland with the moon and a recognition, thereby, of the coincidence of the lunar and female cycles has rationalized the celebration of eland ceremonials in contexts relevant to fertility, especially those rendered by the women attending a girl's first menstruation (see page 100). Compare from the Paleolithic rock shelter of Laussel (page 67), the symbolic figure of *The Women with the Horn* (Figure 109).

170. Profile of a Bushman eland dancer.

The hunter's need to kill in order to live is justified in this legend as an institution of the First Being himself; and the god's ambiguous relationship both to the animal slain and to its killing is our clue to what in literary criticism would be termed the anagogical meaning of the tale. The arrow shot at those butchering his eland turns back and nearly strikes the god himself, while in the second telling of his tale, it is he who is the first to attempt the kill. In the first version he went off to find honey; in the second, to get poison. The apparent equivalence here of the god's life-giving and death-dealing powers cannot be accidental.

Kaggen's creation of the moon after his eland has been butchered is another significant sign. One shoe had become his eland; the other became the moon: the two being equally endowed with the power of rebirth. Moreover, to procure the required honey or poison, Kaggen left the scene for three days: the moon is three nights dark. And when he returns to find his eland dead, he is through his own act covered with darkness—until the new moon appears.

Patricia Vinnicombe calls attention to the Bushmen's use of blood and fat as components of their paints.[98] Herbert Kühn has suggested that blood and fat may have been ingredients of the paints of the European caves.[99] Thus the act of painting may have been, as Vinnicombe suggests, a ritual act of restitution in the very sense of the restitution and multiplication of Kaggen's eland in the second version of his legend. "It seems reasonable," she writes, "to postulate that the Bushman *artist* played an important role in this propitiation ceremony, and that by recreating visible eland upon the shelter walls, Man the Hunter was reconciled with Kaggen the Creator, thereby restoring the balance of opposing forces that was so necessary for the well-being of the Bushman psyche. Through the eland, the Bushman established and maintained communication with his god. Through the eland, the eternal cycle of sacrificing life in order to conserve and promote life, was ritually expressed."[100] In sum, the mythological eland sacrifice, of which every hunting kill is a duplication, is the inexhaustible vessel out of which the bounty of the great god's world proceeds. And every hunter, in his sacrificial killing, is in the role of Kaggen himself, identified with the animal of his kill and at the same time guilty, as the god is guilty, with the primordial guilt of life that lives on life.

171. Opening stage of a night of trance dancing. Having gathered on the danceground, a few women of the camp have built a fire and, clapping time, have begun humming. A few men, each hunched tightly forward, have already begun circling around them with short tight steps. Others will presently join the circle, and the dance may continue all night.

172. One of the dancers (center) has been overcome by the energy known as *ntum*, a hot uprush from the pit of the stomach, up the spinal cord, to the brain.

According to a Kung Bushman legend of Botswana, published in 1975 by Marguerite Anne Biesele:

A woman named Be was alone in the bush one day in Namibia, when she saw a herd of giraffes running before an approaching thunderstorm. The rolling beat of their hooves grew louder and mingled in her head with the sound of sudden rain. Suddenly a song she had never heard before came to her, and she began to sing.

Gauwa (the great god) told her it was a medicine song. Be went home and taught the song to her husband, Tike. They sang and danced it together. And it was, indeed, a song for trancing, a medicine song. Tike taught it to others, who passed it on.[101]

Kung medicine songs are thought to be endowed with a supernatural potency known as *ntum*. In the Mythological Age of the Beginning, quantities of this power were put by the great god into a number of things: medicine songs, ostrich eggs, certain plants and fruits, the sun, falling stars, rain, bees, honey, giraffes, aardvarks, blood, redwing partridges, and fires made in certain situations; also into certain persons, who might function, then as medicine men and healers. *Ntum* is not personified, nor invoked in prayer. Undifferentiated, it varies in force in the various things it informs: beneficent in some, always strong, but in some things dangerously so. *Ntum* is so strong in the great god that should he approach an ordinary mortal, like a lightning bolt his *ntum* would kill the man. The Kung call *ntum* a "death thing"; also, a "fight." "These are expressions," states Lorna Marshall, "frequently used by the Kung for anything strong or dangerous: the sun, for example, is also a 'fight' and a

'death thing.'"[102] Potent medicine men, on the other hand, can meet and face Gauwa down, hurling insults of the grossest kind at him when, in trance, they are curing those whom the god has afflicted; for the power of their own *ntum* is, at such times, enhanced.

The supreme occasion for the activation of *ntum* is the trance dance, performed by the males of the small bands to the sharply rhythmed clapping and wordless chanting of the women. The exertion of the tirelessly circling dancers heats their medicine power, which they experience as a physical substance in the pit of the stomach.[103] The women's singing, the men say, "awakens their hearts," and

eventually their portion of *ntum* becomes so hot that it boils. In the report of Lorna Marshall: "The men say it boils up their spinal columns into their heads, and is so strong when it does this that it overcomes them and they lose their senses."[104] The resemblance of this description to reports from India of the rising of the Kundalini is amazing.

It is generally during the period of the approach of this crisis that the work of healing is undertaken. It is then also that the medicine man can challenge Guawa. His body is indestructible. He can walk into the fire, pick up burning brands, and rub them over his body. A younger dancer may go wild when he first breaks into

174. The spirit of the visionary voyager has just returned to his inert body, which has been lying in the condition known as "half death." The moment is a delicate one and, if failed, may result in full death (see page 96). His friends, who have been watching for this critical moment, are here ministering to a safe return.

173. The entranced member is lowered to the ground. His spirit has departed on the visionary journey from which there is derived direct knowledge of invisibles and their world (see page 96).

this experience. As reported by Richard B. Lee: "He plunges into the fire, runs off into the dark, struggles when restrained, kicks, squirms (perhaps injures himself), and finally falls into the comatose state called 'half-death.' "[105]

Ordinarily a danceground is chosen only a few yards from the encampment, and typically dances commence when a handful of women light the central fire, sit in a tight circle around it, and begin to sing, clapping time. Eventually, a few of the men stray in behind them, to circle with short, heavy stamps in a single line, which, from time to time turns about to circle the other way. Strings of rattles around the men's ankles stress the beat.

Their rhythms are complex, built into 5- and 7-beat phrases. And their body postures are tight, hunched forward, arms close to the sides, slightly flexed. Others join the round, and as the night runs on, those approaching trance begin to concentrate intently.

"They look down at their feet," states Lee, "or stare ahead without orienting to distractions around them. The body is tense and rigid. Footfalls are heavy, and the shock waves can be seen rippling through the body. The chest is heaving, veins are standing out on neck and forehead, and there is profuse sweating." Trance supervenes some 30 to 60 minutes later, either gradually or of a sudden. If

gradually, the trancer staggers; other men come to his aid and lead him around until he shouts and falls down, comatose, in the state of "half death." The sudden trance, on the other hand, is announced by a violent leap or somersault and instant collapse. "It is noteworthy," Lee remarks, "that many of the older medicine men, with years of experience in trance states, do not go through the 'half-death' phase. . . . The discipline displayed by these older men is the result of years of training, during which they learn to bring their reactions under control."[106]

The gaining and maintaining of control over the force of *ntum* is the first requirement of this rite, since it is only when brought under human direction that the force can be applied to healing. Its heat is simultaneously activated and held in check, not only by the dancer himself, but also communally, through the ritualized dancing and songs of the group, where the control, as well as the excitation, is governed by the clapping, singing, and pacing of the whole affair by the women.

The contrast of male and female roles in this rite reflects, as Marguerite Biesele observed, a consistent symbolism in the mythic and social assignments of the sexes. Women gather plant foods, and their power and prestige are linked to their role as providers of this resource. Men are hunters and have to do with arrows, arrow poison, spears, quivers, and other hunting gear. The female is associated with childbirth, menstruation, breastmilk, the gathering of plants, solidarity of the nuclear family, the moon, and the origin of water. Men control lightning with animal horns, and their potency is associated with the sun, semen, heat, trance dancing, and the origin of fire.

"Trancers," Biesele observed, "seem to flirt with the dangerous heat of the fire, coming as close to it as they possibly can in the effort to make the *ntum* boil within them."[107] If it boils up too quickly, however, they go into trance before they can cure; hence those feeling it coming too soon draw back and cease dancing for a while. "Significantly," she noticed, "women offer such men water with which to cool off. Women also watch to prevent insensate trancers from burning their bodies in the fire."[108]

Generally, as Lorna Marshall also has seen, the attributes associated with women are thought to be antithetical to those of men; yet in the cooperative rapture of the trance dance, the two combine, as she has observed, "with such precision that they become like an organic being. And in this close configuration—together—they face the gods."[109]

*   *   *

When the Kung dancers break and pass into the state of half-death, their spirits fly along threads of spider silk to the sky. These are the ways of passage of the gods and spirits of the dead between earth and heaven.[110] Marguerite Biesele has published the rendered account of one such spiritual astronaut:

"When people sing, I dance. I enter the earth. I go in at a place like a place where people drink water. I travel a long way, very far. When I emerge, I am already climbing. I'm climbing threads, the threads that lie over there in the south. I climb one and leave it, then I climb another one. Then I leave it and climb another. . . . And when you arrive at God's place," he told her, "you make yourself small. You have become small. You come in small to God's place. You do what you have to do there. Then you return to where everyone is, and you hide your face. You hide your face so you won't see anything. You come and come and come and finally you enter your body again. All the people who have stayed behind are waiting for you—they fear you. You enter, enter the earth, and you return to enter the skin of your body. . . . And you say 'he-e-e-e!' That is the sound of your return to your body. Then you begin to sing. The *ntum*-masters are there around. They take powder and blow it—Phew! Phew!—in your face. They take hold of your head and blow about the sides of your face. This is how you manage to be alive again. Friends, if they don't do that to you, you die. . . . You just die and are dead. Friend, this is what it does, this *ntum* that I do, this *ntum* here that I dance."[111/112]

175. Two male dancers, silhouetted in the dawn, whirl before their audience. The session, which began at sundown, has run through the night as a dream shared by all.

It is thus entirely possible that the flying figures in the Bushman paintings, known as "flying bucks" or *alites*, may represent, not only spirits of the dead, but also those in flight of the living trancers in half-death, and that such scenes in the painted sanctuaries as those of the Sebaaieni Cave, where there is one such *ales* flying, are to be interpreted, as Harald Pager has suggested, as "the Bushman's idea of their 'eternal hunting grounds,' "[113] to the everlasting scenery of which the great *ntum* masters in their half-death states pay visits three or four times a month.[114]

Neither Vinnicombe nor Pager has found anywhere in the Drakensberg, however, anything like the figure of a looked straight before him, while the two front feet held limp in front of him suddenly moved and pointed downwards to the earth.

" 'Please, how high is the sea?' " Klara asked.

"Mantis lifted his head, looked up and raised his long front feet to point at the cloudless blue sky. I could not make sense of the questions or Mantis's positive response to them. Klara had never been to the sea. We were at that moment some thousand miles from the nearest coastline and she was to die, alas, without ever seeing the sea. Yet her attitude of extreme reverence, the strange shape of Mantis, his uncanny responsiveness to the sound

mantis, and Pager remarks that "there is no mantis cult among contemporary Bushmen and there is no objective evidence of Bushmen or Hottentots having worshipped this insect in the past."[115]

Laurens van der Post, however, who was born and raised in South Africa, recalls very well the tales of his old black nurse, Klara, who had had a Bushman mother and who, on one occasion, went down on her knees before a mantis in the grass, "bowing to it with her hands folded in front of her like a Christian at prayer."

"Calling it a name I had not heard and cannot remember," he recalls "she begged the Mantis in a low hissing voice, 'Please, how low is the sea?' To my amazement the head of the Mantis turned and he

of worship on her tongue, and her extreme delight at the outcome made an impression I was never to forget."[116]

Van der Post had the advantage, of course, of a child's unreformed sense of wonder, as well as appreciation of little things, and the idea of an extraordinary insect as manifestation or messenger of an unknown god was neither incredible to him nor absurd. "With all that," he could write of Mantis fifty years later, "there was something curiously human about his face. Its heart shape, pointed chin, high cheek bones and yellow skin—I realize now how like a Bushman's that face was. Besides, his eyes were extraordinarily big and bright, as if capable of extra perception."[117]

176. In this masterpiece from the Sebaaiene Cave, in the Ndedema Gorge of the Drakensberg Range, a procession of mythic "antelope men" passes mysteriously above a panorama of earthly hunting, fighting, dancing, and domestic scenes. Left of center in the left panel is the *ales*, or "flying buck," reproduced above as **177c**.

Alites ("flying bucks") are envisionments of spirits, almost certainly those of the dead, and possibly those of trance dancers flying from their bodies. "There was a belief," states Harald Pager, "that the souls of the dead fly through the air." And he illustrates this point with an arranged display of forty-five *alites*, selected from eighteen sites in the Ndedema Gorge. The series of examples reproduced above (**177**) is abridged from that presentation.[11] Pager calls attention to the range from nearly human to bird and antelope forms. Immediately apparent in a number of the more human of the figures is the resemblance of their posture—arms held back and a forward pitch of the body—to the stance of Kung trance dancers.

178. Harald Pager describes the "antelope man" as "a human being whose legs and/or arms terminate in hooves. Most *antelope men* also have antelope heads," he adds, "but this feature alone is not considered sufficient for identification."[12] Some have argued that such figures represent disguised hunters, but hooved legs and arms do not support this reading. Pager points out that "antelope men" are larger than the human figures in these paintings and more grandly dressed. "The arithmetic mean of the sizes of all human figures in the Ndedema sample," he observes, "is 91 mm, while for the *antelope men* it is 248 mm. Moreover, the majority of human figures are depicted naked, while only four of the eighty-eight *antelope men* are without habiliment. All the others wear either karosses and leggings, or what appear to be tight-fitting fur garments. . . . Leggings in particular are hardly ever depicted on an 'ordinary' man. All *antelope men* wear body ornaments, often in elaborate quantities. That these figures do depict some extraordinary beings is without doubt and their significance is perhaps contained in an account given to Frobenius by a Bantu who said that the paintings of humans with animal heads were the figures of dead men."[13]

D. N. Lee and H. C. Woodhouse, two authors cited by Pager,[14] write of the *alites* as representing spirits of the dead, citing in support of this view a belief that "Bushmen were formerly springbok and were changed into human beings by the creative power of the *mantis*"; also the idea that "the spirit of a Bushman houses itself in the body of an animal as it goes to the eternal 'Bokveld'." Pager joins to these statements a third, reported by Bleek,[15] that antelopes seen near Bushman graves are the spirits of the dead.

Why, then, do we find no mantis in the paintings? The answer must lie in the distinction between the "feared," unutterable names and the "human" names of the gods. The painted caves and shelters were in some sense sanctuaries, addressed, like the Bushman dances and other ritual observances, to the conjuring of *ntum*. A sacred place is one in which such rituals are performed, and the sanctuaries of Old Stone Age art were evidently such places. Their imagery, therefore, is of an order appropriate to the exaltation of consciousness, whereas folktales, told for amusement or even for instruction, are turned, as it were, toward the world. The god comes to view in them in his "human," apparently harmless, form, to play the clown for his people's enjoyment; and the appearance of any such radically reduced burlesque of a divinity in a sacred place would be incongruous.

The folktale, on the other hand, is for enjoyment, and since the best kind of enjoyment is in release from tension, the tales best loved are of the carnival kind, where the feared god appears in carnival form, as an insect, together with a company of incongruous little players: his wife, a dassie; their daughter, an eland; his adopted daughter, a porcupine; his sister, a blue crane; his grandson, an ichneumon; and his niece, a little springbok, swallowed by an elephant (like Red Ridinghood by the wolf), whom he then must rescue. To each a special manner of speech has been humorously assigned, imitating the shape of the mouth of the kind of animal represented. The curious

179. Rock painting of the women's Eland Dance in celebration of a girl's first menstruation. From Fulton's Rock in the Drakensberg.

The boys' Rite of the First Kill and the girls' Rite of the First Menstruation are their respective rites of passage to maturity. The girl is thought to be charged with a force that must be defended both from the sun's rays and from contact with earth.[16] Head covered with a kaross, she is carried on a kinswoman's back to a shelter apart, where the women, removing their own karosses, perform the Eland Dance to an eland song that is among the most ancient of Kung musical expressions. (Compare the eland/moon identification in the legend on page 91.) At the end, the girl is washed, anointed with eland fat, and painted on her forehead and cheeks with designs the meanings of which have been lost.[17]

180. A Kung Eland Dance today, photographed by Lorna Marshall.

"click" language of the Bushman is played upon with all sorts of bizarre additions and alterations of accent. Nor do all the tales of this carnival have to do with the burlesqued great god and his friends. As everywhere in the universally enjoyed, ageless heritage of the animal fable, one of the most popular themes is of the outwitting of the great by the small—best of all and usually, by some clever counterpart of our European Reynard the Fox. For example:

Jackal, out hunting, one day arrived at Lion's house and, seeing the lion's wife there, asked: "Good lady, where is your husband?" "My husband is a great man," she replied, "not to be spoken of by such as you." "Softly, proud lady," Jackal cautioned, "your husband is my servant." And he trotted away.

When Lion arrived, his wife greeted him contemptuously. "You are nothing. Jackal was here. He told me that you are his servant." Amazed, he demanded, "Where is that fellow now?" And she answered, "Oh, very likely in the bush close by, awaiting your return, for I think he requires your service." "I shall show you something today, dear wife, that will stop your foolish words," Lion said; and he left to look for Jackal.

181. String figures, or "cat's cradle" games, are of a world-wide distribution. The precise figure here displayed by this young Kung Bushman wife is known in Hawaii as *Ma-ha-lii-lii* and *Pu-kau-la;* in Ireland as the "Ladder" and the "Fence"; and in Nigeria, among the Yoruba, as the "Calabash Net." An example of this same figure recorded from the Osage tribe of Oklahoma was called by the collector "Osage Diamonds."[18]

He found him asleep in the bush and roughly roused him. "Jackal, you told my wife that you wanted to see me; so now follow me!" Waking, Jackal replied: "Ah! 'Tis the voice of my lordly friend. Alas, good friend, I am blind, and being blind I stumbled upon your house unwittingly. I cannot see and therefore cannot follow you." "Then I shall carry you," Lion said. And he took the jackal on his back.

Now Jackal had concealed with him hornets and bees, and as they approached Lion's house he released them, so that they attacked his mount, and Lion, on reaching the house, ran before his wife in great pain, while Jackal lashed him with a whip and goaded him on. "Faster! Faster! Do as I bid, you knave!" And as they sped past the house, Jackal called to Lion's wife: "Aha, proud lady! So your husband is a great man, not to be spoken of by such as I! Nevertheless, he is my servant, as I told you. See how I ride and beat him!"

And the lion's wife, humiliated, turned away.[118]

182. In tales told for enjoyment the gods put off their majesty and become transformed through the magic of the story-teller's art into entertainers. The Kung tell tales of a mythical past which they consider to have been actual, not mythical. The "old old people" of that imagined time passed on what they had been taught by the Creator, and the old have transmitted this teaching to the young even until today.[19]

LIVING PEOPLES
OF THE
EQUATORIAL FORESTS

The Pygmies of the African rain forest (**183**), and the mysterious Tasaday of the Philippines (**184**: first discovered in 1971 still dwelling in their ancestral caves) represent at opposite ends of the Afro-Asian equatorial belt a quality of human life in accord with nature that has enchanted everyone who has written of them. Not fear, but an easy confidence in the unfailing bounty of the Lord of their forest is the characteristic ground-feeling of their very casually organized societies. Fear, on the other hand, incredulity, and bewilderment overcome them at the forest's edge, where the uninterrupted space of the sky and plains opens out before their eyes. Hardly could a contrast be greater than that between the worlds and world-views of the jungle and the plains.

Map 26. The peoples treated in this chapter, as representing the mythologies and folkways of the simplest hunters and gatherers of the Old World tropical forests, are: (1) the Pygmies of the Congo Basin; (2) the Tasaday of the Philippines; and (3) the Andamanese of the Bay of Bengal. Other peoples of about the same culture stage include: (4) the Hill Chenchu of southern India; (5) the Veddas of Sri Lanka; (6) the Selung and (7) Semang of the northern Malay Peninsula; and (8) the Mimika of New Guinea. The folkways and mythologies of these differ in detail, of course, from those of the three societies here treated. However, in the main they are equivalent and, indeed, any two or three of them might have been chosen to represent the profoundly sweet and melancholy message to us of our own, forgotten, deepest memories of the wilderness.

The Forest Song of the Pygmies

A small boy, alone in the forest, heard such a beautiful song that he went to see who was singing and, discovering a bird—the Bird of the Most Beautiful Song in the Forest—he brought it back to the camp to be fed. His father was annoyed at having to give food to a mere bird, but, the boy pleading, the bird was fed. Next day its song was heard again, and

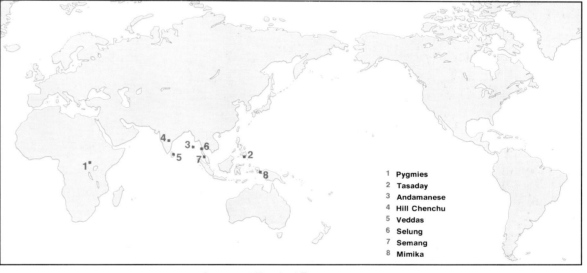

Map 26. Local Foraging Tribes of the Old World Tropical Forests

the boy again returned with it to the camp. The father was more annoyed than before, but again the bird was fed. Then a third day, and again the song! This time, taking the bird from his son, the father told him to run along; and when the boy was gone, the man killed the bird, and with the bird he killed the song, and with the song, himself. He dropped dead, completely dead, and was dead forever.[119]

Colin Turnbull, who returned with this fable from one of his long stays among the Pygmies of the Ituri forest, tells of the forest voice of a marvelous instrument called the "molimo," to which he was introduced at the close of his first visit. Three of the leading hunters had taken him into the forest to make sure, as they said, that he would return. They were going to make him "of the forest." With a rusty arrow blade they cut tiny vertical

slits in the center of his forehead and over each eye, gouged from each a little flesh, and rubbed a black ash-paste into the cuts. And it was later that same evening, while the men were singing, that he first heard the molimo.

"First I heard it call out of the night from the other side of the Nepussi river . . . ; it sounded like someone singing but it was not a human voice. It was a deep, gentle, loving sound, sometimes breaking off in a quiet falsetto, sometimes growling like a leopard. As the

men sang their songs of praise to the forest, the molimo answered them, first on this side, then on that, moving around so swiftly and silently that it seemed to be everywhere at once.

"Then, still unseen, it was right beside me, not more than two feet away, on the other side of a small but thick wall of leaves. As it replied to the song of the men, who continued to sing as though nothing were happening, the sound was sad and wistful, and immensely beautiful. Several of the older men were sitting near me, and one of them, without even looking up, asked me if I wanted to see the molimo. He then continued singing as though he didn't particularly care what my reply was, but I knew he did. I was so overcome by curiosity that I almost said 'yes'; I had been fighting hard to stop

The Rain Forest Domain of the Pygmies

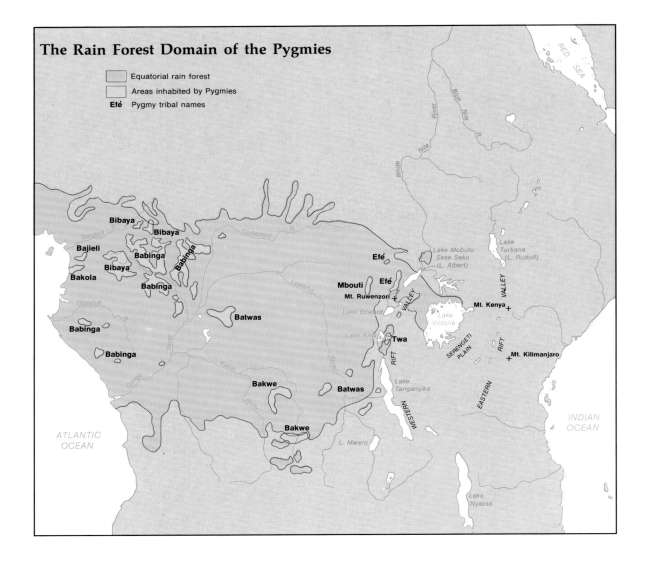

☐ Equatorial rain forest
☐ Areas inhabited by Pygmies
Efé Pygmy tribal names

myself from trying to peer through the leaves to where it was now growling away almost angrily. But I knew that Pygmy youths were not allowed to see it until they had proved themselves as hunters, as adults in Pygmy eyes, and although I now carried the marks on my forehead I still felt unqualified. So I simply said, no, I did not think I was ready to see it.

"The molimo gave a great burst of song and with a wild rush swept across the camp, surrounded by a dozen youths packed so tightly together that I could see nothing, and disappeared into the forest. Those left in the camp made no comment; they just kept on with their song, and after a while the voice of the molimo, replying to them, became fainter and fainter and was finally lost in the night and in the depths of the forest from where it had come." [120]

The contrast of the two worlds and of the ways of life and thought of these Pygmies and the Bushmen could hardly be more extreme. Ethnologically, both are classified as hunters and gatherers. They are the true "primitives" of Africa, surviving from Old Stone Age times in the ways of their fathers and grandfathers. However, one is of the sunburnt plains, the other of the deep forest. The Bushman, dependent utterly on the miracle of rain

Map 27. Lake Victoria, with the great Serengeti animal plain, Rift Valley, and Kenya highlands to the east, Tanzania to the south, and the Mountains of the Moon (Mount Ruwenzori) to the west, marks the general area of the first appearances of the running humanlike apes of the plains that evolved into *Homo habilis* and eventually into the present human race. The return of the ancestors of the Pygmies to the forest was, therefore, a secondary development, like the return to the sea of the ancestors of the whales. The forest received them, prehuman arboreal skills were recovered, and for untold millennia, until well into the first millennium A.D., these little "singers and dancers of God" (as they have been called) were the sole inhabitants of their wilderness.

185. The forest itself provides all the materials necessary for a life-style come to rest on a level of late Paleolithic technology. Impermanent leaf-thatched huts are raised and struck as the little groups of thirty or more move about.

186. Deep-forest hunting is a very different affair from hunting on the plains. A party sets out with nets and lances for a day's catch.

and on the killing of animals for his life, is dominated by an enduring sense of the tension of opposites—hunter and hunted, drought and rain, female and male, life and death; whereas the forest-dwelling Pygmies, at home in a rain-soaked jungle rich in roots, leafage, and fruits, are sustained substantially by the vegetal abundance, into which they enter with a sense of accord, and of which the animals are a natural part. "The forest is a father and mother to us," said Turnbull's old initiator, Moke; "and like a father and mother it gives us everything we need—food, clothing, shelter, warmth . . . and affection. Normally, everything goes well, because the forest is good to its children, but when things go wrong there must be a reason . . . .

"Normally everything goes well in our world. But at night when we are sleeping, sometimes things go wrong. Army ants invade the camp; leopards may come in and steal a hunting dog or even a child. If we were awake, these things would not happen. So when something big goes wrong, like illness or bad hunting or death, it must be because the forest is sleeping and not looking after its children. So what do we do? We wake it up. We wake it up by singing to it, and we do this because we want it to waken happy.

Then everything will be well and good again. So when our world is going well then also we sing to the forest because we want it to share our happiness." [121]

It is impossible to extract from the fragments of lore and custom reported of the Pygmies any secure idea of what the missionary Paul Schebesta, of the order of the White Fathers, called Pygmy Theology. However, the contrasts with what we know of the Bushman forms give clues. For example, though both races are appreciative of the values of dance and song, their applications of these arts are very different. There is no trance dancing reported of the Pygmies; no trance flights; no healing. Though the dances are named "chimpanzee dances," "elephant dances," and so on, their character is rather of free pantomime than of a strictly maintained form intended to launch the participants into exalted spiritual states. "A chimpanzee dance that I saw," states Father Schebesta, "demanded considerable histrionic ability on the part of the performers. Only men and boys take part in it. They proceed through the entire camp with slow serpentine movements, their faces working in weird grimaces. The eldest of the group, armed with bow and arrow, represents the hunter, who lurks behind a bush or tree, and takes aim at the revel-

lers. Off goes the arrow, while the dancers scatter, roll about the ground, grin and roar. The drama is rehearsed again and again to the accompaniment of the thunder of the drums." [122]

Turnbull tells of a honey-gathering dance: "The men and women divided, and while the men pretended to be honey gatherers, dancing in a long curling line through the camp, looking up with exaggerated gestures as if searching for some sign of bees, the women danced in another long line through the trees at the edge of the camp, pretending they were the bees. The two lines gradually came closer and closer together, the women singing in a soft, rhythmic buzz, buzz, buzz, while the men pretended to hear but still not to see them. Then the women seized burning logs of wood and attacked the men, tapping the logs on their heads so that a shower of sparks fell over them, stinging them like the sting of the honeybee. At that they all gathered up the embers, and where some of the younger men had been building an elaborate hearth of special woods and special leaves, moistened to just the right extent, they lit the great honey fire. There was no flame, but dense clouds of smoke billowed upward. Men blew on their honey whistles, women clapping hands, and everyone burst into the song of magic that would travel with the smoke and call the bees to come and make more honey." [123]

These are very different affairs from the trance dances of the Bushman. A very different affair, also, from the Bushman's hunt is that of the Pygmy. It is a hunt with nets, in which the women as well as the men participate. One hears little or nothing of that severe ritual separation of the male and female sectors that is basic to Bushman life. Nor do we hear of anything comparable to the Bushman reverence for the animal slain. Turnbull, for example, tells of the killing in the course of a general hunt of a sindula: an animal, not much larger than a small dog, which had broken through one of the nets. A youngster of about thirteen had speared it, pinning it through the belly to the ground, and the little beast, full of fight, was doubled up, biting at the shaft with its sharp teeth. One of the men put another spear through its neck, but it still writhed and fought. A third spear pierced its heart, and the little beast expired. "They stood around," states Turnbull, "in an excited group, pointing at the dying animal and laughing. One boy, about nine years old, threw himself on the ground and curled up in a grotesque heap and imitated the sindula's last convulsions. The men pulled their spears out and joked with one another about being afraid of a little animal like that, and to emphasize his point one of them kicked the torn and bleeding body. Then Maipe's

187. The Pygmies are superb hunters. Here they have killed a gorilla twice the size of any two of them.

188. Through a section of the forest a long net is being laid, into which the animals are driven by the noise of the whole encampment—men, women, and children—closing in unseen through the dense tropical growth.

mother came and swept the blood-streaked animal up by its hind legs and threw it over her shoulder into the basket on her back." [124]

The Pygmies, in Father Schebesta's terms, "do not feel a consciousness of sin . . . . They are not troubled by fears through guilty conscience." [125] They are not, that is to say, troubled as the Bushmen are by the necessity to kill in order to live. Nor, in the present instance, was there any sign of compassion—any shared suffering with the animal—such as in the Bushman rites is apparent in every stage of what, for them, is an intensely ritualized act of sacrifice. There is no enduring Pygmy art celebrating the outstanding animals of their forest. Their address is, rather, to the forest itself, of whose bounty the animal slain to be eaten is a product. For there is a presence informing their forest, one of the names of which is

Man of the Forest. Another name, alluding to its guardianship of the dead, whose spirits inhabit the dark places, is Gate of the Abyss. Hunters' prayers are addressed to this presence, who may then go before them, opening the way, dropping leaves as signs. An elephant trumpets. "Tore must have struck him," they say. And away they go to the kill. As a thanks offering they will lay a piece of its flesh on some leaves. [126]

*   *   *

The informing spirit of their forest is known to the various Pygmy camps variously; as Tore, Arebati, Epilipili, Baatsi, or simply as Father or Grandfather, with the comment that no one really knows the name. When asked about "creation" by investigators in whose own mythology this concept is important, a Pygmy of the

Oruendi camp replied that Epilipili, who had always existed, was the one who created all things. In this account his image was somewhat confused, however, with that of Aporofandza, the First Man. [127] In the Nduye camp, where the Creator's name was unknown, he was pictured as an aged being with a long beard which, when swung to and fro, created hurricanes, thunderstorms, and damaging rains. He was Lord of the Lightning and the Rainbow: the latter was a huge serpent, and both were greatly feared. But here again there was a tendency to attribute some of the god's qualities to the First Man, who in turn was identified with the moon, [128] and the moon with the chameleon, who climbs the highest trees. [129]

The people of the Maseda camp called their counterpart of this figure Baatsi. He dwelt above and was Lord of the Dead, dangerous when offended. Incense offerings were addressed to him. In the words of one informant: "When the fire is kindled and the leaves cause a thick smoke, we say: 'Grandfather, Great Father, let matters go well with me; for I am going into the forest!' Or when the fire is lighted on the occasion of a storm and the smoke rises, it is done so that Baatsi may see it and smell the incense. Then we call upon him, saying: 'Father, your children are afraid. Cause the wind to cease; for your children here are many, and behold, we shall die.' Baatsi sees our plight and hears our cry, stretches forth his arms, and thereupon the storm flees." Others declared, however, that the smoke worked of itself. "The incense chases the clouds away." Also the sound of the segbe-pipe, an instrument carved from the wood of a tree struck by lightning, was interpreted by some as itself frightening the wind away, but by others (or even the same informant, if asked on another occasion), as heard by Baatsi, who then attends to the work to be done.[130]

The essential question here is of the power of the Pygmy rites. Are their apparent effects due to the action of a god, or are they thought to work of themselves? The Pygmy term for their power is *megbe*, which is approximately a counterpart of the Bushman *ntum*; and like *ntum*, *megbe* inheres with especial force in certain animals, plants, and things. Crabs possess it, for example. It ascends with the rising smoke of the incense ceremony, where it may attract bees, move the clouds away, or rouse the Lord of the Forest to action. Living individuals make use of it in their lifetimes, and at death a part of man's portion is passed on to his son. "It is to receive this," states Schebesta, "that the eldest son bends down over the dying father and puts his mouth against his. The transmission is believed to take place through the mouth . . . . The other part goes with the dead."[131] It may happen, however, that the son's part may escape, in which case it becomes a worm and eventually dies.

There is a second spiritual element, which leaves the body through the nose and is carried to the Lord of the Dead by flies or bees. And there is, finally, a third part, known as the *lodi*, which remains with the body and is visualized as a shadowlike, thin apparition. It can also appear in dreams. It may assemble and dwell with other *lodi* in certain meeting places in the forest. And there is a diminutive special variety, known as *mbefe*, which in legends appear as tricky little forest imps. These serve as spirit gamekeepers of the Forest Lord. When a child, newly born, died in the Koukou camp, Father Schebesta was told, "He has become a *mbefe*." And on another occasion he was told that every person who dies becomes a Tore,[132] a counterpart of that supreme power which has just been described as the creator of all things, and who has been always in existence.

Curiously, it turns out that in one of the published legends, this same Tore had a mother, who now was dead. It had been in that once-upon-a-time, of which we all know from our fairy tales, that she had been given charge by Tore of his fire, to keep watch of it while he—who had just made for himself a swing of liana—would go whirling above the forest tops to great distances. One of his names, in fact, in recognition of this activity, is the One Who Swings To And Fro Above the Abyss.

One day it happened that when Tore was enjoying his swing, a Pygmy, lost in the forest, chanced upon the fire while the old mother was dozing, stole it, and fled. But the mother, wakened then by the cold, cried out in alarm to her son, who, flying on his swing, easily caught the Pygmy and returned the fire to its place.

The little thief, on reaching his camp, related the adventure, and one of his brothers, stronger than he, determined to attempt it. The old mother was again sleeping, but again, when she woke to the cold and cried, her son came swinging over the forest and recovered the precious flame.

But now there was an exceedingly powerful Pygmy named Doru, greatly endowed with *megbe*, who, on hearing of these two failures, clothed himself in the feathers of a raven [a sacred, magically potent bird] and began to hop and then to fly "as high as to the heavens and as far as to the horizon." He winged his way to the fire, and again the old mother was dozing. She woke to the cold a third time, and a third time called to her son, who again came flying on his swing. But the pursuit, this time, went differently, over mountain and valley, up to the sky and down to the abyss, until Tore, exhausted, grabbing hold of a treetop, called ahead in anguish: "Doru, Doru, my brother, we are born of the same mother and are of equal birth!" But the birdman had flown on and, at the Pygmy camp, was already sharing out the fire, for which he was being richly rewarded. Everybody was giving him a maid to wife, and the joy of the camp was great.

Not long thereafter, however, people began to die, one after another. For Tore, having

189. Two animals having been trapped, the men perform a dance of joy, but also of gratitude to their Forest and its bountiful Lord.

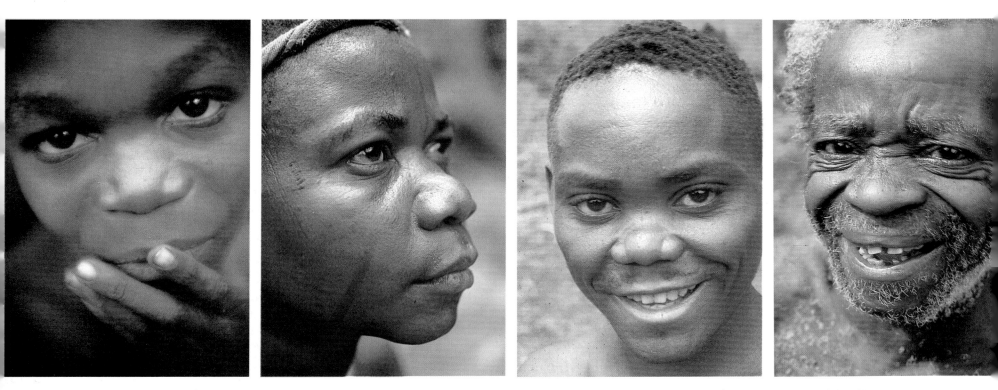

A gallery of Efé Pygmies, photographed by Jean-Pierre Hallet:

190. A six-year-old boy listening to a story.

191. A young woman, no more than eighteen years old. Girls are mature by the age of nine at the latest.

192. A young man of thirteen. The males also mature by the age of nine.

193. An older man, about fifty-five years old.

194. Two young women.

Carleton Coon (see pages 41–43) states: "We know nothing about these little people, except that they have lived in the equatorial forests of Africa for as long a time as is covered by the records of history."[20]

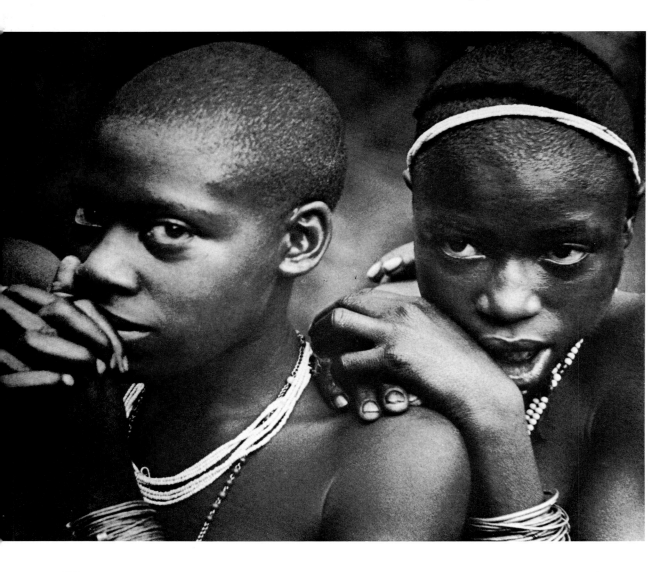

failed in his wild pursuit, while clinging still to the branches of his tree, had called out to his mother, who had not replied. When his strength returned, therefore, he went to seek her. And there, at the place where their fire had been, she lay dead of the cold. "For this," then said he in the bitterness of his grief, "the people shall die."

So the people now had the fire, but death had come, and the Age of the Beginning was ended.[133]

Apparently, then, as in the Bushman world, so also in this of the Pygmies, the ultimate metaphysical term is not what our theologians would call the Godhead, but an undifferentiated power, which in the Kalahari is experienced as *ntum*, and here, in the forest, as *megbe*. This power dwells in all things, in some more evidently than in others; supremely, but not uniquely, in such imagined Creators as Tore Baatsi, or, in the Kalahari, Kaggen; yet, in a gifted human being its portion may become so augmented that he may challenge and even outpoint the presumed Godhead.

* * *

In the legend of Doru's outwitting of Tore, there are three themes, besides that of the elevation of a magician's power to the potency of a god's, which are of worldwide distribution: (1) the Fire Theft, (2) the Origin of Death, and (3) the End of the Mythological Age. Themes 1 and 2 are not often combined, as here, but 2 and 3 frequently are; and Schebesta gives a number of examples from his Pygmy repertory. In the simplest, the blame is shared by a toad and a frog.

Muri-muri [another name for Tore] had given a pot to the toad, telling him not to break it, for death was shut up inside. The toad met a frog who offered to help carry the load, and though the toad for a moment hesitated, the pot was heavy and he let the other take charge—with a warning, however, to be careful. The frog hopped away with the pot, but let it fall. It broke, death escaped from it, and that is why people die.[134]

From the Pygmy camp in Apare comes the strange legend of how, in the Beginning, there was only Masupa, who created for himself two sons and a daughter, one of the sons, ancestor of the Pygmies, the other, of the Negroes. He would speak unseen to them, and he gave them one commandment: never to try to see him.

Masupa lived in a large hut, apart, from which the sounds could be heard of hammering and forging. [The legend, that is to say, cannot date from earlier than the knowledge in this area of iron, c. A.D. 500.] That was an altogether happy time, with no need to work. Or at least, the two sons had no such need. To the daughter the daily task had been given of fetching water and gathering firewood, to be placed at Masupa's door, and since she was burning to know what the one she was serving looked like, one evening, as she set the waterpot down, she decided to wait and see. She hid behind a post, and when Masupa's arm reached out for the pot, she saw it, richly adorned.

Masupa was enraged. He informed his children that he now would leave them and that the days of their ease were ended. He gave them weapons and tools, taught them the use of the forge and of other things necessary for their maintenance; and, especially angry with his daughter, he told her that she would henceforth be a toiling wife and bring forth her children in pain. Then secretly he left them, passing downstream along the banks of the river, and no one has seen him since.

Death came with the death of the woman's first child two days after its birth. She had named him, with a premonition, Death Is Coming. And no one has escaped death since.[135]

Another version of this theme struck Schebesta with especial force as suggesting a myth with which he had been long familiar. It was told by an eighty-year-old member of the Maseda camp, who declared that he had heard it from his father. "At that time," states Schebesta, "any Biblical influence on the Pygmies was out of the question."[136] (Compare Frobenius' comment on the Bassari creation myth reproduced on page 14.)

A deity with the help of the Moon created Baatsi, the first man. [The Moon of this legend is female; the name of the deity we do not learn; and Baatsi, it is recalled, was in another legend recorded from this camp the name of the Creator himself.] The body was made by kneading, then clothed with a skin, blood was poured in, and the man lived. His Creator then whispered in his ear: "You will live in the forest and beget children. Tell them of my command, that they may eat of all the trees of the forest but one, the Tahu tree." Baatsi indeed begat many children and, having warned them of the one forbidden thing, departed to rejoin his Creator in the heavens. But a pregnant woman one day was filled with a craving for the forbidden fruit and so worried her husband that he finally crept secretly into the deep forest, plucked the fruit, quickly peeled it, and hid the peel beneath leaves. The Moon, however, who had seen, told the Creator, who was so incensed that he cursed the human race to die.

"I could not believe my ears," states Schebesta. "That was the Creation story of the Bible."[137] And another Catholic father, the French Jesuit Henri Trilles, who during his time with the Pygmies

195. Five Efé girls being taught the movements of a dance by an older woman (with a baby on her back!). Music, dance, and mime are the arts thorough which the Pygmies give expression to their characteristic communal joy in existence.

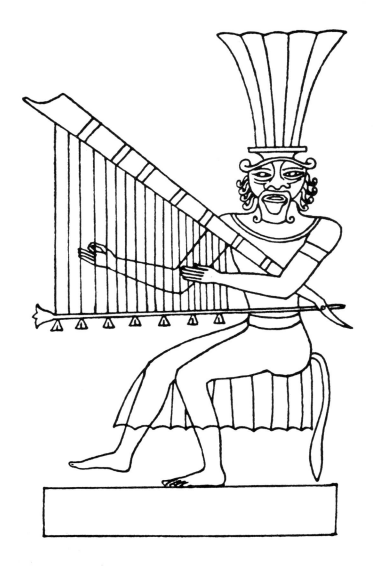

196. Bes. a god of the Egyptian folk tradition, patron of music and dancing and of children. Represented always full-face (which in Egyptian art is exceptional), he first appears c. 2000 B.C.—on mirrors, ointment jars, and other articles of feminine use—apparently inspired by Pygmies brought for entertainment from the source-lands of the Nile.

197. Three Pygmy "dancers of God." Twelfth-Dynasty Egypt, c. 1950 B.C. Cairo Museum.

also recorded a version of this legend, regarded it as a demonstration of the truth of the account in Genesis 2 and 3, interpreting both texts literally, as variant chronicles of the same prehistorical event.[138]

Pygmy dancers, known as the Little Dancers of God, were already appreciated in Pharaonic Egypt as early as the Sixth Dynasty (c. 2350 B.C.), as we know from the reading of a now-famous letter engraved on a façade of the tomb of the Prince Herkhuf of Elephantine. The letter was sent by the Pharaoh Pepe II (Neferkare), at the time still a child, in response to word from the prince that he was bringing from the forests of the south a living Pygmy dancer.

"You announce in your letter," states the Pharaoh's order, "that you have brought from the Land of Trees and from the Land of Spirits, a Pygmy Dancer of God, similar to the one whom the Conservator of Divine Seals, Ba-Wes-Djed, brought from Punt during the days of King Isosi. . . . Hail to the Dancer of God, to the one who rejoices the heart of Pharaoh, to the one for whom King Nefer-

kare, who lives eternally, sighs. . . . When you bring him to the ship, choose reliable men to keep watch on both sides, lest perchance he should fall into the water. . . . When he sleeps at night, post ten stout fellows to sleep alongside him. My Majesty yearns mightily to see this Pygmy. See that you bring the Pygmy alive, hale and sound, to my palace, and then My

Majesty will confer on you far higher awards than those given to the Conservator of Divine Seals in the days of King Isosi."[139]

In the Egyptian Museum in Cairo there is a little sculptural piece of three such Pygmies dancing (Figure 197), from the period of the Twelfth Dynasty (twentieth century B.C.). And in the time of Queen

198. Efé boy playing the bow harp (ndomu), an important instrument in ancient Egypt associated with the god Bes. The Efé harp has five strings, more are used by non-Pygmy tribes. Usually played solo, it may also appear in ensembles.

199. Efé girls in a dance without meaning, but one filled with joy in being.

Hatshepsut (1501 to 1480 B.C.), expeditions were still being sent up the Nile to the Land of Punt: there is, on a wall of her temple at Deir el Bahari, a bas relief representing the queen of that land in a procession. So that, if, as Jean-Pierre Hallet reminds us, the Pygmy legend of the forbidden fruit suggests some sort of link with the Bible, the influence may have passed, not from Genesis (a relatively late text) to the Pygmies, but from the Land of Trees, down the River Nile to the Pharaohs, out of one of whose palaces Moses came.

Yet it may also have come the other way, for, as Father Schebesta has noted, in Pygmy legends " a very strong Negro influence must be reckoned with."[140] These are not primordial tales, but secondary and late. The element of Masupa's forge, for example, betrays a knowledge of iron, while the fact that the two sons of the god—a Pygmy and a Negro—had nothing to do but sit around in the paradisiacal age while their sister hauled wood and water, speaks for an already assumed male superiority. Indeed, this disfranchisement of the female is clearly a leading function of the Pygmy legend, as it is also of the Bible story. And appropriately, in Schebesta's report of his first hearing of the tale while in the Pygmy camp in Apare, he declares:

"I was just chatting with a circle of my little friends, when a group of panting women came into the camp, their bent shoulders laden with bundles of firewood, which were almost heavy enough to kill them. Involuntarily, I allowed a sarcastic remark to pass my lips about the lords of creation who sat there lazily smoking and yawning while their wives

were doing such heavy work. 'It's their own fault,' said one of them, rousing himself. 'They have sinned.' " And the legend then was related of the daughter and two sons of Masupa.[141]

There is some evidence, on the other hand, of an earlier stratum underlying the mythic lore of these Pygmies, from a period when the position of women was not the same as today. We have already seen that the creator, Tore, had a mother. Mothers antecede their sons, not only temporally, but also, in a symbolic sense, ontologically. And Turnbull tells of watching an extraordinary festival in which the Pygmy women not only joined the men in singing the molimo songs, but at times even took the lead.[142] The high moment was of a dance performed around the molimo fire by two females—a skinny, red-eyed crone and a young matron. Their performance climaxed when the old dame went into the flames and, whirling and kicking, scattered the fire in all directions. It became, then, the part of the men to gather back the brands and, themselves dancing in a circle, to return the fire to life. Twice again this occurred, after which the women withdrew and the men were alone.

"There is an old legend," states Turnbull at this juncture, "that once it was the women who 'owned' the molimo, but the men stole it from them and ever since the women have been forbidden to see it. . . . There is another old legend which tells that it was a woman who stole fire from the chimpanzees, or, in yet another version, from the great forest spirit."[143] The Fire Theft again—by a female! Fire is the forest's greatest gift, while the voice of the forest is the molimo.

The men were still singing when the old woman returned, alone, with swift and agile strides. She held in her hands a long roll of the twine used for making hunting nets, and while the men sang on, she moved about among them, knotting a loop around each singer's neck, until all

200. Giant *ato* tree, as a percussion instrument, its winged buttress roots being natural sound boxes; usually three men play to accompany dancing girls.

201. Men's flute ensemble, each flute of a single tone. Melody improvised, three octave range.

were tied; whereupon, their singing ceased and Moke (Turnbull's initiator) spoke. "This woman," he said, "has tied us up. She has bound the men, bound the hunt, and bound the molimo. We can do nothing." Another of the company then declared that they each had now to admit that he was bound, and to give the woman something as a token of the men's defeat. And when a certain quantity of food and cigarettes had been agreed upon, the old dame went solemnly about among the men again, untying them, and as each was untied he began again to sing. When all were in song, the molimo was free, and the crone departed.[144]

The mythic ground of this stunning ritual is in every detail evident, and in contrast, furthermore, to the lessons of the current myths. The image and mystery of life are represented by two women, circling at opposite poles a central sacred fire: one a crone, the other in the beauty of mature youth. Eye to eye across the blaze, each was the past or future of the other. But it was the crone, alone, who entered the fire, kicking its embers about, to be taken up, restored to the fire, and preserved in flame by the men. Then it was she, again, who brought them twine for the knotting of their hunting nets and, in a telling moment of silence, had them all tied in her power. The allegory is obvious. She released them of her own free will to perform the works with which she had charged them: the handling of the nets of the hunt and the maintenance of life's fire, of which she was the sole mistress and bestower.

As Turnbull has shown, the characteristic Pygmy hunt is a hunt with snares and nets, in which both women and men and even children participate. Such may have been the oldest hunting style of the plant-gathering people of this forest—which is situated, by the way, immediately to the west of that high plateau where the earliest human races are now supposed to have appeared. The hunting bow was a much later, Capsian-age invention. Hence, the Bushman hunt, with its poisoned arrows and associated rites, is of a later culture stage than the Pygmy hunt. The two are representative of the earliest known orders of living and of mythic thinking: the one infected with anxiety, in constant need of ecstatic release; the other inspired, rather, with joy and a confident, childlike participation in the natural bounty of its world, the wonder of which is rendered in the voice of the molimo, responding to its Pygmies' songs of praise.

These, then, are two contrary orders of life, determinant of the life-styles, mythologies, and rites of the most primitive peoples known: one, of the widespreading animal plains, the other of the sheltering forest. They were not arrived at by reason, but are grounded in fundamental experiences and requirements touching very deep levels of the psyche. In contrast, such questioning as "Who made the world?" "Why?" "How?" and "What happened to make life so difficult?" belongs to a plane of consciousness much closer to the surface of things than those deeps from which the controlling images of these two orders of life arose, not reasoned but compelled. Such questions spring from the moralizing intellect, asking for information, meanings, and justifications. And the responses to them in the way of explanatory origin myths may not represent in any significant way the more recondite, unspoken requirements and assumptions of a people. Moreover, as just seen, such an origin myth may be intentionally contrived to confirm such vested privileges as, for example, those certified to the "lords of creation" by the fable of the Tahu tree.

Thus two distinct, though tightly interlocked, strata of myth are to be recognized: one grounded, as dreams are, in the deepest level of the psyche; the other fantasized and controlled by interested parties who, ironically, may in the end come to believe, themselves, in their theologized mythologies.

202. A family of the cave-dwelling Tasaday: Bilangan, the father, his wife, Etut, and (clockwise) a boy not yet named, Lobo, Lolo, and Natek.

Ancestral Caves of the Tasaday

The mystery of the Tasaday of Mindanao is unsolved. Had this little cluster of less than thirty souls actually continued into the twentieth century A.D. a way of life and thought of 50,000 B.C.? Or had they, for some reason, reverted? When discovered, June 7, 1971, they were true gatherers, not even hunters. Toads and frogs, tadpoles and crabs, grubs, rats, and lizards were the meat items of their menu. Biking (a starchy potatolike tuber), wild yams, palm piths, bamboo shoots, and various fruits were their mainstays. Food was eaten, either raw, baked inside leaf wrappings, or roasted in hot coals from fires made with fire sticks.[145] Their occasional stone tools were readily fashioned from the pebbles of their stream and could be affixed with rattan bindings to crude handles (see Figure 29, page 31). Thorns, also, were used. The most serviceable implement was a sort of stone scraper of a kind found throughout the Philippines in archeological strata of Late Paleolithic dates.[146] And they inhabited three caves in a limestone conglomerate, 400 or 500 feet above a creek that provided all their frogs, tadpoles, and crabs, as well as water. The caves were reached by climbing up vines or roots, and the grace and ease of the Tasaday's arboreal skills were as amazing as those of the African Pygmies. Indeed, like the Pygmies, they were true forest children, absolutely at home and at peace in the protection of their wilderness; equally ill at ease and afraid at even the sight of an open plain.[147]

The evidence of their language is interesting. It is of the Malayo-Polynesian family, the immense reach of which extends from Madagascar in the west to Easter Island in the east, and from New Zealand in the south to Taiwan and Hawaii in the north. Within this great linguistic lineage, the closest relative to the dialect of the Tasaday is the language of the nearby Blit, who are not, today, hunter-gatherers, however, but agriculturalists. When, then, did the parting of the Tasaday from these now more advanced neighbors occur? A loss from the language of about 20 percent of its Blit-shared words has been estimated to indicate a separation from each other of some 700 to 900 years, from about A.D. 1100 to 1300. And this is additionally interesting because, at that time, there were strong Indian influences present in

203. Among the vines, rattans, and descending roots in front of the Tasaday caves, Lolo sits snug and at ease.

the Philippines and at least three words in the Tasaday vocabulary have been recognized as perhaps derived from Sanskrit or some Sanskrit-related tongue; namely, Tasaday, *diwata*, meaning "good, great, or godlike man or spirit" (Sanskrit, *devata*, "a divinity or god, divine being, or image of a god"); Tasaday, *mu-lan*, meaning "to plant" or "putting something in the ground" (Sanskrit, *mūl*, "to strike root, to be rooted," and *āmūmulat*, "to plant, to transplant, or to grow"); and Tasaday, *sawa*, meaning "spouse" (Sanskrit, *sava*, "a generator, offspring, progeny").[148]

The Tasaday were not an inbred group; they had been, before discovery, in touch with other forest tribes, notably the Tasafang and Sanduka, from which at least two of the wives had come.[149] Moreover, the two or three adolescents occasionally talked of going in search of wives. The surprisingly different hair types also be-

tokened a mixing. They varied from straight and thick to soft and curly, also to wavy and coarse; there was even one fair-skinned child whose hair was straw-brown and straight.[150]

In spite of all these inconclusive signs of possible outside influences, however, the overwhelming impression that the Tasaday made upon everyone who first saw them was of an authentic Middle Paleolithic cave community. And the evident implication of the few fragments known of their myths and legend tells of their having remained in the caves from of old, as at the place of their beginning; the caves having been assigned to them by their ancestors, of whom they talked a great deal. Their separation from the Blit, then, and from such other possibly related tribes as the Higa-onon, Sanduka, Tasafang, Ubu, and Tboli, would have had to have been not of the Tasaday from the others, but of the others from these caves of their common ancestors.[151]

They told of a godlike man named Bebang, who was the first person on earth. He had two wives, Fuweh and Sidaweh, and all three had been Tasaday. Bebang was owner of the top part of the caves and Sidaweh of the lower part.[152] "Our ancestors," one of the young men, named Balayam, declared, "said a person came to them in their sleep and said he was the owner [of the forest] and that our mountain is Tasaday Mountain. He owned the mountain. He told that to our ancestors and they told us."[153] "Our fathers and our fathers' fathers lived here. We never heard of Tasaday living anywhere else."[154] "My father's father told my father, and my father told me," this young man said again, "that we can roam in the forest in daytime, but must come back to the cave at night. It is always safe there."[155] "Our ancestors said never to leave this place. They had a good dream that said if we

204. Balayam, the leading bachelor of the group, springs from the big cave to his own.

205. Lolo's younger brother, Lobo, climbs on a swinging vine 100 feet long.

stayed we would not get sick. We have a little sickness—like coughing—but nothing bad."[156]

There was a bird about as big as a hand, with brown body and white head and tail, that they called *le mokan*, whose appearance they took as a warning not to venture from the cave.[157] Also, in general, going out by night was dangerous: "It has thorns, snakes, leeches, things you cannot see," said Balayam. "And you might slide off a cliff or steep hill. In the daytime we can see these things, and our bird warns us; when it calls, we stay still. My father told me that. If you go out when the bird calls, something bad may happen—a branch may fall on you, or you may fall down yourself, or a snake may bite you."[158]

When asked what they most feared, the answer given was, "Thunder! . . . . The big word . . . . The worst thing . . . . We are afraid of it."[159] And when asked about their reckoning of time, a young woman, Dul by name, replied, "We count from one to ten moons." "What is a moon?" "It is when the moon comes and then goes away." "Where does it go?" "We don't know."[160]

There were two stories told by Balayam that may or may not have been learned

206. Udelen, one of the young married men, rests in the waters of the stream below the caves.

from somewhere else. The first was of a small cave that his ancestors had carried on bamboo poles when they traveled. They would stop, set up the cave, and search for food. But they returned one time to find that the cave had grown into a large cave that they could not carry, and they decided to stay there forever. Was this the site of their present home? Balayam did not make that clear.[161]

The other story was of a man named Ogoo, who carried a stick that he swirled in a stream until a hair clung to it. The direction in which the hair pointed led to people, and Ogoo went after them. He pointed his stick at people and their fingers and limbs fell off. (The neighboring Tboli had this story too, and it strikingly resembles the Australian theme of the

pointing stick; see Figure 107, page 66.) Balayam said that his father had effected a cure for this, and that after that the cave grew big and Ogoo came no more.[162]

It is not much of a mythology, but what motifs there are represent standard stock: the voice of thunder; a lunar reckoning of time; the auspices of a warning bird; the notice of a mystic Owner of the Forest, announced to the ancestors in dream; a First Man, with two wives; the authority of the ancestors; a variant of the pointing-stick motif; and finally, a legend of a period of folk wandering, which is in conflict with the other legend of a residence in the Tasaday caves from the beginning. And curiously, the image of the small cave carried on bamboo poles and set down at Tasaday, where it remained and became enlarged, is not unlike the biblical story of

the folk wandering in the wilderness, bearing with them the Ark of the Covenant, which in Jerusalem was made permanent in the Temple.

The Tasaday are monogamous and expressed shock at the suggestion of the possibility of sharing or exchanging wives. They had no special marriage ceremony. "We all gather round the new couple and say, good, good, beautiful, beautiful, that's all." And how long does a couple stay together? "Until their hair turns white."[163] Indeed, the Tasaday had no rituals whatsoever. If one of them died in the forest, the body was left there, cov-

207. The Tasaday take turns twirling a fire drill to ignite dried moss.

208. Mahayag, successful at last, exhibits the blazing moss to his son, Biking.

115

ered with leaves. If someone died in the cave, the body was carried into the forest and left. And nobody wanted to speak any more of the one who had died. "What is it happens to any person when he dies? What happens to that, in him, which was living?" "The *sugoy* (the 'spirit') goes away, goes out—then you are dead." "And where does this spirit go?" "We don't know." "Where did it come from to start with?" "We don't know that either,"[164] Another view was expressed, however; namely, that the souls of the dead reside in treetops.[165] Balayam proposed that "The soul may be the part of you that sees the dream . . . . I dream," he said, "but I don't know where it ends or starts." The word for both the dream and the seer of dreams was *lomogul*.[166] There was some talk of fairies: rock fairies, stream fairies; and when a rash appeared on the neck of one of the company of visitors, it brought a laugh and he was told that a fairy had urinated on him there.[167] It was observed that the Tasaday always kept their genitals covered, and one explanation was that this was for protection against witches. Another view, however, was that the protection was against insects, leeches, thorns, and raspy vines.[168] When a child was born, the only accompanying requirement was that the father either bury the placenta or hang it in a certain tree—not too high and not too low—where the Tasaday always put placentas. Was it the custom, then, to visit this tree from time to time? "No. Once it is put there, that is all we do."[169]

209. The "big bird," the helicopter, touches down on the bamboo-and-sapling platform made to receive it. When it was first seen, and then arrived, most of the Tasaday fell to the ground in terror.

210. After receiving from one of their native visitors (a hunter and herb-gatherer named Dafal) some metal tools and elementary instruction in their use, the Tasaday learned from him to make pounders of bamboo and rattan with which to hack the starchy pith from sections of Caryota palm. John Nance photographed these implements in use and observed: "Several men often worked together with the L-shaped pounders to break loose and shred the pith in the sections of halved palm. Each man put one foot on the ground and the other atop the wood to hold it steady."[21]

The whole history and prehistory of tool use in the rain forests of Southeast Asia—where, for millennia, implements of stone hardly advanced beyond the "chopper" stage—remains, and will ever remain, unknown; for the availability of wood—and especially of bamboo, which is infinitely practical—has left nothing for the archeologist to recover and analyze. Indeed, it was recognition of this fact that Leo Frobenius characterized the historical role of tropical cultures, in relation to those of the stone-age north, as being an "invisible counterplay" whose contribution to the development of the early arts of civilization could not be tangibly documented, but only deduced—as, for example, in his recognition that the sudden appearance in Cro-Magnon art of carved stone figurines implied a probable influence from a region abounding in wood (see page 129).

With respect to government—the social order and authority—the attitudes were equally casual. Asked who was the headman, "Nobody," came the answer. "Who decides who does what?" "We do as we like."[170] And the atmosphere of harmony and ease among the group was amazing. "The best people I've ever seen anywhere are the Tasaday," was the comment of one of the visitors; and he later added: "Where did *we* take the wrong turn?"[171]

One more insight into what might well be called the archetypology of their mythic imagination deserves mention, namely, their almost immediate deification of the genial and devoted official, Manuel Elizalde, Jr., the conductor of the discovering expedition, who became, thereafter, their protector and the sponsor of the establishment of their forest as a national sanctuary. They named him Momo Dakel Diwata Tasaday: "great or big man, god (*diwata*) of the Tasaday"; or perhaps, "who brought good fortune (*diwata*) to the Tasaday."[172] "This is what our ancestors had been telling us," one of them was overheard to say, one night. "It has come true. As our ancestors said it, we should stay in this place of ours and a good man will come to us, and that is Momo Dakel Diwata Tasaday. Now it seems that our fathers are not dead, because the father we have now is more than our fathers; for he gives us knives and puts things on the necks of the women. The big surprise that we can't understand is the coming of Momo Dakel Diwata Tasaday in that big bird [*manukdakel*, the helicopter]. When we first saw Momo Dakel Diwata Tasaday he had few companions, now he brings many, which shows his love and gives us more help."[173]

Balayam had had a dream, one night, when Elizalde had been sleeping with the Tasaday in their cave. "I had a dream . . . that I was on my way to look for *biking* and to make a trap. I saw a small white boy on top of the mountain, sitting on the stone. He said to me: 'Balayam, don't stop making traps and looking for *biking*.' I think this was the spirit of Momo Dakel Diwata Tasaday, whose feeling goes with us in whatever we do."[174] "All of us are now the sons of Momo Dakel Diwata Tasaday," said another of the chatting company, "including you, Kuletaw. Even you old women. We must always continue to look for the food that we eat, so that Momo Dakel Diwata Tasaday may see it and taste it."[175]

"We have much to learn from the shy, innocent, lovable people Nance discovers for us," wrote Lewis Mumford in comment on John Nance's book *The Gentle Tasaday*; "above all, what it means to be truly human, the lesson that 'advanced,' 'civilized,' scientifically progressive man has almost forgotten."[176]

211. Elizalde, who discovered the Tasaday and is idolized by them as a messiah, is here surrounded by five of the children.

The tantalizing question of the innocence of those utterly primitive cave dwellers—in contrast, for example, to the savage reputation of the almost equally primitive Andamanese—acquires a new complexion in the light of Nance's observation that they are probably the descendants of a company from the coast which fled into the jungle (not more than ten, nor less than four, centuries ago) to escape pursuit and capture by pirates. "Most researchers," Nance declares, "have estimated their presence inside [the forest] at from 400 to 1000 years. . . . Studies of tribal folk living nearby outside the forest suggest why people may have sought sanctuary in the forest centuries ago."[22] They are, therefore, of a regressed, not primary, primitivity; they know how to make fire, but otherwise lack the elementary inventions even of the age of stone. As Nance remarks: "The Tasaday, who did not dominate their environment, were as close to nature as any people known in modern times."[23]

Although considerable controversy continues to surround the "discovery" of the Tasaday, their lifestyle, whether authentic or reconstructed, remains appropriately metaphorical of a particular state of cultural development.

Map 28. On Mindanao, the large southernmost island of the Philippines, is the forest home of the Tasaday. Some 2500 miles to the west are the islands of the Andamanese. But if the character of "man at one with nature," as represented in the shy cave dwellers of the Philippine forest sanctuary, has suggested to many the innocence of the idyll of man before the Fall, a very different judgment has generally been given of the Andamanese, whose custom it was, for millennia, to slaughter every ship's company that the gods of their monsoons would occasionally toss onto their beaches. Occupied by the British in 1857 and by the Japanese in 1942, the Andaman Islands are now a colony of India, and the native population has all but disappeared.

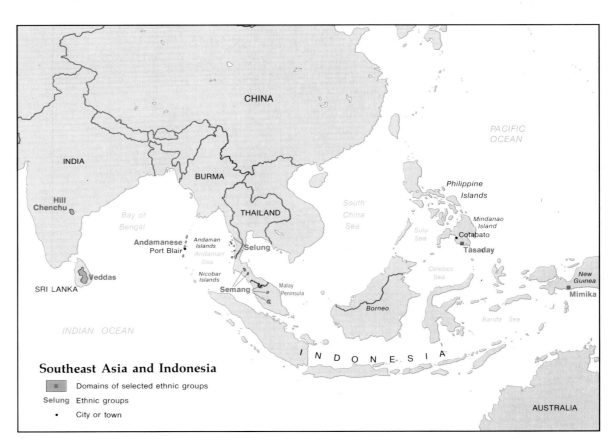

Southeast Asia and Indonesia

- Domains of selected ethnic groups
- **Selung** Ethnic groups
- • City or town

117

The Andaman Islanders

If the Tasaday, when discovered, were the only people on earth still inhabiting caves, the Andamanese were of the very few with no method of making fire. What fires they had were carefully tended in their villages and carried with them on journeys, kept alive in wood that could smoulder long without turning to ashes or breaking into flame.[177]

In contrast, however, with the "gentle Tasaday," who knew nothing of weapons, even weapons of the hunt, nothing of enemies or of fighting, but only the refuge of their caves, the Andamanese, on their strip of islands off the southern tip of Burma, enjoyed such a reputation for ferocity that, although their beaches lay in the way of sea-lanes traversed for millennia by the merchantmen of China, Borneo, India, the Persians, Arabs, Romans, and finally, Portuguese and Dutch, they remained innocent of history until the British, in 1857, took it upon themselves to put a stop to their murdering of shipwrecked crews by occupying the islands. It was then found that they had no

way of working stone. Their tools were of wood, shell, and bone, but also bits of iron gathered from shattered ships. And they carried extraordinarily beautiful long bows, with two sorts of arrow: one, with a detachable head fixed by a thong to the shaft, which would quickly bring an animal up short when shot in the thick jungle; the other, long and fine, for shooting fish (see Figure 212). They also had harpoons for the seahunting of porpoises and dugongs from outrigger canoes.

In language, the Andamanese were isolated from all other people. Physically, however, they are classified as Negritos. An Asian race of pygmy stature and Negroid traits of skin, hair, and face, the males average 4 feet 10½ inches tall, and the females, 4 feet 6 inches. Their name, from the Malay *Handuman*, was derived, apparently, from that of the popular monkey warrior, Hanuman, of the Sanskrit *Rāmāyana*. Other, widely separated peoples, known also as Negrito, are the Semang of the Malay Peninsula, the Tapiro of New Guinea, and the Aeta of some of the high mountain districts of the Philippines. And there are other indications, as well, of what must have been a very early Negrito substratum underlying a large part of the Southeast Asian quarter of the globe. But only the Andamanese, on their island chain, remained uncontaminated by perceptible outside influences until the middle of the nineteenth century; and so they have been generally taken to represent, in their mythology and customs, a truly primitive stage of development of the human race.

In 1952, however, Lidio Cipriani, excavating at a place marked on the maps as Bee Hive Hill but today called, in Hindi, Goal Pohar, uncovered in a prodigious kitchen midden (the accumulation of which "may easily have required," as he states, "a period of no less than 4000 to 5000 years") unquestionable evidence of a distinct threshold of acculturation at some very early date. Cutting through the great mound, he found, from the top to a depth of about 6 inches, chips of broken bottles, rifle bullets, pieces of iron, and the like; then, through the greater part of the midden to within 3 feet of the bottom, the bones of pigs, pottery shards, crab legs that had been used as smoking pipes, and clamshells well-preserved; finally, through the last 3 feet, no pig bones or pottery, no crab-leg pipes, but clamshells that were heavily calcined, showing that they had been exposed directly to the fire. His conclusion:

212. Posed photograph from the period of Radcliffe-Brown's visit to the Andamans (1906 to 1908) exhibiting the extraordinarily beautiful Andamanese long bow and its two kinds of arrow: the long for shooting at fish, the short for the jungle.

"The Andamanese, on their arrival did not know pottery. Previous to its introduction, food was roasted in the fire or in hot ashes; later it was boiled in pots . . . . The first Andamanese pottery is of good make, with clay well worked and well burned in the fire. The more we approach the upper strata, the more it undergoes a degeneration. . . . Bones of *Sus andamanensis* [the Andamanese pig] begin to appear later than pottery. They become more frequent, the more we approach the top levels. The inevitable conclusion would seem to be that the ancient Andamanese knew neither pottery nor the hunting of pigs. It is likely that both pottery and domesticated *Sus* were introduced by one and the same people . . . . Human burials," Cipriani states further, "occasionally took place in the kitchen-middens; however, only the skull and the long bones were placed in the grave, after having been preserved in the huts for some time, as is still done in the Nicobars. These skulls and bones show the same physical characteristics as the present day Andamanese. No traces of cannibalism were found." Further: the pigs, now wild in the islands, arrived probably as a domesticated species. And finally: "There are indications of cultural connections between the Andamans and the Nicobars, allowing the supposition that a common foreign influence, of as yet unknown origin, spread to both groups of islands."[178]

According to A.R. Radcliffe-Brown, at the time of his visits and researches (from 1906 to 1908, half a century before the extinction of these people), there was one essential belief that underlay the whole of their social and mythological order; namely, of a power thought to be dangerously present in certain foods (pig, tortoise, and dugong), as well as in people at the moments of their life crises (birth, pubescence, marriage, and death), and in anyone who had recently killed another. The native technical term referring to an immediate presence of this power in any person or thing was *ot-kimil*, meaning "hot." "In its various uses," declares Radcliffe-Brown, "the word *ot-kimil* denotes a condition of danger due to contact with that power on the interaction of the different manifestations of which the well-being of the community depends."[179]

There were, however, certain persons, male and female, who were supposed to have come into some sort of possession or mastery of this power. They were known as *oko-jumu*, a term meaning literally "one who speaks from dreams," or "dreamer."

They were supposed to be able to communicate with spirits while awake, as well as in dream; to cause and to cure disease; to prevent bad weather by the recitation of charms against the sea spirits and even against the great deities of the southwest and northeast monsoons, Tarai and Biliku; to have knowledge of the magical powers of minerals, plants, and certain animals; and to be fully acquainted with the personages of the myths. Each will have come into possession of his power in any one or more of three recognized ways: (1) by dreams, (2) by dying and returning to life, or (3) by meeting and consorting with spirits in the jungle.

213. Lacking the shell fishhook (otherwise well known throughout the Pacific), the Andamanese turned their great bows and longest arrows to the harvesting of fish.

In sum, then, according to Radcliffe-Brown, the following are the implicit beliefs underlying the Andamanese ceremonial order:

"(1) There is a power or force in all objects or beings that in any way affect the social life. (2) It is by virtue of this power that such things are able to aid or harm the society. (3) The power, no matter what may be the object or being in which it is present, is never either essentially good or essentially evil, but is able to produce both good and evil results. (4) Any contact with the power is dangerous, but the danger is avoided by ritual precautions. (5) The degree of power possessed by anything is directly proportioned to the effects that it has on the social life. (6) The power in one thing may be used to counteract the danger due to contact with the power in some other thing." And finally: "(7) If an individual comes into contact with any thing and successfully avoids the danger of such contact (as, for instance, in such experiences as give to the *oko-jumu* his super-normal powers), he becomes himself endowed with power of the same kind as that with which he is in contact."[180]

Thus, as among the Pygmies and the Bushmen, so here among the Andamanese, there is an informing power that is recognized as inherent in things in differing degree. It is known as *megbe* to the Pygmies, *ntum* to the Kung Bushmen, and *ot-kimil* to these Southeast Asian islanders. Of the Tasaday, nothing quite comparable is reported, unless something of the kind be implicit in their (possibly Sanskrit) term *diwata*. They expressed fear of thunder, night, and the open plain. Talking with foreign visitors early in the 1970s, they avoided speaking of the dead. Safety was felt in the forest by day, in the cave by night, and in ancestral custom, though nothing of a ceremonial order has been recorded of them. In summary of the lesson of the Andamanese interpretation of *ot-kimil*, Radcliffe-Brown states in conclusion: "The society itself is the chief source of protection to the individual; the spirits are the chief source of danger."[181] And this would seem to hold in a general way, as well, for the Tasaday, Bushmen, and Pygmies.

For the Andamanese, protection was given principally by ceremonial ornamentation and ceremonial acts. White clay and red paint designs on the body, scarification, the wearing of certain protective leaves and of ornaments made from the bones of feared animals, or, in the case of a widow in mourning, the skull of her deceased husband—such were the ornamental counteragents to the "heat," *ot-kimil*, of a spiritual threat.[182] And of ceremonial acts, there were two of especial force: weeping and the dance. The former was never a spontaneous personal expression, but always a rite, demanded by custom, in which the two essential elements were the weeping and the embrace. It was seen to have been practiced when two friends or relatives met after having been for some time parted; likewise, at peacemaking ceremonies between tribes; at weddings, when the relatives wept over bride and groom; at initiation ceremonies, where the female relatives wept and the initiate remained

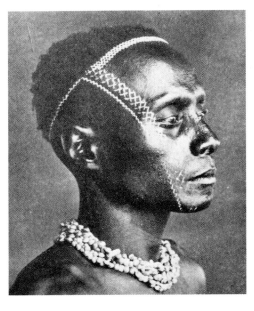

214. The ornamental "snake" pattern in white clay, here shown on the face, might be carried to the chest and back, the outside of the arms, and the front and back of the legs. It was used to decorate brides and grooms, corpses, and the dancers at initiations and mourning ceremonies.

215. (opposite) Posed photograph, taken by A. R. Radcliffe-Brown between 1906 and 1908, that suggests something of the variety of traditional whole-body patterns, executed in white clay (*odu*) by the women, who paint themselves and their male relatives. The clay is mixed in a wooden dish or shell and applied with the fingers. The women compete in the creation of new and interesting designs. The same clay—but applied differently—is used to indicate bereavement and for initiation rites.

216. Two villages, terminating a tribal conflict, celebrate a peacemaking dance.

217. Village huts surround the oval danceground. The sounding board in the mid-foreground was struck by the song leader's foot while the men danced, circling in file. Seated behind the sounding board, the women kept time, clapping their thighs.

passive; at death, when friends and relatives embraced the ornamented corpse and wept; when the bones of a dead man or woman were recovered from the grave; and at the end of mourning ceremonies, when the mourners wept with their friends who had not been mourning.[183]

The dance, on the other hand, was enjoyed as a common nightly entertainment, as well as practiced formally as a feature of both peacemaking and war ceremonials, initiatory pig-eating and turtle-eating rites, or at the termination of mourning. The eight or ten open-fronted family shelters of a typical Andamanese village (Figure 216) were set up around an elliptical dance area, at one end of which was a sounding log aslant, to be struck by the foot of the male song leader. And, as among the Bushmen, so here: the women, sitting on the ground, clapped time and sang in chorus (here, however, not clapping their hands but their thighs, with their legs out straight before them), while the men danced round and round, for some five or six hours a night. "In the dance of the Southern tribes," states Radcliffe-Brown, "each dancer dances alter-

nately on the right foot or on the left. When dancing on the right foot, the first movement is a slight hop with the right foot, then the left foot is raised and brought down with a backward scrape along the ground, then another hop on the right foot. These three movements, which occupy the time of two beats of the song, are repeated until the right leg is tired, and the dancer then changes·the movement to a hop with the left foot, followed by a scrape with the right and another hop with the left. The arms were held out straight in front, thumb and forefinger of one hand interlocked with those of the other, and as a man danced, he remained in one spot for a time, then advanced a yard or two around the dancing ground."[184] There was in these dances no trend toward trance, as among the Bushmen; nor do we read of anything comparable either with the symbolic Pygmy dance of the two women, young and old, or with their imitative honey-hunting mime. The value, rather, was simply of a rhythmic form, and the effect, a sense of social unification: a force to stay the individual in his daily confrontations with the powers of the wilderness, the sea, the animals slain to be eaten (pig, tortoise, and dugong), the mysterious powers of the life-passages from birth to death, and the spirits, then, of the dead.

The chief divinity in the mythology of

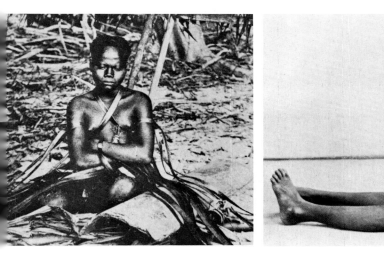

218. A girl decorated with protective pandanus leaves at the time of her first menstruation sits for three days in a special hut in a required posture. No longer a child, she will now receive a new name, a "flower name," after some plant or tree in bloom at the time. The two staves aslant behind her are for her to lean back upon in sleep, for she is not to lie down during the whole term of this period (some two weeks) of her meditation on her new estate.

219. Young woman wearing her sister's skull as a protective, or curative, amulet. Certain substances and objects—white clay, red paint, shells, bones, pandanus, and certain other leaves and woods—were believed to give protection against the "heat" (*kimil*) of dangerous conditions, times, and foods. Among such were illness, storms, the end of the rainy season, murder, menstruation, marriage, death, birth, and the initiate's first eating of pork, turtle meat, or dugong.

these little people was a personification of the northeast monsoon, named, in the various dialects, Biliku, Bilika, Bilik, or Puluga, whose character, in keeping with that of the stormy season itself, was tricky and temperamental, at once beneficent and dangerous. Sometimes envisioned as a great spider, Biliku was usually female. The milder southwest monsoon, personified as Tarai, might then be her husband, with the birds, the sun, and the moon, their children. The moon could sometimes turn into a pig—which is an association (pig=moon) that immediately suggests that at least some of the motifs of this apparently very primitive hunting-and-gathering mythology must have been derived from the Southeast Asian mat-

rices of the earliest known planting and pig-domesticating cultures. The mythology was never systematized by an established priesthood, and so, a number of versions have been recorded of practically all its characters and events. Indeed, every *oko-jumu* had his own collection of tales and might, on different occasions, give completely different versions of the same episode.[185] And yet, a number of constant themes emerge as a background against which all the legends play. All deal with the time of the Ancestors, when Biliku, Bilika, Bilik, or Puluga, lived on earth. And all recognize that that period ended when a broken tabu roused the deity's wrath; a catastrophe immediately followed, and the world became as now known. We may review the myths with a view to this classic order.

Myths and Tales of the Andamanese

In the Beginning

In from the sea came floating a big joint of bamboo of a kind that does not grow in the Andamans. [Joints of this kind drift ashore from Burma, to be picked up and made into buckets.] The bamboo split and there came forth from it, like a bird from its egg, an infant, the First Man, whose name was Jutpu, "Alone". As a child he built a little hut for himself and made a little bow and arrow. As he grew he made bigger huts and bigger bows and arrows, until one day he found a piece of quartz and scarified himself. Then he felt alone and from an ants' nest took clay which he molded into a woman's shape. She became alive. Her name was Kot, "Clay". The two settled at Teraut-buliu, where Alone fashioned other people of clay, who became the Ancestors. He taught them to make canoes, bows and arrows, to hunt and to fish. Clay, meanwhile, taught the women to make baskets, nets, mats, belts, and to use clay to paint patterns on the face and body.[186]

Other storytellers had it, either that Alone emerged from the buttressing root of a tree and cohabited directly with an ants' nest, or that the First Man was not Alone, but the southwest monsoon, Tarai, whose wife was the woman of clay, and their progeny, the wind, the storm, the sky, and the foam of a rough sea.[187]

A fundamentally different mythology is apparently represented in a legend in which it was a female, Lady Crab, who came floating in from the sea, already pregnant, like the joint of bamboo from which the First Man, Alone, was born. And it was she who then bore the Ancestors.[188] (Compare the North Australian

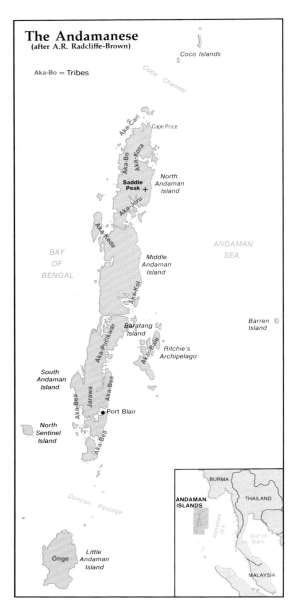

The Andamanese
(after A.R. Radcliffe-Brown)

Aka-Bo = Tribes

Coco Islands

Coco Channel

Cape Price

Saddle Peak +

North Andaman Island

BAY OF BENGAL

ANDAMAN SEA

Middle Andaman Island

Baratang Island

Barren Island

Ritchie's Archipelago

South Andaman Island

Jarawa

● Port Blair

North Sentinel Island

Duncan Passage

Önge

Little Andaman Island

BURMA

ANDAMAN ISLANDS

THAILAND

Gulf of Siam

MALAYSIA

Map 29. 207 islands: the largest three—North, Middle, and South—being known together as Great Andaman. Tribal customs, north to south, were increasingly archaic.

legend of Old Woman, I.2: 140.) But according to others, for whom the First Man was Tomo, meaning simply Ancestor, it was he who, on noticing Lady Crab swimming in the ocean near his home, called to her; and she, coming ashore, became his wife.[189] Or yet again, from others we have it that Tomo's wife was Mita, the dove. Tomo invented bows, arrows, and canoes; Mita, nets and baskets. And it was she who discovered the ritual uses of white clay and red paint.[190] By some it is said that Tomo, after his death, went to live in the sky, where it is always daylight and the weather always fine. When people die, according to this version of the world, their spirits go up to the sky and live with Tomo.[191]

There were some who thought of Tomo as the Creator, connecting him with the Sun, whose wife was the Moon;[192] whereas, for others, the Moon was a male, and the Sun, his wife. When this Moon Man is crossing the sky, his tongue hangs out (sometimes more, sometimes less), which is all that we ever see of him.[193] Or the Creator might be the northeast monsoon—Biliku, Bilika, Bilik,

or Puluga—who, after creating the world, fashioned Tomo as the First Man, black, like the Andamanese, but much taller and bearded. And having taught Tomo what to eat and how to live, Puluga created Lady Crab to be his wife.[194]

There is a prominent series of myths in which the First Man is a monitor lizard. This large, prolific reptile can swim in water, walk on land, and climb trees, and was thus the obvious local candidate for the classic mythological role of master of the three worlds.

Sir Monitor Lizard, out fishing one day, saw floating a piece of black wood, which he brought home and placed above the fire to dry. Then he sat down to fashion an arrow. While bending over this work, he heard someone behind him laugh. The wood had turned into a woman, who became his wife.[195]

More often it is Lady Civet Cat who is Sir Monitor Lizard's wife.

In the days before his marriage, when he had just completed his initiation rites, Sir Monitor Lizard went into the jungle to hunt pig and, climbing a dipterocarpus tree, got somehow caught up there by his genitals. Lady Civet Cat, recognizing his plight, climbed up and released him. The two married, and the Ancestors are their children.[196]

The Wild-Pig Hunt

The earliest Andamanese knew neither pottery nor the pig. Both were imported c. 3000 B.C., and the prominence of the feral pig in their myths shows that an associated (Neolithic or Bronze Age) mythology must also have been brought in at that time. The pottery deteriorated, the domesticated pigs ran wild, and, as the mainland mythology fell apart, a number of its elements became absorbed into the local hunting-and-gathering traditions.

The curious tale just told, for example, of Sir Monitor Lizard rescued by Lady Civet Cat, carries an uncanny suggestion of the great Near Eastern, Bronze Age cycles of Attis, Adonis, Tammuz, and Osiris—those killed, castrated, and resurrected fertility gods, who in many of the legends were not only killed or castrated by a boar (Attis was even hung on a tree), but also restored to the world by the power of a goddess whose animal counterpart or vehicle was the lion. In the Andamans, the civet cat was the only possible animal candidate for the role of this leonine goddess. The association, furthermore, of female magic with these Andamanese legends of the pig hunt also is suggestive of myths of the age of the Great Goddess of Many Names—as, for instance, in the following adventure, of a time when Bilika, dwelling on earth, was married to the pig hunter, Porokul.

Having gone into the jungle to hunt, Porokul killed his pig and started home. But,

when he came to the creek in front of his hut, he was unable to cross with the burden. Bilika was inside asleep. Her children were outside, playing; and when they saw their father's predicament, they ran into the hut to tell their mother. Bilika came out, lay down on the bank, stretched out one leg so that it reached to the other shore, and Porokul, with his pig, came safely home on the bridge of his wife's offered limb.[197]

The Andamanese have a number of other legends likewise treating of magic in association with the pig. For example:

At first there were no pigs, until Lady Civet Cat invented a new game. She made the Ancestors run on all fours and grunt. Those playing the game became pigs and ran off into the jungle. Whereupon, the lady herself became a civet cat.[198]

Do we think here of Homer's Circe, who turned men into swine?

The pigs had no ears, noses, or eyes. They just roamed around the village and the people ate a great many of them. But they were such a nuisance that Lady Dove bored holes in their heads for ears, eyes, and nostrils; whereupon, they ran off into the forest, where they have remained.[199]

The first pig caught in the jungle had neither eyes, ears, nor a mouth. When its captor put it on the fire, it swelled in the heat and suddenly six holes were blown through its head, making eyes, ears, and nostrils. Then it perceived that it was being burnt, jumped from the fire, and ran off. The hunter flung a large leaf, which struck it as it plunged into the sea, where it became a dugong with the leaf as its flippers.[200]

A huge turtle came swimming to a camp by the sea and called, "Bring out your canoes and catch me!" Then it swam away with the people following. And when they were far from land, it suddenly turned, upsetting them. The men became turtles, and their canoes were transformed into a reef.[201]

It is evident that the animals that were used by the Andamanese as food—the pig, dugong, and sea-turtle—occupy in the legends a very different place from those such as the civet cat, monitor lizard, and dove, to whom the active roles are assigned. The latter had no value as food or in any other way. They were the little neighbors in the forest, whereas the animals to be killed and eaten were felt to be transformed men. Moreover, there was an even deeper, a mythic association by which their flesh—particularly that of the pig—was rendered dangerous, "hot," *otkimil*; for the moon could turn into a pig and appear in this form in the jungle.

A hunter, deep in the jungle one day, happened upon the moon in the form of a pig and, mistaking it for a pig, shot it with an arrow. Sir Moon then cut off that hunter's head and, leaving it in the jungle, carried the body aloft and consumed it.[202]

An association of the pig with the moon, and the moon with a severed head, is a combination familiar through much of the range of the early swine-herding cultures of Asia and Europe. The Irish poet W. B. Yeats, in his play *A Full Moon in March* (that is, the full moon of Easter and the Resurrection), has presented an interpretation of this complex derived from traditional Irish sources. Monthly, the moon dies into the sun, to be reborn three nights later. The last crescent of its vanishing and first of its reappearance are compared in Melanesia (according to John Layard)[203] to the two curving tusks on either side of the black face of a sacrificed boar—the skull of which is to be preserved. In the Andamans (according to Radcliffe-Brown),[204] the natives ''were formerly in the habit of preserving as trophies the skulls of pigs and turtles that were killed in the chase,'' even going so far, in some tribes, as to encase every skull carefully in a wrapping of basketwork (Figure 220). The evidence thus seems to indicate that when the domesticated pig arrived in the Andamans, c. 3000 B.C., there likewise arrived an associated mythology of death and resurrection.

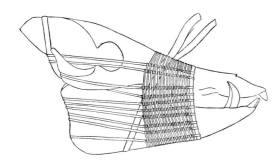

220. Pig's skull encased in basketwork as a hunting trophy and relic. Jarawa tribe, South Andaman. The pig and pig hunt were associated in the Andamans with legends of female magic. There were rules, furthermore, for the slaughtering of pigs and preservation of their skulls. These traditions brought together with the pigs from the mainland (c. 3000 B.C.), not only regressed in the islands to a hunting-and-gathering level of folk belief, but also became in part applied to the other two animals of the local hunt, the sea-turtle and dugong.

We cannot, therefore, assume (as did Radcliffe-Brown) that these Andamanese stories of the pig hunt and of pigs are truly native to the islanders and as primitive as their culture. They are the fragments, rather, of a mainland mythology which has regressed—that is, run wild like the pigs themselves, and, like the associated pottery, has deteriorated, breaking up, as it were, into shards. But there is a creative work here evident, also, in that the imported material has been imaginatively adapted to the life and features of the islands. The local animals available to assume the imported mythic roles were few: besides a number of birds and insects and a few kinds of bat and rat, only the moni-

tor lizard, a much smaller tree lizard, and the civet cat. Fish of the sea, wild pigs, sea-turtles, and dugongs were of a different class since they were used as food. (Yet the crab and the shrimp, for some reason, were found acceptable for mythic roles.) The tall dipterocarpus tree was given the place of a sort of *axis mundi*; and in all parts of the islands there were specific sites pointed out by the tribes as the place where Biliku had lived when on earth. Ananda K. Coomaraswamy has noted the process of adaptation by which imported mythologies generally are adapted to local landscapes and conditions. Using a term derived from the Icelandic (where a people from the European mainland, on entering an uninhabited island, made it their own), he has called this mythologizing process, *land-nam* (''land taking'').[205] Native landscapes, plants, and animals are assigned archetypal mythological roles, and the whole local scene with its plant and animal life is transmuted, thus, into metaphor.

The Fire Theft

Some twenty-odd versions of the Fire Theft were recorded from the various tribes, and they conform generally to the usual pattern of the tale, as comprising four components: (1) the Fire Hoarder (some miserly deity, personage, people, or animal species); (2) the Clever Thief (human or animal trickster); (3) the Flight (frequently a relay race); and (4) an epochal transformation with negative as well as positive results: usually the end of the Mythological Age.

At first the Ancestors lacked fire. Bilika, however, had a pearl shell and red stone, which she could strike together to make sparks. One day when she had fallen asleep by her flame, she woke to see Sir Kingfisher stealing it and flung at him the pearl shell, which cut off his wings and tail. Diving into the water, he carried the fire to Bet-ra-kuku, where he gave it to someone who passed it on to the Bronze-winged Dove, who distributed it to the rest. Sir Kingfisher, however, had been turned into a man.[206]

A second version had it that when Biliku woke, Sir Kingfisher swallowed the fire, the flung pearl shell cut off his head, and the fire came out of his neck. The Ancestors got the fire and Sir Kingfisher was turned into a bird.[207] Or again:

Bilik [now a male], when he woke, threw a lighted brand that struck Sir Kingfisher on the neck where the bird now has a patch of red feathers. And Bilik was so enraged by this theft that he left the earth for the sky.[208]

Sir Prawn, according to other accounts, was the one who first had fire. Some dry leaves had broken into flame.

Sir Prawn fell asleep by his flame and Sir Kingfisher, making off with it, built a fire with which to cook fish and then himself fell asleep. Sir Dove then stole that fire and gave it to the people.[209]

Sir Prawn was so big that he could go into the deepest water without a canoe. One day, when the Ancestors provoked him, he flung his fire at them and they turned into birds and fishes. Sir Prawn himself then turned into a prawn.[210]

There are a number of other, completely different versions of the origin of fire, for example:

Dim-dori [a kind of fish] fetched fire from the Place of Departed Spirits and, throwing it at the people, burned and thus marked them. They plunged into the sea, becoming varicolored fish, and Dim-dori himself then turned into a dim-dori.[211]

There was a Hill of Fire, at which somebody had shot an arrow, which Sir Kingfisher then found burning. He would not share his fire with the others, and so, that night they all came and stole it.[212]

The Catastrophe

There is a kind of cicada in the islands that ''sings'' during the twilight hours of morning and evening; also when it is picked up. And there were prohibitions both against killing it and against making any loud noise during its morning or evening song. (One thinks of the Egyptian scarab, symbolic of the rising sun.) Other acts offensive to Biliku were the melting of beeswax and the eating of certain plants. And as in Genesis 3, so here: It was the breaking of one of the god's tabus that terminated the Mythological Age.

In the Beginning it was always day, until Sir Monitor Lizard found a cicada in the jungle. The Ancestors watched as he rubbed it between his palms; and when it cried, he crushed it. Immediately, darkness fell, and the Ancestors tried to get day back. They made torches, danced, and sang. First a Kotare-bird sang; then a Bumu-beetle, the Bulbul, and the Koio-bird sang. But day did not return. Sir Ant then sent up a song, and lo! the morning! Day and night have been alternating ever since.[213]

At first there were no birds or fish. But at play one evening, the Ancestors made a noise while the cicadas sang and a cyclone turned them all into birds, fish, turtles, and jungle beasts.[214]

Other legends tell of a deluge.

When the Ancestors refused to give a portion of their honey to the Kipoterawat-bird, it became so angry that it intentionally made a noise when the cicadas sang, and immediately such a rain fell that the sea swelled over the land. Lady Dove saved the fire in a cooking pot as the Ancestors climbed a dipterocarpus tree. And when the waters subsided, Lady Charami-lebek [a bird that lives in the tallest treetops] let down a vine on which they all descended.[215]

There was also a great drought, which in the only recorded version is rendered as a comical animal tale.

It began when a woodpecker found a honeycomb in the hollow of a tree and, while enjoying it, noticed a toad below wistfully watching. Lowering a vine, he invited the toad to attach a basket in which to sit, and, this done, hauled him up. But when the basket reached the honeycomb, he let go, and down dropped the toad—who was so enraged by this trick that he drank up all the rivers on the islands, to the whole world's great distress. The revenge so delighted him that he began to dance for joy, and as he danced, the water poured out of him and the drought ended.[216]

The Separation of Heaven and Earth is an elementary theme of world mythology. In the little cycle of tales of Bilika and Porokul, when they were living at Purum-at-chafe, the Separation seems to have occurred shortly before the adventure of the crossing of the stream.

Porokul made a long bow with which to shoot pigs in the jungle. The sky at that time was near the earth, just above the trees. When he had finished making the bow, he lifted it and its top struck the sky, which rose to its present position, where it remained.[217]

A related theme is of the departure and separation of the Creator from his creation. This appears in another legend from the same tribe as the last. Here the Creator, Bilika, is a male and his wife is Mita, the Bronze-winged Dove. They are living at a place called Poron-et-cho and have a child.

The Ancestors had been eating Bilika's special plants and he was now furious. To learn who the culprits were, he went about smelling people's mouths, and when he found someone who had eaten of the forbidden vegetables, he cut that person's throat. This performance incensed the Ancestors and, coming all together, they killed both Bilika and Mita. Maia-burto [a kind of fish] then carried away their child to the northeast, and it is that child who now lives in that quarter and sends storms.[218]

In a related legend from another tribe, where the name of the deity is Pulugu, the sex again is masculine and the temperament outrageous.

The Ancestors were living along the eastern coast of Henry Lawrence Island, with Pulugu dwelling apart on a little island offshore. They had been digging up his yams and other special plants and, in a passion, he came down on them, destroying their huts and possessions. So they told him to disappear, to get out of this world. "We do not want you here. You are always angry," they told him. So he left and moved away, to the northeast.[219]

The most elaborate of the collected tales is altogether exceptional in that two of the chief food animals, the dugong and the crab, play leading roles.

Sir Dugong had invited everybody to a dance, and Lady Civet Cat warned Sir Tree Lizard that there would be a bird at the party who was going to pick a quarrel with him. "Oh, I don't care," Sir Tree Lizard replied. "I can handle anybody." So when the quarrel started, everybody was afraid. To halt it, Sir Dugong stepped in and caught Sir Tree Lizard by the arm, but was thrown aside with such force that he fell into the sea and became a dugong. A monster called Kochurag-boa was flung into the jungle. Sir Tree Lizard tossed everybody, one after another, into the jungle

221. Photograph, 1883, from the collection of the Royal Anthropological Institute of Great Britain and Ireland. Within this communal dwelling each family had its portion, as (among other tribes) around the village dance ground each family its hut (see **216**).

or the sea, where they became birds, beasts, and fishes. Then he went home and covered himself with red paint in observation of a custom to be followed by any man who had killed another.

When told what had occurred, Sir Crab went to Sir Tree Lizard, pretending to be sick and to need some protective paint to put on his upper lip, where, when breathing, he would inhale its healing strength. His host, who had no more, suggested, "You'd best take some off me." But when Sir Crab brought his nose to the painted arm, he bit into the shoulder and could not be shaken off. Sir Tree Lizard died. Then the Ancestors attacked Sir Crab, but his skin was so hard they were unable to kill him. So they threw him into the sea, where he became a crab. And Sir Tree Lizard's mother, on seeing her son dead, became so angry that she deliberately cut down one of Puluga's special plants, who, in wrath, sent a storm that wiped out everybody in that place.[220]

The Landscape Mythologized and the Origin of Death

One function of mythology is to open through the forms of the known world a sense of the mystery informing all things (page 8); and within such tight little worlds as those of the simplest hunting-and-gathering tribes, this end is served through a mythologization of the local landscapes (land-nam, see page 123). Every possible detail has attached to it the legend of some imagined event, which, though "past," is thus kept simultaneously "present."

The Ancestors brought a turtle into camp and, since Biliku was sitting there, they asked if she would have some. She declined, but when they left their catch unattended, she ate it all and fell asleep. Returning, they realized what had happened and set out to find another turtle. Biliku woke and, seeing them paddling at sea, called to be taken aboard. "No, indeed!" they called back. "You ate our turtle." This made her angry, and she began throwing her pearl shells at them. Two missed and returned to her feet, but the next hit the boat, transforming it and everybody in it into a rocky reef that is still there. Biliku then set a stone on the water and stepped onto it, to float across the inlet. Halfway, however, both she and her stone went down, and they are now two rocks, still to be seen.[221]

At first, there was only one big island. An ant, however, made a turtle net, caught in it an immense fish and attached a line to its tail; whereupon the fish, plunging to break free, repeatedly struck the island and broke it to pieces.[222]

Originally, people did not die. However, when young Yaramurud went to hunt pig for his mother and returned from the jungle with none, she brought out some pork she already had, and he, preparing to carve, cut himself, and his mother watched him die. "You are

now dead," she then said. "Get out of here!" She carried him into the jungle, where she buried him and returned home.

But he, too, returned. "Mother," he said, "I wasn't dead. Why did you bury me?" She was sure that he was dead and buried him again. Again he returned. A third time she buried him and a third time he returned. Finally, she took him to a dumla-tree in which there was a big hole, kicked the tree, and said, "Now you go in there!" In he went. "Are you all the way in?" she called. "Yes," he answered. "Then tell me how the spirits talk." "To kit," he replied; for that is how they talk. Then she knew that he was among the spirits. "Oh my child," she said, "you are now finished. You will never again come back."

But as a spirit he did come back to see his brother, who was building a hut; and when he saw his brother, he killed him. "You see what has happened!" the mother said then to the people. "We shall all now die, as these two have died."[223]

222. G. E. Dobson, who photographed this group in 1872, calls attention to the woman in the center with a round object on her left shoulder. This is her late husband's skull, decorated with red paint and fringes of wood fiber, to be carried about until she obtains another husband. The man standing upper left (nicknamed Jumbo by Europeans) had recently shot through the heart a sailor "taking liberties" with an Andamanese young woman.

APPENDIX

ENDNOTES

PROLOGUE

Text

[1]Fritjof Capra, *The Tao of Physics* (Berkeley, Calif.: Shambala, 1975), p. 56; citing M. P. Crosland (ed.), *The Science of Matter* (Baltimore: Penguin, 1971), p. 76.

[2]Ibid., pp. 80–81.

[3]Ananda K. Coomaraswamy, "Literary Symbolism," in Roger Lipsey (ed.), *Coomaraswamy, Selected Papers*, 2 vols., Bollingen 89 (Princeton, N.J.: Princeton University Press, 1977), vol. 1, p. 324.

[4]Natalie Curtis, *The Indians' Book: An Offering by the American Indians of Indian Lore, Musical and Narrative, to Form a Record of the Songs and Legends of Their Race* (New York: Harper & Brothers, 1907), p. 96.

[5]*Holy Bible*, Genesis 1, Revised Standard Version (New York: Thomas Nelson & Sons, 1953).

[6]*Brihadaranyaka Upanishad*, 1.4.1–5, translated by Joseph Campbell.

[7]John S. Mbiti, *African Religions and Philosophy* (Garden City, N.Y.: Doubleday, Anchor, 1970), pp. 19–129.

[8]Leo Frobenius, *Volksdichtungen aus Oberguinea*, vol. 1, *Fabuleien Drier Volker* (Jena, Germany: Eugen Diederichs, 1924), pp. 75–76.

[9]J. A. Moerenhaut, *Voyage aux Iles du Grand Océan*, 2 vols. (Paris, 1837), vol. 1, pp. 419–423; translated by A. Forander, *An Account of the Polynesian Race; Its Origins and Migrations*, 3 vols. (London, 1880), vol. 1, pp. 221–223.

[10]Curtis, op. cit., p. 315.

[11]Frank Russell, "The Pima Indians," in *26th Annual Report of the Bureau of American Ethnology, 1904–1905* (Washington, D.C.: Government Printing Office, 1908), pp. 206–230, 277.

[12]Translation by Joseph Campbell, based on L'Abbé Brasser de Bourbourg, *Popul Vuh: Le Livre Sacré et les mythes de l'antiquité Americaine* (Paris: Aug. Durand, 1861), pp. 7–13, with corrections from Adrian Recinos, Delia Goetz, and Sylvanus G. Morley, *Popul Vuh: The Sacred Book of the Ancient Quiché Maya* (Norman: University of Oklahoma Press, 1950), pp. 81–84.

[13]J. W. Schopf, "The Evolution of the Earliest Cells," *Scientific American*, vol. 239, no. 3 (1978), pp. 100–138.

[14]David Pilbeam, "Recent Finds and Interpretations of Miocene Hominoids," *Annual Review of Anthropology*, 1979, pp. 333–334.

[15]David Pilbeam, *The Ascent of Man* (New York: Macmillan, 1972), p. 48.

[16]Oswald Spengler, *The Decline of the West*, 2 vols. (New York: Alfred A. Knopf, 1926), vol. 1, p. 166, abridged.

[17]Curtis, op. cit., p. 96.

[18]Spengler, op. cit.

[19]Carleton S. Coon, *The Origin of Races* (New York: Alfred A. Knopf, 1966), p. 259.

[20]Ibid., pp. 259, 284; with addition from Richard E. Leakey and Roger Lewin, *Origins* (New York: E. P. Dutton, 1977), p. 86.

[21]Konrad Lorenz, *Vom Weltbild des Verhaltungsforschers* (Munich: Deutscher Taschenbuch, 1968), pp. 75–76.

[22]Leakey and Lewin, *Origins*, p. 205.

[23]Ibid., p. 203.

[24]Pilbeam, *The Ascent of Man*, p. 155.

[25]Raymond A. Dart, "Some Aspects of the Significance of the Australopithecine Osteodontokeratic Culture," named by title but not reprinted in Anthony F. C. Wallace, *Selected Papers of the Fifth International Congress of Anthropological Ethnological Sciences* (Philadelphia: University of Pennsylvania Press, 1960), p. xix. See also R. A. Dart, "The Makaprensgat Australopithecine Osteodontokeratic Culture," in J. Desmond Clark (ed.), *Third Pan-African Congress on Prehistory: Livingstone, 1955* (London: Chatto & Windus, 1957), pp. 161–171.

[26]Oswald Spengler, *Der Mensch und die Technik* (Munich: C. H. Beck'sche, 1932), p. 14.

[27]Wolfgang Köhler, *The Mentality of Apes* (London: Routledge & Kegan Paul, 1925; New York: Random House, Vintage, 1959). Jane Van Lawick-Goodall, *In the Shadow of Man* (Boston: Houghton Mifflin, 1971).

[28]Köhler, op. cit., Vintage ed., p. 92.

[29]Ibid.

[30]Spengler, *Der Mensch und die Technik*, p. 7.

[31]F. C. Howell, "Hominidae," in Vencet J. Maglis and H. B. S. Cooke (eds.), *Evolution of African Mammals* (Cambridge, Mass.: Harvard University Press, 1978), p. 192.

[32]Pilbeam, *The Ascent of Man*, p. 188.

[33]William Howells, *The Pacific Islanders* (New York: Charles Scribner's Sons, 1973), p. 182.

[34]Ibid., p. 177; Coon, op. cit., p. 412.

[35]*San Francisco Chronicle*, March 27, 1972, p. 2.

[36]Ibid.

[37]Howells, op. cit., pp. 112, 132–133, 146–148.

[38]Ibid., pp. 130–131, 149.

[39]Ibid., p. 187.

[40]Coon, op. cit., p. 408.

[41]Howells, op. cit., pp. 146–155; citing, among others, N. W. G. MacIntosh, "Recent Discoveries of Early Australian Man," *Annals, Australian College of Dental Surgeons*, vol. 1 (1967), pp. 104–126, and "The Talgai Cranium," *Australian Natural History*, vol. 16 (1969), pp. 189–195. Also, A. G. Thorne, "The Racial Affinities and Origins of the Australian Aborigines," in D. J. Mulvaney and J. Golson (eds.), *Aboriginal Man and Environment in Australia* (Canberra: Australian National University Press, 1971), pp. 316–325.

[42]Howells, op. cit., pp. 128–129., Also, David and Ruth Whitehouse, *Archaeological Atlas of the World* (San Francisco: W. H. Freeman, 1971), pp. 206–207.

[43]Richard S. MacNeish, "Early Man in the New World," *American Scientist*, vol. 64 (May–June 1976), p. 317.

[44]Ibid. See also Richard S. MacNeish, "Early Man in the Andes," *Scientific American*, vol. 224, no. 4 (1971), pp. 36–46.

[45]W. W. Crook and R. H. Harris, "A Pleistocene Campsite near Lewisville, Texas," *American Antiquity*, vol. 23, no. 3 (1958), pp. 233–246.

[46]M. de M. C. Beltrao, "Datacaos arqueologicas mais antigas do Brasil," *Anais da Academia Brasileira de Ciências*, vol. 46, no. 2 (Rio de Janeiro, 1974).

[47]D. E. Puleston, "Richmond Hill: A Probable Early Man Site in the Maya Lowlands," paper presented at the Forty-First International Congress of Americanists, Mexico City, 1974.

[48]L. Aveleyra, "The Primitive Hunters," in Robert Wauchope (ed.), *Handbook of Middle American Indians*, 13 vols. (Austin: University of Texas Press, 1964–1973), vol. 1, pp. 384–412.

[49]J. F. Epstein, "The San Isidro Site: An Early Man Campsite in Nuevo León, Mexico," *Anthropological Papers of the University of Texas*, no. 1 (1969).

[50]R. D. Simpson, "The Calico Mountains Archaeological Project," in W. C. Schulling (ed.), *Pleistocene Man at Calico* (San Bernardino, Calif.: San Bernardino County Museum Association, 1972).

[51]C. Borden, "Frazer River Archaeological Project Progress Report," *Anthropological Papers*, no. 1 (Ottawa, Canada: National Museum, 1961).

[52]J. F. V. Millar, "Archaeology of Fisherman's Lake, N.W.T." Ph.D. dissertation, University of Calgary, Alberta, Canada, 1968.

[53]MacNeish, "Early Man in the New World," p. 317.

[54]Ibid., p. 320.

[55]Hansjurgen Müller-Beck, "On Migrations of Hunters across the Bering Land Bridge in the Upper Pleistocene," in David M. Hopkins (ed.), *The Bering Land Bridge* (Stanford, Calif.: Stanford University Press, 1967), p. 40.

[56]Cited and discussed by W. S. Laughlin, "Human Migrations and Permanent Occupation in the Bering Sea Area," in Hopkins (ed.), *The Bering Land Bridge*, p. 437.

[57]Ibid., p. 446.

[58]Ibid., p. 410.

[59]J. L. Giddings, *The Archaeology of Cape Denbigh* (Providence, R.I.: Brown University Press, 1964).

[60]H. M. Wormington, *Ancient Man in North America*, rev. 4th ed. (Denver: Denver Museum of Natural History, 1957), p. 209.

[61]Helge Larsen and Froelich Rainey, *Ipiutak and the Arctic Whale Hunting Culture*, Anthropological Papers of the American Museum of Natural History, New York, vol. 42 (1948), p. 146.

[62]Leo Frobenius, *Erlebte Erdteile*, vol. 7, *Monumenta Terrarum*, 2 aufl. (Frankfurt am Main: Frankfurter Societäts-Druckerei, 1929), pp. 210–219.

[63]Leo Frobenius, *Das Unbekannte Afrika* (Munich: Oskar Beck, 1923), pp. 163–164.

[64]Ibid.

[65]Leo Frobenius, *Indische Reise* (Berlin: Reimer Hobbing, 1931), pp. 222–223.

[66]Henry Fairfield Osborn, *Men of the Old Stone Age*, 3d ed. (New York: Charles Scribner's Sons, 1925), pp. 284–287.

[67]Ibid., pp. 333–347.

[68]Coon, op. cit., pp. 3–4.

[69]Basil Davidson, *Africa in History* (New York: Macmillan, 1968), p. 18.

[70]Ibid.

Captions

[1]Sylvanus G. Morley, *An Introduction to the Study of Maya Hieroglyphics*, Smithsonian Institution, Bureau of Ethnology, Bulletin 57 (Washington, D.C.: Government Printing Office, 1915); *The Ancient Maya*, 2d ed. (Stanford, Calif.: Stanford University Press, 1947), pp. 295–296.

[2]Coon, op. cit., p. 412.

[3]William G. Haag, "The Bering Strait Land Bridge," in Ezra B. W. Zubrow (comp.), *New World Archaeology* (San Francisco: W. H. Freeman, 1974), p. 270.

[4]Gordon R. Willey, *An Introduction to American Archaeology*, 2 vols. (Englewood Cliffs, N.J.: Prentice Hall, 1966), vol. 2, p. 45.

[5]Ibid.

[6]Ibid.

[7]Coon, op. cit., p. 660.

MYTHOLOGIES OF THE PRIMITIVE HUNTERS AND GATHERERS

Text

[1]N. Tinbergen, *The Study of Instinct* (London: Oxford University Press, 1951), p. 38.

[2]Ibid., pp. 36–37.

[3]Ibid., pp. 41–42.

[4]Ibid., p. 50.

[5]William Wordsworth, "Intimations of Immortality," in *Recollections of Early Childhood*, v. 5, ll. 58–66. First published in 1807.

[6]Curtis, op. cit., words of Letakots-Lesa, p. 96.

[7]Osborn, op. cit., pp. 221–222; citing H. Klaatsch, "Homo aurignacenis Hauseri," *Prähistorische Zeitschrift*, vol. 1 (1909), heft 3–4 (1910), pp. 273–338.

[8]M. Boulé, "L'Homme fossile de La Chapelle-aux-Saints," *L'Anthropologie*, vol. 19 (1908), pp. 519–525.

[9]Dorothy Garrod and D. M. Bates, *The Stone Age of Mount Carmel* (Oxford, England: Clarendon Press, 1937).

[10]Osborn, op. cit., pp. 513–514.

[11]Oswald Spengler, *Der Untergang des Abendlandes*, 2 vols. (Munich: C. H. Beck'sche, 1923), vol. 1, p. 216.

[12]Ralph S. Solecki, "Shanidar IV, a Neanderthal Flower Burial in Northern Iraq," *Science*, vol. 190 (November 28, 1975), pp. 880–881.

[13]Ibid., p. 881.

[14]Ibid.

[15]Edward B. Tylor, *Primitive Culture*, 6th ed., 2 vols. (London: John Murray, 1920), vol. 1, p. 458. First published in 1871.

[16]Van Lawick-Goodall, *In the Shadow of Man*, pp. 279–280.

[17]Emil Bächler, *Das alpine Paläolithikum der Schweiz im Wildkirschli, Drachenloch und Wildenmannlisloch*, Schwizerische Gesellschaft für Urgeschichte, Monographien zur Ur- und Frühgeschichte der Schweiz, vol. 2 (Basel, Switzerland: Birkhauser, 1940), p. 260.

[18]André Leroi-Gourhan, *Les Religions de la préhistoire* (Paris: Press Universitaires de France, 1964), pp. 31–36.

[19]Bächler, op. cit., p. 151.

[20]Ibid., pp. 152–156.

[21]Ibid., p. 155.

[22]Giambattista Vico, *La Scienza Nuova* (giusta l'edizione del 1744 con le varianti dell'edizione del 1730), vol. 1 (Bari, Italy: G. Laterza & Figli, 1928), p. 118, par. 333; translated by T. G. Bergin and M. H. Fische, *The New Science of Giambattista Vico* (Ithaca, N.Y.: Cornell University Press, 1968), p. 118.

[23]James George Frazer, *The Golden Bough*, 1-vol. ed. (New York: Macmillan, 1922), p. 386.

[24]C. G. Jung, *The Archetypes of the Collective Unconscious*, translated by R. F. C. Hull, vol. 9:i in *The Collected Works of C. G. Jung* (New York: Pantheon, 1959), p. 155.

[25]*Webster's New International Dictionary*, 2d ed. (Springfield, Mass.: G. & C. Merriam, 1937).

[26]Frazer, op. cit., p. 50.

[27]Leroi-Gourhan, op. cit., pp. 142–143.

[28]Vico, op. cit., p. 86, prop. 184.

[29]J. W. von Goethe, *Faust*, part 2, act 1, sc. 5, ll. 6272–6274, translated by Joseph Campbell:

> The spell of dread is the best part of man.
> Though the world may fend him from
> this feeling,
> Once seized, he senses deeply the
> Tremendum.

[30]André Leroi-Gourhan, *Treasures of Prehistoric Art* (New York: Harry N. Abrams, n.d.), fig. 73, caption.

[31]Ibid., pp. 144, 146.

[32]Ibid., p. 147.

[33]Ibid., p. 110.

[34]Ibid., p. 118.

[35]Ibid., p. 144.

[36]Ibid., p. 112.

[37]Ibid., pp. 370–371. See also Leo Frobenius, *Kulturgeschichte Afrikas* (Zurich: Phaidon, 1923), pp. 84–85, and Felix Trombe and Gabriele Dubuc, "Le centre préhistorique de Ganties-Montespan (Haute-Garonne)," *Archives de l'Institute de paleontologie humaine*, memoire 22 (1947).

[38]Leroi-Gourhan, *Treasures of Prehistoric Art*, p. 313.

[39]Ibid., p. 316.

[40]Ibid.

[41]Abbé Henri Breuil, *Four Hundred Centuries of Cave Art* (Montignac, France: Centre d'Etudes et Documentation Préhistoriques, 1952), pp. 134–136.

[42]Leroi-Gourhan, *Treasures of Prehistoric Art*, p. 316.

[43]Ibid.

[44]Ibid., p. 51.

[45]Geza Roheim, *Psychoanalysis and Anthropology* (New York: International Universities Press, 1950), p. 131.

[46]S. Giedion, *The Eternal Present*, vol. 1, *The Beginnings of Art*, Bollingen 35, 6.1 (Princeton, N.J.: Princeton University Press, 1962), p. 470.

[47]Ibid., p. 469.

[48]J. G. Lalanne, "Découverte d'un bas-relief à répresentation humaine dans les fouilles de Laussel," *L'Anthropologie*, vol. 22 (1911), pp. 257–260. See also J. G. Lalanne and Jean Bouyssonie, "Le Gisement paléolithique de Laussel," *L'Anthropologie*, vol. 50 (1941–1946), pp. 1–163.

[49]Giedion, op. cit., p. 470.

[50]Leroi-Gourhan, *Treasures of Prehistoric Art*, p. 47.

[51]Alexander Marshack, *The Roots of Civilization* (New York: McGraw-Hill, 1972), p. 335 and n. 17.

[52]Leroi-Gourhan, *Treasures of Prehistoric Art*, p. 315.

[53]Curtis, op. cit., p. 96.

[54]The bas-relief was revealed to today's world through the work of three distinguished archeologists: Dorothy Garrod, Susanne de Saint-Mathurin, and Germain Martin. See S. Saint-Mathurin and D. Garrod, "La Frise sculptée de l'abri du Roc aux Sorciers à Angles-sur-Anglin (Vienne)," *L'Anthropologie*, vol. 55 (1951), pp. 413–425. Also, Breuil, op. cit., pp. 334–335, fig. 404.

[55]Giedion, op. cit., pp. 477–481.

[56]Leroi-Gourhan, *Treasures of Prehistoric Art*, p. 347.

[57]Franz Hančar, "Zum Problem Venusstatuetten im Eurasiatischen Jungpaläolithikum," *Prähistorische Zeitschrift*, vol. 30–31 (1939–1940), heft 1–2, pp. 85–156.

[58]Ibid., pp. 118–121. Also, Alfred Salomny, *Jahrbuch für Prähistorische und Ethnographisch Kunst* (Leipzig: IPEK, 1931), pp. 1–6.

[59]Chester S. Chard, *Northeast Asia in Prehistory* (Madison: University of Wisconsin Press, 1974), p. 27.

[60]Ibid., pp. 20–26.

[61]*Webster's New International Dictionary*, op. cit., p. 2301, *shaman*.

[62]Marshack, op. cit., p. 231.

[63]Herbert Kühn, *Auf den Spuren des Eiszeitmenschen* (Wiesbaden, W. Germany; F. A. Brockhaus, 1953), pp. 91–94, abridged.

[64]Ibid., p. 96.

[65]Eugen Herrigel, *Zen in the Art of Archery*, translated by R. F. C. Hull (New York: Pantheon, 1953), p. 20.

[66]Ananda K. Coomaraswamy, "Svayamātrnnā: Janua Coeli," in Lipsey (ed.), *Coomaraswamy, Selected Papers*, vol. 1, p. 483.

[67]Breuil, op. cit., pp. 152–157.

[68]Ibid., pp. 170–171.

[69]Ibid., p. 170.

[70]Ibid., p. 234.

[71]Ibid., p. 170.

[72]Kühn, op. cit., pp. 94–95.

[73]Leroi-Gourhan, *Treasures of Prehistoric Art*, p. 367.

[74]Frobenius, *Kulturgeschichte Afrikas*, pp. 65–69.

[75]Hans-Georg Bandi, "The Rock Art of the Spanish Levant," in H. G. Bandi, H. Breuil, et al., *The Art of the Stone Age*, translated by Ann E. Keep (New York: Crown, 1961), p. 98.

[76]Leo Frobenius, *Atlantis: Volksmärchen und Volksdichtungen Afrikas*, 12 vols. (Jena, Germany: Eugen Diederichs, 1921–1928), vol. 1, *Volksmärchen der Kabylen*, pp. 64–69.

[77]Ibid., pp. 70–71.

[78]Henri Lhote, "The Rock Art of the Maghreb and Sahara," in Bandi, Breuil, et al., *The Art of the Stone Age*, pp. 125, 127.

[79]Ibid., p. 147.

[80]Frobenius, *Atlantis*, vol. 1, p. 11.

[81]James Mellaart, *Catal Huyuk: A Neolithic Town in Anatolia* (New York: McGraw-Hill, 1967), p. 19.

[82]Lhote, op. cit., p. 121.

[83]Philip E. L. Smith, "Stone Age Man on the Nile," *Scientific American*, vol. 235, no. 2 (August 1976), p. 38.

[84]Henri Lhote, *The Search for the Tassili Frescoes*, 2d ed., translated by Alan Houghton Brodrick (London: Hutchinson, 1973), p. 127.

[85]Herodotus, *The Persian Wars*, translated by George Rawlinson (New York: Modern Library, 1942), book 4, i 83.

[86]Lhote, *The Search for the Tassili Frescoes*, pp. 128–132.

[87]Leo Frobenius, *Erythräa; Länder und Zeiten des heiliges Königsmordes* (Berlin-Zurich: Atlantis-Verlag, 1931), p. 295.

[88]Ibid., p. 296.

[89]E. Goodall, "Styles in Rock Paintings," in Clard (ed.), *Third Pan-African Congress on Prehistory: Livingstone, 1955*, pp. 295–299.

[90]Patricia Vinnicombe, *People of the Eland* (Pietermaritzburg, S. Africa: University of Natal Press, 1976), p. 151.

[91]F. Bleek, *The Mantis and His Friends: Bushman Folklore* (Oxford, England: Blackwell, 1924), pp. 1–5, condensed.

[92]Lorna Marshall, "!Kung Bushman Religious Beliefs," *Africa*, vol. 32, no. 3 (1962), p. 227.

[93]Ibid., p. 223.

[94]Ibid., p. 226.

[95]Ibid., pp. 228–229.

[96]Vinnicombe, op. cit., p. 181, n. 21.

[97]J. M. Orpen, "A Glimpse into the Mythology of the Maluti Bushmen," *Cape Monthly Magazine*, no. 9 (1874); reprinted in *Folklore*, no. 30 (1919), pp. 143–145; summarized in Vinnicombe, op. cit., pp. 176–177; further abridged here.

[98]Vinnicombe, op. cit., p. 180.

[99]Kühn, op. cit., pp. 30–32.

[100]Vinnicombe, op. cit., p. 181.

[101]Marguerite Anne Biesele, *Folklore and Ritual of !Kung Hunter-Gatherers*, thesis presented to Harvard University, Department of Anthropology, Cambridge, Mass., 1975, p. 1.

[102]Lorna Marshall, "The Medicine Dance of the !Kung Bushmen," *Africa*, vol. 39, no. 4 (October 1969), pp. 350–352.

[103]Richard B. Lee, "The Sociology of the !Kung Bushman Trance Performances," in Raymond Prince (ed.), *Trance and Possession States*, Proceedings of the Second Annual Conference of the R. M. Bucke Memorial Society, Montreal, 1966, p. 42.

[104]Marshall, "The Medicine Dance of the !Kung Bushmen," p. 352.

[105]Lee, op. cit., p. 47.

[106]Ibid., pp. 39–42.

[107]Biesele, op. cit., p. 13.

[108]Ibid., pp. 150–151.

[109]Marshall, "!Kung Bushman Religious Beliefs," p. 251.

[110]Ibid., p. 242.

[111]Biesele, op. cit. p. 168.

[112]Ibid., pp. 160–161.

[113]Harald Pager, *Ndedema: A Documentation of the Rock Paintings of the Ndedema Gorge* (Graz, Austria: Akademische Druk und Verlagsanstalt, 1971), p. 341.

[114]Lee, op. cit., p. 38.

[115]Pager, op. cit., p. 338.

[116]Laurens van der Post, *The Heart of the Hunter* (New York: William Morrow, 1961), pp. 163–164.

[117]Ibid., p. 168.

[118]E. W. Thomas, *Bushman Stories* (London: Oxford University Press, 1950), pp. 59–60.

[119]Colin M. Turnbull, *The Forest People: A Study of the Pygmies of the Congo* (New York: Simon & Schuster, Clarion, 1962), p. 83.

[120]Ibid., pp. 24–25.

[121]Ibid., p. 92.

[122]Paul Schebesta, *Among Congo Pygmies*, translated by Gerald Griffin (London: Hutchinson, 1933), p. 200.

[123]Turnbull, op. cit., pp. 226–227.

[124]Ibid., p. 101.

[125]Paul Schebesta, *Revisiting My Pygmy Hosts*, translated by Gerald Griffin (London: Hutchinson, 1936), p. 201.

[126]Ibid., pp. 175–176.

[127]Ibid., p. 172.

[128]Ibid., p. 171.

[129]Ibid., p. 169.

[130]Ibid., pp. 173–174.

[131]Ibid., pp. 189–190.

[132]Ibid., p. 175.

[133]Ibid., pp. 182–184.

[134]Schebesta, *Among Congo Pygmies*, p. 238.

[135]Schebesta, *Revisiting My Pygmy Hosts*, pp. 177–179.

[136]Ibid., p. 179.

[137]Ibid., p. 180.

[138]Henri Trilles, *L'Ame du Pygmée d'Afrique* (Paris: Editions du Cerf, 1945).

[139]As cited in Jean-Pierre Hallet, *Pygmy Kitabu* (New York: Random House, 1973), p. 92.

[140]Schebesta, *Revisiting My Pygmy Hosts*, p. 196.

[141]Ibid., p. 177.

[142]Turnbull, op. cit., pp. 146–155.

[143]Ibid., p. 154.

[144]Ibid., p. 155.

[145]John Nance, *The Gentle Tasaday* (New York: Harcourt Brace Jovanovich, Harvest, 1977), pp. 22, 121–123, 133, 271.

[146]Ibid., pp. 51, 54, 67, 140–141, 215, 306–307.

[147]Ibid., pp. 281, 411–412.

[148]Ibid., pp. 21, 71, 238–239, 401–402, 404.

[149]Ibid., pp. 118, 150, 156.

[150]Ibid., p. 64.

[151]Ibid., pp. 269, 279.

[152]Ibid., pp. 23, 226–227.

[153]Ibid., p. 62.

[154]Ibid., p. 112.

[155]Ibid., p. 98.

[156]Ibid., p. 112.

[157]Ibid., p. 99.

[158]Ibid., p. 118.

[159]Ibid., p. 58.

[160]Ibid., p. 320.

[161]Ibid., p. 277.

[162]Ibid., p. 278.

[163]Ibid., p. 131.

[164]Ibid., p. 389.

[165]Ibid., p. 23.

[166]Ibid., p. 118.

[167]Ibid., p. 397.

[168]Ibid., p. 24.

[169]Ibid., p. 392.

[170]Ibid., p. 116.

[171]Ibid., pp. 217–219.

[172]Ibid., pp. 238–239.

[173]Ibid., pp. 167–168.

[174]Ibid., p. 165.

[175]Ibid., p. 167.

[176]Mumford's comment appears on the cover of the paperback edition of Nance, op. cit. Additional information can be found in John Nance, *Discovery of the Tasaday* (Hong Kong: Vera Reyes, 1981).

[177]A. R. Radcliffe-Brown, *The Andaman Islanders*, 2nd printing, enlarged (London: Cambridge University Press, 1933), p. 42.

[178]Lidio Cipriana, "Excavations in Andamanese Kitchen-Middens," in *Actes du IVᵉ Congrès International des Sciences Anthropologiques et Ethnologiques* (Vienna, 1952), tome 2, pp. 250–253.

[179]Radcliffe-Brown, op. cit., p. 308.

[180]Ibid., p. 306.

[181]Ibid., p. 307.

[182]Ibid., pp. 254–276.

[183]Ibid., pp. 239–246.

[184]Ibid., pp. 129–130.

[185]Ibid., p. 187.

[186]Ibid., p. 192, a legend of the Aka-Bo tribe.

[187]Ibid., pp. 192–193, legends of the Aka-Jeru.

[188]Ibid., p. 196, from the Aka-Bea.

[189]Ibid., from a South Andaman tribe.

[190]Ibid., p. 195, an A-Pučikwar tale.

[191]Ibid., an A-Pučikwar belief.

[192]Ibid., p. 142.

[193]Ibid., p. 143, from the A-Pučikwar.

[194]Ibid., p. 196, from a South Andaman tribe.

[195]Ibid., pp. 193–194, a legend of the A-Pučikwar.

[196]Ibid., p. 193, from the Aka-Kol.

[197]Ibid., p. 199, from the Aka-Kede.

[198]Ibid., p. 218, from the Aka-Kede.

[199]Ibid., an A-Pučikwar tale.

[200]Ibid., a North Andaman legend.

[201]Ibid., pp. 218–219, from the Aka-Čari.

[202]Ibid., pp. 141–142, from the Aka-Jeru.

[203]John Lyard, "The Making of Man in Malekula," in *Eranos-Jahrbuch 1948* (Zurich, Switzerland: Rhein-Verlag, 1949), p. 235.

[204]Radcliffe-Brown, op. cit., p. 247.

[205]Ananda K. Coomaraswamy, *The Rg Vedas as Land-náma-bók* (London: Luzac, 1935).

[206]Radcliffe-Brown, op. cit., pp. 202–203, from the Aka-Kede.

[207]Ibid., p. 201, from the Aka-Jeru.

[208]Ibid., pp. 203–204, an A-Pučikwar legend.

[209]Ibid., p. 202, from the Aka-Čari (or, possibly, from the Aka-Kora or Aka-Jeru).

[210]Ibid., p. 207, from the Aka-Čari.

[211]Ibid., p. 204, from the Aka-Bale.

[212]Ibid., p. 202, from the Aka-Jeru.

[213]Ibid., pp. 213–214, an A-Pučikwar tale.

[214]Ibid., p. 208, a legend of the Aka-Kol.

[215]Ibid., pp. 207–208, from the Aka-Kede.

[216]Ibid., pp. 222–223, from the Aka-Bea.

[217]Ibid., pp. 199–200, from the Aka-Kede.

[218]Ibid., p. 200, from the Aka-Kede.

[219]Ibid., pp. 200–201, from the Akar-Bale.

[220]Ibid., pp. 208–209, from the Akar-Bale.

[221]Ibid., pp. 197–198, an Aka-Jeru tale.

[222]Ibid., p. 217, from the A-Pučikwar.

[223]Ibid., pp. 216–217, from the Akar-Bale.

Captions

[1]For a detailed and illustrated treatment of these mysterious figurines, see Miguel Covarrubias, "Tlatilco: Archaic Mexican Art and Culture," *DYN: The Review of Modern Art*, vols. 4–5 (December 1943), pp. 40–46.

[2]Van Lawick-Goodall, *In the Shadow of Man*, pp. 214–217.

[3]For accounts of these two finds, see Ralph S. Solecki, *Shanidar: The First Flower Burial* (New York: Alfred A. Knopf, 1971), pp. 176–200, 227–238.

[4]Van Lawick-Goodall, *In the Shadow of Man*, pp. 279–280.

[5]Baldwin Spencer and F. J. Gillen, *The Native Tribes of Central Australia* (London: Macmillan, 1899; reprinted with preface, 1938), pp. 331–334.

[6]Breuil, op. cit., pp. 164–169.

[7]Frobenius, *Das Unbekannte Afrika*, pp. 36–41 and plate 8.

[8]Frobenius, *Erythräa*, pp. 309–310.

[9]Ibid., p. 310.

[10]Pager, op. cit., p. 344.

[11]Ibid., p. 342.

[12]Ibid., p. 340.

[13]Ibid., p. 341.

[14]Ibid.; citing D. N. Lee and H. C. Woodhouse, "Rock Paintings of 'Flying Bucks'," *South African Archaeological Bulletin*, vol. 19, no. 75 (1964), pp. 71–74, and "More Rock Paintings of 'Flying Bucks'," ibid., vol. 23, no. 89 (1968), pp. 13–16.

[15]W. H. I. Bleek and L. C. Lloyd, *Specimens of Bushman Folklore* (London: George Allen, 1911), p. 431.

[16]James George Frazer, "Between Heaven and Earth," in *The Golden Bough*, 1-vol. ed. (New York: Macmillan, 1922), chap. 60, pp. 595–667.

[17]Lorna Marshall, *The !Kung of Nyae Nyae* (Cambridge, Mass.: Harvard University Press, 1976), pp. 179, 244, 277–278.

[18]Ibid., pp. 351–353; citing and discussing Caroline Furness Jayne, *String Figures: A Study of Cat's Cradle in Many Lands* (New York: Charles Scribner's Sons, 1906), pp. 24–27.

[19]Ibid., p. 53.

[20]Coon, op. cit., p. 652.

[21]Nance, *Discovery of the Tasaday*, p. 103.

[22]Ibid., p. vii.

[23]Ibid., p. viii.

A NOTE ON THE INDEXES

References to pages, captions, maps, and map captions

In the Place Name Index and the Subject Index, references to pages are page numbers, e.g.,

Barrow (Alaska), 187

which means that a reference to Barrow is to be found on page 187. In both indexes, commas, rather than dashes, are used to indicate separate mentions of a topic in adjacent pages, e.g.,

125, 126

References to captions consist of a boldface caption number (or range of caption numbers), followed by a hyphen and a page number. For example,

254-147

126–130-72

References to maps consist of a boldface capital "M" and map number (or range of map numbers) followed by a hyphen and a page number, e.g.,

M50-255

M44–46-211

Map captions are referred to similarly, but with an additional letter "C," e.g.,

MC29-122

CREDITS AND ACKNOWLEDGEMENTS

PICTURES

ABM = Armando Braun Menendez, Buenos Aires; **AHB** = Abbé H. Breuil, *Four Hundred Centuries of Cave Art* (Montignac, France: Centre d'Etudes et Documentation Préhistoriques, 1952); **AI** = Anthropos Institute, Moravske Museum, Brno; **AMNH** = American Museum of Natural History, New York; **AP** = Associated Press; **ARRB** = A. R. Radcliffe-Brown, *The Andaman Islanders* (London: Cambridge University Press, 1933); **AW** = Achille Weider, Zurich; **BM** = British Museum, London; **EB** = Emil Bächler, *Das alpine Paläolithikum der Schweitz im Wilderkirschli, Drachenlock und Wildenmannlisloch* (Basel, Switzerland: Birkhauser, 1940); **FI** = Frobenius Institute, Frankfurt-am-Main; **GA** = George Armstrong; **HH** = Hans Hinz, Basel; **HL** = Hermitage Museum, Leningrad; **HP** = Harold Prager, *Ndedema: A Documentation of the Rock Paintings of the Ndedema Gorge* (Graz, Austria: Akademische Druk und Verlagsanstalt, 1971); **HVL** = Hugo von Lawick; **JNM** = John Nance/Magnum, New York; **JPH** = Jean Pierre Hallet, Los Angeles; **JR** = John Reader, London; **JV** = Jean Vertut, Issy-Les-Moulineaux, France; **LB** = Lee Boltin, New York; **LM** = Laurence Marshall, Cambridge, Mass.; **MAI** = Museum of the American Indian/Heye Foundation, New York; **MH** = Musée de l'Homme, Paris; **MSGL** = Musée de St. Germaine en Laye; **NRFL** = N. R. Farbman/*Life*, New York; **PKRL** = Peter Kain, London/Richard Leakey; **PRM** = Pitt Rivers Museum, London; **RAI** = Royal Anthropological Institute of Great Britain and Ireland, London; **SEPA** = Scala/Editorial Photocolor Archive; **SI** = Smithsonian Institution, Washington, D. C.;

PROLOGUE

1 Museo de La Plata, Argentina; **2** SEPA; **3** MAI; **4** SEPA; **5** Eliot Elisofon/Time-Life, New York; **6** Delmar Lipp, Museum of African Art, SI; **7** BM; **8** MAI; **9** AMNH; Evolution Charts: GA; **10** GA/Museum Trustees of Kenya, Nairobi; **11** GA/MH; **12** GA/SI; **13** GA/MH; **14–17** GA; **18** LB; **19** Tartarsky/Design Photographers International, New York; **20** Tim White, University of California at Berkeley; **21** PKRL; **22–24** JR; **25** PKRL; **26–27** JR; **28** JNM; **29** Panamin/AP; **30** GA; **31** AMNH; **32** BM; **33** Department of Anatomy, University of Sydney, Australia; **34** Chris Stringer, Department of Paleontology, British Museum of Natural History, London; **35** AMNH; **36** Axel Poignant, London; **37** Dacre Stubbs, *Prehistoric Art of Australia* (New York: Charles Scribner's Sons, 1974); **38** GA; **39** AMNH; **40** GA; **41** AMNH; **42** GA; **43** AMNH; **44–45** GA; **46** AMNH; **47** Texas Memorial Museum, Austin; **48** GA; **49** ABM; **50** The Art Institute, Chicago; **51** GA; **52–55** AMNH; **56–57** HL; **58–59** AMNH; **60** BM; **61** Wilfred Thesiger, London; **62–63** The University Museum, Philadelphia; **64–65** LM.

MYTHOLOGIES OF THE PRIMITIVE HUNTERS AND GATHERERS

66 AW; **67** Gillett G. Griffin, Princeton, N.J.; **68** Cherel Ito; **69** AMNH; **70** HVL; **71** Franz Coray; **72** Institute de Paleontologie Humaine, Paris; **73** GA; **74** MH; **75–76** Ralph S. Solecki, Department of Anthropology, Columbia University; **77–78** BM; **79** HVL; **80** Knocher Magazine, Frankfort Schadel Steinkiste; **81** Toni Nigg; **82** Museum, St. Gallen, Switzerland; **83** EB; **84** AMNH; **85** EB; **86–87** National Museum of Hungary, Budapest; **88** JV; **89** Collection Bégouën, Paris; **90** AW; **91** HH; **93** JV; **94** André Leroi-Gourhan; **95** AW; **96** HH; **97–98** Caisse National des Monuments Historiques & Sites, Paris; **99** AW; **100** AHB; **101** AW; **102–103** JV; **104** A. Rosenfeld, Australian Institute of Aboriginal Studies, Canberra; **105** JV; **106** AW; **107** AMNH; **108** AW; **109** MH; **110** AW; **111–112** Musée de Cluny, Paris; **113** JV/GA; **114** MSGL; **115–116** AI; **117** Alain Roussot, Bordeaux; **118** Natural History Museum, Vienna; **119** MH; **120** AI; **121** Musée des Antiquités Nationales, Paris; **122** Institute of Archaeology, Brno; **123** AI; **124** Nina Ellinger, Copenhagen; **125–130** Institute of Archaeology of The Academy of Sciences of the U.S.S.R., Leningrad; **131** AHB; **132** AW; **133** Herbert Kühn, *Auf den Spuren des Eiszeitmenschen* (Wiesbaden, W. Germany: F. A. Brockhaus, 1953); **134** JV; **135** Jean Gausson, Neuvic-sur-L'isle, France; **136–137** JV; **138** FI; **139** AW; **140** Museo Ethnologico de Morella y del Maestrazgo, Spain; **141** Graham Clark, *The Stone Age Hunters* (London: Thames & Hudson); **142** Herbert Kühn, *Rock Art of Europe*; **143–144** FI; **145–155** Documents Henri Lhote's Expedition, Paris; **156** FI; **157** National Cultural History Museum, Pretoria; **158** FI; **159** National Museums and Monuments of Rhodesia, Umtali; **160** LM; **161** NRFL; **162** LM; **163** HP; **164** LM; **165** HP; **166** Henri P. Junod, *Art of Africa* (Johannesburg: Shuter & Shuter); **167** LM; **168** Constance Stuart/Black Star, New York; **169–170** LM; **171** Seeliger/Stern/Black Star; **172–173** LM; **174–175** Richard B. Lee, Toronto; **176–178** HP; **179–181** Lorna Marshall, Cambridge, Mass.; **182** NRFL; **183** JPH; **184** JNM; **185** P. Muller/Hao-Qui, Paris; **186** Colin M. Turnbull; **187** Noël Baliff, Paris; **188–189** Elisofon Archives, Museum of African Art, SI; **190–193** JPH; **194** George Rodger/Magnum; **195** JPH; **196** E. A. Wallis Budge, *The Gods of the Egyptians* (London: Methuen, 1904); **197** Cairo Museum; **198–201** JPH; **202–211** JNM; **212** ARRB; **213** RAI; **214** ARRB; **215** PRM; **216–219** ARRB; **220** Baldwin Spencer and F. J. Gillen, *The Native Tribes of Central Australia* (London: MacMillan, 1899); **221–222** RAI.

MAPS

Map 7. Based on information adapted from J. L. Bischoff and R. J. Rosenbauer, "Uranium Series Dating of Human Skeletal Remains from the Del Mar and Sunnyville Sites, California," *Science*, vol. 213 (August 28, 1981), pp. 1003–1005; "Little Spring, Florida—A Unique Underwater Site," *Science*, vol. 203 (February 16, 1979), p. 609; M. Penkala, *A Correlated History of the Far East (An Atlas)* (The Hague, Netherlands: Mouton, 1966); D. J. Clark, *The Prehistory of Africa* (New York: Praeger, 1970); W. Bray and D. Trump, *The American Heritage Guide to Archaeology* (New York: American Heritage, 1970); B. M. Fagan, *People of the Earth*, 3rd. ed. (Boston: Little Brown, 1980); and J. Hawkes, *Atlas of Ancient Archaeology* (New York: McGraw-Hill, 1978; used with permission of Rainbird Publishing Group, London).

Maps 9, 10, 11, 12. From Hansjurgen Müller-Beck, "Paleohunters in America: Origin and Diffusion," *Science*, vol. 152 (May 27, 1966), pp. 1191–1210.

Map 13. Based on information adapted from G. R. Willey, *An Introduction to American Archaeology*, vol. 1 (Englewood Cliffs, N.J.: Prentice-Hall, 1966); *American Heritage Pictorial Atlas of United States History* (New York: American Heritage, 1966); R. S. MacNeish, "Early Man in the New World," *American Scientist*, vol. 64 (May-June 1976), pp. 316–327; Henry P. Walker and Don Bufkin, *Historical Atlas of Arizona* (copyright © 1979 University of Oklahoma Press, Norman, Oklahoma); and Warren A. Beck and Ynez D. Haase, *Historical Atlas of New Mexico* (copyright © 1969 University of Oklahoma Press, Norman, Oklahoma).

Map 14. Based on information adapted from H. G. Bandi, *Eskimo Prehistory* (Fairbanks: University of Alaska Press, 1969), and David M. Hopkins (ed.), *The Bering Land Bridge* (Stanford, Calif.: Stanford University Press, 1967).

Map 15. Based on information adapted from Andreas Lommel, *Prehistoric and Primitive Man* (Feltham, Middlesex: Hamlyn Publishing Group, 1967).

Maps 16, 17, 18. Based on information adapted from Carleton S. Coon, *The Origin of the Races* (New York: Alfred A. Knopf, 1962).

Map 20. Based on information adapted from David Whitehouse and Ruth Whitehouse, *Archaeological Atlas of the World* (London: Thames & Hudson, 1975).

Map 21. Based on information adapted from Hans-Georg Bandi, Henri Breuil, et al., *The Art of the Stone Age* (New York: Crown, 1961; copyright © Holle and Co., Verlag, Baden-Baden, W. Germany; used by permission of Crown Publishers Inc.).

Map 22. Based on information adapted from David Whitehouse and Ruth Whitehouse, *Archaeological Atlas of the World* (London: Thames & Hudson, 1975), and Hans-Georg Bandi, Henri Breuil, et al., *The Art of the Stone Age* (New York: Crown, 1961; copyright © Holle and Co., Verlag, Baden-Baden, W. Germany; used by permission of Crown Publishers Inc.).

Map 24. Based on information adapted from Henri Lhote, *The Search for the Tassili Frescoes*, 2d ed., translated by Alan Houghton Brodrick (London: Hutchinson, 1973; copyright © Editions Arthaud, Paris, 1958).

Map 25. Based on information adapted from: Hans-Georg Bandi, Henri Breuil, et al., *The Art of the Stone Age* (New York: Crown, 1961; copyright © Holle and Co., Verlag, Baden-Baden, W. Germany; used by permission of Crown Publishers Inc.), and Andreas Lommel, *Prehistoric and Primitive Man* (Feltham, Middlesex: Hamlyn Publishing Group, 1967).

EXTRACTS

From Emil Bächler, *Das alpine Paläolithikum der Schweitz im Wildkirschli, Drachenloch und Wildenmannlisloch*, Schwizerische Gesellschaft für Urgeschichte, Monographien zur Ur- und Frühgeschichte der Schweiz, vol. 2 (Basel, Switzerland: Birkhauser, 1940), used with permission.

From André Leroi-Gourhan, *Treasures of Prehistoric Art* (New York: Harry N Abrams, n.d.), used with permission.

From Abbé Henri Breuil, *Four Hundred Centuries of Cave Art* (Montignac, France: Centre d'Etudes et Documentation Préhistoriques, 1952), used with permission of L'Office Départemental du Tourisme de la Dordogne, Perigeaux, France.

From S. Giedion, *The Eternal Present*, vol. 1, *The Beginnings of Art*, Bollingen 35, 6.1 (Princeton, N.J.: Princeton University Press, 1962; copyright © 1962 by The National Gallery of Art), used with permission.

From Herbert Kühn, *Auf den Spuren des Eiszeitmenschen* (copyright © 1956 F. A. Brockhaus, Wiesbaden, W. Germany), used with permission.

From Laurens van der Post, *The Heart of the Hunter* (New York: William Morrow, 1961), used with permission.

From Colin M. Turnbull, *The Forest People: A Study of the Pygmies of the Congo* (New York: Simon & Schuster, Clarion, 1962), used with permission.

From Paul Schebesta, *Among Congo Pygmies*, translated by Gerald Griffin (London: Hutchinson, 1933), and *Revisiting My Pygmy Hosts*, translated by Gerald Griffin (London: Hutchinson, 1936), used with permission.

From John Nance, *The Gentle Tasaday* (New York: Harcourt Brace Jovanovich, Harvest, 1977), used with permission.

From A. R. Radcliffe-Brown, *The Andaman Islanders*, 2d printing, enlarged (London: Cambridge University Press, 1933), used with permission.

Grateful acknowledgment is made to the following for their noted contributions to this volume: John A. Van Couvering, the American Museum of Natural History, for providing current research, accurate data, and conceptual insights on geological, archaeological, and anthropological prehistory; Ian Tattersall and David Thomas (assisted by Lori Pendleton), the American Museum of Natural History, for supplying additional prehistorical data as needed.

Editorial Director: *Robert Walter*

Associate Editor: *Hugh Haggerty*

Designer: *Jos. Trautwein/Bentwood Studio*

Picture Editor: *Rosemary O'Connell*

Permissions Editor: *Cynthia Beckett Ortega*

Copyeditor/Indexer: *Leonard Neufeld*

Illustrator: *George Armstrong*

Maps and Charts: *Cartographic Services Center of R. R. Donnelley & Sons Company:*

Map Design: *Sidney P. Marland* III

Map Research, Compilation, and Project Coordination: *Luis Freile*

Map Drafting and Production: *David F. Stong*

Design, Drafting, and Production of the Two Evolution Charts: *Jeannine M. Schonta*

Type Composition by *Typographic Art, Inc.*

Printing and Binding by *Royal Smeets Offset B.V., The Netherlands*